RADICAL PHILOSOPHY

2.17
Series 2 / Winter 2024

Impunity in times of genocide **Brenna Bhandar**	3
Shields and the genocide in Gaza **Neve Gordon**	10
Terrestrial uprisings and living alliances **Paul Guillibert**	23
By all means **Peter Hallward**	34
The transformation of everyday life **Interview with Kristin Ross**	51
Exchange: Apathy and the neoliberal university **Justin Cruikshank and Nathaniel Barron**	61

REVIEWS

Alberto Toscano, *Late Fascism: Race, Capitalism and the Politics of Crisis* **Danny Hayward**	69
Naomi Klein, *Doppelganger: A Trip into the Mirror World* **Ashley Bohrer**	77
Richard Seymour, *Disaster Nationalism: The Downfall of Liberal Civilization* **Luke De Noronha**	83
Elsa Dorlin, *Self-Defense: A Philosophy of Violence* **Chrys Papaioannou**	88
Vincent Bevins, *If We Burn* **Neal Harris**	91
Paul Rekret, *Take This Hammer: Work, Song, Crisis* **Dante Philp**	94
Grant Kester, *The Sovereign Self* and *Beyond the Sovereign Self* **Steyn Bergs**	97
John Lennon, *Conflict Graffiti: From Revolution to Gentrification* **Kyle Proehl**	100
Sjoerd van Tuinen, *Philosophy of Mannerism* **Debjyoti Sarkar**	103
Camille Robcis, *Disalienation: Politics, Philosophy, and Radical Psychiatry in Postwar France* **Gary Genosko**	106
Mario Tronti, 1931-2023 **Matteo Mandarini**	110

Editorial collective
Brenna Bhandar
Victoria Browne
David Cunningham
Isabell Dahms
Lucie Mercier
Robert Nichols
Hannah Proctor
Rahul Rao
Chris Wilbert

Engineers

CC BY-NC-ND
RP, Winter 2024

ISSN 0300-211X
ISBN 978-1-914099-06-9

Impunity in times of genocide
Brenna Bhandar

For over a year, the world has been conscripted as an 'involuntary witness' to the ongoing genocide of Palestinians. With no shortage of legal rulings and academic opinions on the illegal nature of the particular and gross forms of violence the Israeli state is inflicting on the people of Palestine, and now, Lebanon, the question of impunity looms large. Attempts to grasp the juridical structures that produce impunity, and relatedly, the psychic-social entanglements with this radical state of exception from responsibility, are taking place at multiple scales. At the level of individuals and communities engaged in solidarity work, the last years have engendered a state of profound psychosomatic disorientation – and indeed, heartbreak – in the midst of relentless political organising.[1] The idea that taking political (and legal) action should in some ways make one feel hopeful that a change in course is possible – particularly as it relates to intensive lethal violence – has been challenged by the brazen performance of impunity by Israeli politicians, soldiers and citizens. How is one, literally and metaphorically, to swallow, to digest, to comprehend, the ability of Israel, the U.S. and its other imperial backers, to slaughter and destroy Palestinian life with apparent freedom, in the face of continued Palestinian resistance and mass political mobilisations against the genocide? How is one to understand the intensification and expansion of Israel's theatre of brutality in the face of repeated judgments issued by the International Court of Justice, multiple UN General Assembly resolutions, and the recently issued ICC warrants for the arrest of Netanyahu and Gallant?

At the level of the state, the enjoyment with which large swathes of people greet expressions and acts of impunity (transmitted across borders at dizzying speed via social media platforms) seems to be a major driver of recent electoral outcomes, whose consequences reverberate globally. Trump's 2016 exclamation that 'I could stand in the middle of Fifth Avenue and shoot somebody, and I wouldn't lose any voters, OK?' now seems like a quaint understatement, given his electoral victory in the aftermath of several criminal convictions and civil losses relating to fraud, bribery and sexual assault. While any sort of definitive diagnosis is beyond the scope of this short commentary, the juridical-political sphere is producing forms of impunity that have consequences for a world gripped by the conjoined forces of rising fascism and intensified climate change, both cause and effect of multiple and interlocking crises. Impunity, it seems, is becoming the psycho-juridical basis for a new world (dis)order.

Within a juridical framing of Israel's conduct, international lawyers have cautioned that the impunity with which Israel continues to act threatens the very legitimacy of the post-war international legal order. While Palestinian legal scholars have enumerated the ways in which international laws have acted as an alibi for Israel's settler colonial project,[2] the South African charge of genocide has prompted a renewed reckoning with the potential – if foundationally flawed – power of this international legal order to give meaning to its twentieth century prohibitions on genocide, the annexation of territory by force, and related forms of mass human rights violations. Steadfast critics of the international legal order have had to pause, even if only out of respect for Palestinians and others looking to the court to lend legal force to political efforts to end the genocide. Additionally, the basic fact is that there is currently no other legal-political discourse that would impel a nation state to stop arming Israel, or to assert political pressure on Israel to end its occupation. The question of the enforceability of the ICJ rulings, which are legally binding on the parties to the case, raises another set of problems and potentialities for confronting the problem of impunity. Where and how can these forms of international law be enforced, and what is the relationship between political movements such as the BDS campaign, and mechanisms for political and economic sanction embodied in international law? How does one contend with a liberal human rights order that is designed to produce impunity for all that lies outside of its orbit, namely the political economy of the war machine and settler colonial extractivism? In what follows I outline three tentative rationales for why impunity is a central feature of the current conjuncture: i) impunity is produced by the founding violence of the colonial nation state, and remains central to its settlement project; ii) the colonial nation-state and its settler citizens are the paradigmatic subjects of a primordial and absolute right to self-defence; and iii) the excess pleasure found in the masculinist performance of impunity that is overwhelmingly present in contemporary politics.[3]

I

> 'The law is haunted by impunity.'[4]
>
> Zahid R. Chaudhary

The OED defines impunity as the 'exemption from punishment or penalty'; and in a weaker sense, as 'exemption from injury or loss as a consequence of any action; security.' Israel enjoys impunity in both senses, evidenced by the fact that no meaningful sanctions have been imposed on it as a consequence of its flagrant and ongoing breaches of international law. That Israel enjoys impunity is not solely a result of its existence as a European colonial project that has the full backing of the west. As Zahid R. Chaudhary has argued, drawing on the work of Derrida, modern law itself produces impunity through the very self-authorising force that constitutes its foundations.[5] Derrida, in 'The Force of Law: Mystical Foundations of Authority' seemed to have, without referencing it as such, described the violence of the founding moments of settler colonies:

> Yet, the operation that amounts to founding, inaugurating, justifying law, to making law, would consist of a *coup de force*, of a performative and therefore interpretive violence that in itself is neither just or unjust and that no justice and no earlier and previously founding law, no pre-existing foundation, could, by definition, guarantee or contradict or invalidate.[6]

While Derrida goes onto to examine the injustice inherent to the act of rendering a judgment (as in a legal decision or ruling), this passage articulates the inauguration of the founding moment of settler colonial rule. This is embodied in proclamations of discovery and assertions of title that are built on both the interpretive violence of recognising Indigenous rights[7] – in the same moment they are subordinated to colonial rule – and the fiction that the inauguration of a colonial legal order is based on anything else but its own pronouncement. As Chaudhary writes, '[t]his prior violence that establishes the law necessarily enjoys impunity'.[8] While the founding violence of settler colonies inaugurated genocidal violence against Indigenous peoples,[9] it is also the case that juridically, this dispossession is a silence 'walled up' as Derrida writes, in the 'violent structure of the founding act'.[10]

The founding violence of the modern (colonial) legal order becomes the basis for quotidian and spectacular, individual and state-level, particular and gross forms of impunity. That much of the individual private property ownership in settler colonies is essentially founded on theft,[11] or that contemporary forms of massive accumulation of wealth by individuals are structured by the law,[12] offer evidence for this claim. Chaudhary notes that the rise of neoliberal rationality during the Cold War era also witnessed expanded forms of state violence with impunity in the name of 'stamping out impunity' (consider, for instance, the rhetoric surrounding the American 'war on drugs'). There are thus at least two forms of impunity that structure the juridical sphere: the foundational forms of impunity that inaugurate a legal order itself; and the continuous reiteration of impunity in the form of police and military power that seeks to grapple with revolt and resistance (crisis), a power that is often deputised to civilian-settler subjects.

In the international sphere, Third World Approaches to International Law (TWAIL) scholarship has excavated the colonial origins of the modern international legal system, showing how the cards are structurally overdetermined to be stacked against the perpetually 'subalternised' Global South.[13] Given contemporary international law's genealogy, it is not difficult to understand how Global South countries are routinely disadvantaged in this sphere. International economic law sedimented neocolonial trade relationships through instruments such as the GATT and WTO.[14] The particular ways in which the 'colonial present' manifests in the era of decolonisation, however, requires us to consider more carefully the specific forms of (neo)colonialism that have been prohibited by international legal instruments, as well as the meaning of their repeated violations. Israel stands indicted of the crime of genocide, has been found to be violating the prohibition of apartheid, and its occupation of Palestinian lands that extend beyond the 1967 Green Line, has been found to be illegal, its intention to permanently annex them laid bare. On 21 November 2024, the International Criminal Court issued arrest warrants for Netanyahu and Gallant, 'for crimes against humanity and war crimes committed from at least 8 October 2023 until at least 20 May 2024.'[15] Significantly, in its press release, the ICC states that while arrests warrants are 'classified as secret' (in order to protect witnesses and safeguard the investigation) the Chamber decided to release the information 'since conduct similar to that addressed in the warrant of arrest appears to be ongoing …'. Several European states (Hungary and France) and of course the United States have offered Netanyahu immunity on their territorial soil. In light of the above, we can consider how foundational impunities produced by the modern legal order persist in contemporary forms, and also, in the face of explicit legal indictments and advisory opinions that have found Israel to be in violation of laws prohibiting the most grave, explicit and direct forms of violent human rights abuses.

There are at least three explanations (however partial) for why Israel continues to act with complete impunity, in the face of three rulings (two contentious cases, one advisory opinion[16]) of the International Court of Justice in 2024 alone. The first judgment of the ICJ, handed down on 26 January 2024, found that the risk of irreparable prejudice to the rights sought, and the urgency of the situation, justified provisional measures. The petitioners had established that Israel was 'committing plausible genocide' and that Israel had to take every necessary action to stop acts that were imperilling the rights of Palestinians to not be subjected to genocide under the Genocide Convention. The second ruling of 28 March 2024 provided for further provisional measures given the worsening humanitarian conditions in Gaza. The third ruling, of 19 July 2024, an advisory opinion, found Israel's occupation of the Occupied Palestinian Territories, as a contiguous territory, to be illegal. The breadth of findings is vast, with Israel in violation of the prohibition on racial apartheid, forcible transfer of Palestinians, exploitation and control of natural resources, the building of infrastructure for the purposes of settlement, and other acts of dispossession that are central to colonisation even though they are not named as such. The Court found that Israel must evacuate all settlers, allow displaced Palestinians to return to their original homes, and that Israel should return all land and property seized since the occupation began in 1967. The Court made a clear statement that Israel owes reparations to anyone who suffered material damage as a result of Israel's unlawful acts during the occupation. In effect, the Court ruled that all of Israel's colonisation activities post 1967 are illegal.[17]

Yet, the impunities that inhere in the founding violence of the state of Israel survive in spite of repeated rulings and UN General Assembly and Security Council resolutions decrying Israel's illegal activities. Unlike the self-authorising force of colonial governments in other settler states, Israel was founded, after the colonial proclamation of Balfour, by the UN Partition Resolution

181. However, as is well known, the 'legal' partitioning of Palestine was accompanied by the mass displacement of 750,000 Palestinians, the widescale destruction of Palestinian villages and communities, extrajudicial killings and what many have duly referred to as the ethnic cleansing of Palestine. This originary and founding violence, the illegal counterpart to the legality of the Partition resolution, which was the condition of its execution, has remained central to Israeli nation-building and statecraft throughout its brief history.

A painfully plain and obvious fact, but one with complex juridical and political consequences, is that the temporality of Israel's creation in 1948, the culmination of a Zionist project modelled on European settler colonialism, is temporally out of joint[18] in relation to other settler colonies that were founded in an era prior to the emergence of contemporary international legal norms that render the key characteristics of settler colonialism illegal. Whereas settler colonialism is *per se* not illegal, many of its core aspects have been prohibited from the early twentieth century onwards. Francesca Albanese, UN Special Rapporteur on human rights in the Palestinian territories occupied since 1967, attempts in her most recent report 'Genocide as Colonial Erasure' to identify Israel's settler colonial ambitions as key components of the commission of genocide. She draws on the work of Indigenous scholars Tamara Starblanket and Leanne Betasamosake Simpson and theorists of settler colonialism to contextualise the genocide as a totality, taking place across Palestine.

The genocidal violence of settler colonies such as Canada continues into the present time but is not justiciable because ultimately, and as indicated in Albanese's report, genocide is mainly conceived of as happening in a time of armed conflict or conventional warfare. The difference between the slow and eliminatory violence of settler colonialism, and the intense, murderous and lethal violence that happens in the context of conventional warfare is glossed by the distinction between 'cultural' genocide and 'physical and biological' genocide.[19] Settler colonialism as a mode of governance, now generalised across post-colonial spaces,[20] is not conceived of as a crime. The catastrophe of climate degradation and extractivism that are lethal for entire populations are part of the necropolitical drive of colonial capitalism, and can only be rendered justiciable as discrete acts that potentially cross a legislative red-line, rather than as a system. This means that while genocide may be recognised as a state crime and individuals may be held responsible for its commission, settler colonialism as a violent modality of governance and accumulation remains outside the purview of the law, embedded as it is in the very formation of many liberal democracies globally.

||

'[A]ny good defense is also an attack.'[21]

Elsa Dorlin

What persists, in the colonial present, is a form of impunity wherein some subjects and nations are entitled to act in self-defence, and those who are not, are rendered definitionally and practically defenceless, and 'killable'. This constitutes a second rationale for how Israel can continue to act with impunity in the face of legal censure. In spite of the fact that an occupying power does not have the right to self-defence in international law, Israel argues that its war on Gaza, the West Bank and Lebanon, is just and legitimate because it 'has the right to defend itself'. Elsa Dorlin exposes the modern legal subject as one defined by his capacity to defend himself, which, as an extension of a Lockean theory of subjectivity, means the right to defend one's property. As many have argued, there is a multi-scalar bind between the proprietorial racial subject and the possessive logic of nationalism. The person who has a right to use violence in his self-defence is the proper subject of a nation that has a primordial, natural right to self-defence; and Israel's repeated mantra, parroted by every western political leader, taps into this civilizational discourse that is a hallmark of colonial modernity. But more than this, it is essential to recognise that the lines between individual, deputised settler violence of the police and the soldier, and the state, are utterly blurred in the colony, and without these forms of deputised violence the settler state could not maintain its sovereign control over Indigenous and native peoples. As settlers rampage across the West Bank, as the villages of Bedouin are repeatedly destroyed, as unimaginable violence is inflicted on Gaza, it is crucial to recall that *this is settler colonialism in its totality,* a lesson taught to the world by the Unity Intifada of 2021.

Dorlin illuminates the meaning of self-defence for people facing genocide. Texts posted by the Jewish Combat Organisation throughout the Warsaw Ghetto, in January 1943, read '[w]e are ready to die to be human'. As Dorlin notes, 'in the most tragic situation imaginable, human dignity required dying with a weapon in hand – to fight, and perhaps survive, but to become, above all, the heralds of life against death'.[22] The history of self-defense in Jewish communities, is tied, as Dorlin writes, 'to their struggles against pogroms, primarily in Russia' from the late nineteenth century.[23] Self-defence becomes the *condition sine qua non* for the assertions of one's humanity when faced with genocidal violence. The Israeli military's release of the drone footage of Yahya Sinwar's final moments, a miscalculated attempt to propagandise its killing of Sinwar, instead became widely reported as a symbol of revolutionary defiance. Sinwar is seen, alone in a bombed-out room, heavily wounded, throwing a stick at a drone moments before he is killed, resisting until the bitter end.

The affirmation of life in the face of certain death, through the forceful act of self-defence, is then, according to Dorlin, transformed in the 1940s into an offensive act by Jewish refugees who, under the auspices of right-wing nationalist Zionists, contributed to the founding of the Jewish state and its founding myths. Tracing the roots of the Israeli martial art krav maga, Dorlin writes that '[t]his new people, fully engaged in the military, celebrated the heroism represented by their shift from defense to offense ... Krav maga symbolises the national ideology of offensive defense, of a war of conquest waged in a context where an army came to define itself as a nation engaged in self-defense, against everyone, in order to survive'.[24]

Offensive acts of violence, which in the political imaginary of the colony are represented as self-defence, not only benefit from impunity, but have taken on different meaning in the symbolic order of the current conjuncture. Illegality and the performance of impunity are a source of enjoyment and pleasure, even an excessive pleasure that bleeds into a sort of ecstasy. This excess can be seen on the faces of each Israeli soldier who has posted recordings, visual evidence, of the commission of war crimes on social media. It is seen in the unbridled laughter and joy that supporters of Trump unleash in response to his threats of criminal behaviour; or indeed, in the fact that so many could cast a vote for a man who is now a convicted felon. What I'd like to suggest here is that in addition to the bad faith and hypocrisy that characterises western denialism of Israel's status as an apartheid state[25] that is committing a genocide, we have moved into a moment where impunity itself is more than foundational to the modern legal order. More than just a shadow counterpart of legality, that which makes our modern colonial legal order viable, is impunity itself becoming the basis for a new world (dis)order?

The notion of legitimating illegal conduct through defiance of laws and legal norms is a tension and dynamic universally familiar to modern legal orders. Indeed, international law scholar Nathaniel Berman argues that appeals to a transcendent set of moral and/or political imperatives in order to justify the violation of international law has been one means of changing international law itself.[26] The Iraq War that began in 2003 is an object lesson in western powers winning support for an illegal war through defiance of international laws, based on an appeal to (offensive) self-defence, security and anti-terrorism. In this moment, it is not simply defiance of international law but the performance of impunity by all levels of the Israeli political system, state organs, settler-citizens and by association their allies and backers, that is setting the world order on a different course. Appealing not to transcendent political values but to god himself, Israeli politicians and military leaders repeat biblical justifications for daily massacres; and Israel's near full-blown mutation into a theocratic, authoritarian state has not yet disrupted the myth of Israeli democracy for westerners. Israel's attempts at moulding IHL to provide cover for genocide seem to have less probative value today than Netanyahu and others' blatant flaunting of the belief that they can continue on course with a blanket exemption from punishment or penalty and with complete security.

This continued performance of impunity in the time of the law runs up against a different temporality, that of anti-colonial struggle. Nasser Abourahme writes that 'there is no chance of grasping this conjuncture without reading it within a historical arc of a renewed war of national liberation that has begun to pose insurmountable challenges to the very logic of settler colonial power in Palestine'.[27] With international law being reordered by the disintegration of long-held distinctions, between 'legal' and 'illegal', 'theory' and 'practice', as Michael Fakhri has argued recently,[28] one may consider how the very foundational forms of impunity baked into the colonial legal order may also be pushed, through the formation of renewed anti-colonial resistance, to the point of collapse.

Brenna Bhandar is a member of the Radical Philosophy *editorial collective.*

Notes

1. See Hannah Proctor, *Burnout: The Emotional Experience of Political Defeat* (London: Verso, 2024).
2. See for instance the work of Noura Erakat, who argues, to take one example, that maintaining the international legal framework enables 'Israel to continue its civilian settlement under the auspices of temporality, demonstrating intent *not* to annex the land, without imposing on the state any duty to withdraw'. *Justice for Some: Law and the Question of Palestine* (Stanford: Stanford University Press, 2019), 84. See also Nimer Sultany, 'The Question of Palestine as a Litmus Test: On Human Rights and Root Causes' 23 *Palestine Yearbook of International Law* (2022), 1.
3. See Zahid R. Chaudhary, 'This Time with Feeling: Impunity and the Play of Fantasy in The Act of Killing', *boundary 2* 45:4 (2018), 82–87. In relation to the Indonesian genocide of the 1960s, Chaudhary explores the psychoanalytic aspects of the performance of impunity in Joshua Oppenheimer's film *The Act of Killing*, including the fantasy of a masculinist will to power.

4. Zahid R. Chaudhary, 'Impunity' in *Political Concepts: a critical lexicon* (December 4 2018), https://www.politicalconcepts.org/impunity-zahid-r-chaudhary/
5. Chaudhary, 'Impunity'.
6. Jacques Derrida, 'Force of Law: The "Mystical Foundation of Authority"' in *Act of Religion* (New York: Routledge, 2002), 241.
7. On the recursive nature of the formation of private property ownership in the colonial settlement of the United States, see Robert Nichols, *Theft is Property! Dispossession and Critical Theory* (Durham: Duke University Press, 2019).
8. Chaudhary, 'Impunity'.
9. See Tamara Starblanket, *Suffer the Little Children: Genocide, Indigenous Nations and the Canadian State* (Atlanta: Clarity Press, 2018); Harry Harootunian, *The Unspoken as Heritage: the Armenian genocide and its unaccounted lives* (Durham: Durham University Press, 2019).
10. Derrida, 'Force of Law', 242.
11. Brenna Bhandar, *Colonial Lives of Property: Law, Land and Racial Regimes of Ownership* (Durham: Duke University Press, 2018).
12. Katharina Pistor, *The Code of Capital: how the law creates wealth and inequality* (New Jersey: Princeton University Press, 2019).
13. See Antony Anghie, *Imperialism, Sovereignty and the Making of International Law* (Cambridge: Cambridge University Press, 2005); and in relation to Palestine specifically, see Ardi Imseis, *The United Nations and the Question of Palestine: Rule by Law and the Structure of International Legal Subalternity* (Cambridge: Cambridge University Press, 2023).
14. Donatella Alessandrini, *Developing Countries and the Multilateral Trade Regime: The Failure and Promise of the WTO's Development Mission* (Portland: Hart Publishing, 2010); Sujith Xavier, Amar Bhatia & Adrian A. Smith, 'Indebted Impunity and Violence in a Lesser State: Ethno-Racial Capitalism in Sri Lanka', *Journal of International Economic Law* 25:2 (2022).
15. 'Situation in the State of Palestine: ICC Pre-Trial Chamber I rejects the State of Israel's challenges to jurisdiction and issues warrants of arrest for Benjamin Netanyahu and Yoav Gallant', ICC press release, 21 November 2024, https://www.icc-cpi.int/news/situation-state-palestine-icc-pre-trial-chamber-i-rejects-state-israels-challenges.
16. Article 65 of the Charter of the United Nations and the ICJ Statute provides in section 1 that the 'Court may give an advisory opinion on any legal question at the request of whatever body may be authorized by or in accordance with the Charter of the United Nations to make such a request.' Article 68 establishes that the statute also applies to contentious cases, which are cases brought by one member state against another.
17. *Legal Consequences Arising from the Policies and Practices of Israel in the Occupied Palestinian Territory, including East Jersualem*, Advisory Opinion, 19 July 2024, I.C.J. Reports 2024.
18. See Nasser Abourahme, *The Time beneath the Concrete: Palestine between Camp and Colony* (Durham: Duke University Press, 2025).
19. Tamara Starblanket, *Suffer the Little Children: Genocide, Indigenous Nations and the Canadian State* (Atlanta: Clarity Press, 2018).
20. Amitav Ghosh, 'European colonialism helped create a planet in crisis', *The Guardian*, 14 January 2022; see also Azad Essa, *Hostile Homelands: The New Alliance between India and Israel* (London: Pluto Press, 2023).
21. Elsa Dorlin, *Self-Defense: A Philosophy of Violence*, trans. Kieran Aarons (London: Verso, 2022), 70–71.
22. Dorlin, *Self-Defense*, 55. Subheading above from Dorlin, 70–71.
23. Ibid., 59.
24. Ibid., 67.
25. Saree Makdisi, *Tolerance is a Wasteland: Palestine and the Culture of Denial* (Oakland: University of California Press, 2022).
26. Nathaniel Berman, 'Legitimacy Through Defiance: From Goa to Iraq', *Wisconsin International Law Journal* 23:1 (2005), 93–125.
27. Nasser Abourahme, 'In tune with their time', *Radical Philosophy* 216 (Summer 2024), 16.
28. Michael Fakhri, 'What's going on?', in 'On international law and Gaza: critical reflections', *London Review of International Law* 12:2 (July 2024), 217–301.

Shields and the genocide in Gaza
Neve Gordon

Both the actual use of civilians as human shields and Israel's efforts to frame civilians and civilian structures as shields have played a central role in the application and justification of violence in Gaza at least since the 2008-2009 war. Yet, following October 7, 2023, Israel has introduced three novel processes related to human shielding: the first involves forcing Palestinian civilians to dress in military uniforms and sending them into underground tunnels as human shields; the second is the casting of practically all civilian structures as 'shielding' structures, and the third includes the invocation of the shielding provisions laid out in international humanitarian law to indict everyone and everything above ground in Gaza as legitimate military targets. Ultimately, all of these different forms of shielding and, more importantly, the accusations of shielding have become tools for perpetuating genocide and for framing the genocide as legitimate.

Before describing these processes, I introduce the central legal provision relating to human shields as it is enshrined in international humanitarian law. I then distinguish between animate and inanimate shields in order to underscore the idea that human shielding operates through a politics of vulnerability, whereby the vulnerable human body ostensibly functions as a tool of moral deterrence. Next, I discuss the changes Israel introduced after October 7. I argue that dressing Palestinian civilians in IDF uniforms and forcing them to serve as shields underscores how Israel has dehumanised Palestinians not merely by depriving them of their dignity, but by reducing them into things. I then trace the way international humanitarian law distinguishes civilian from military 'objects', demonstrating that particularly in urban settings the distinction is not based on what the objects are but on their perceived function within the theatre of political violence. An apartment building is considered a civilian structure, but it might also function as an arms depot and can consequently be indicted as a shield, leading it to lose some protections that international law bestows on 'civilian objects'. I go on to argue that by centre-staging functionality as the primary tool of distinction, international humanitarian law facilitates the extension of Israel's shielding accusation so that hospitals, schools, universities, mosques, bakeries and apartment buildings can all be imagined as shields and therefore as targetable 'military objects'. Moreover, Israel's sweeping charge that civilian structures in Gaza function as shields is, I maintain, informed by the way that physical structures are racialised as Palestinian structures. The two inverse processes—whereby the human becomes a thing and buildings are assigned a race—set the stage for extending shielding to practically every civilian and civilian structure, revealing how the legal provisions that were introduced following the Second World War as part of a new global order committed to 'Never Again' can, paradoxically, be used to provide legal justifications for genocidal warfare.

Shielding and the politics of vulnerability

The bedrock of international humanitarian law (IHL) is the principle of distinction. This principle draws a distinction between civilians and civilian structures that must be protected during war, and combatants and military objects that can be legitimately attacked. IHL defines human shielding as the use of protected people – namely, civilians or prisoners of war – to shield a legitimate military target. The pertinent legal provision states that the use of human shields is a war crime, but also adds that human shields will not render a legitimate military target immune from attack.[1] If a warring party takes into account certain principles, like proportionality, precaution and military necessity, then the killing of human shields used by the enemy can be justified as legal.[2] In other words, it is illegal to use human shields, but it is not always illegal to kill them. Moreover, since it is illegal to utilise human shields, a warring party that kills human shields can assign the blame and legal responsibility for the shields' deaths on the party using them as shields. The underlying logic here is that the illegal use of civilians as shields (namely, as instruments of war) puts in motion the interactions that led to their deaths, and that the bullet or bomb that killed them was merely an effect of their original 'illegal' use as human shields – and thus the blame is placed on the original illegal action.

When thinking of shields in theatres of violence, Nicola Perugini and I have highlighted the differences between animate and inanimate shields.[3] Human shields function as defensive tools, but in a profoundly different way from inanimate shields, such as land mines used to defend a border or anti-aircraft missiles protecting an airfield. Generally speaking, inanimate shields are an integral part of any arsenal: they are built with the objective of being both impenetrable and robust so as to protect military targets, and they have been used in war since time immemorial. Their particular physical or technological capacities determine their function as instruments of protection within armed conflict; and, because they are inanimate, they rarely raise moral dilemmas. By comparison, human beings would seem an unlikely choice for a shield, since as embodied beings made of flesh and blood they can easily be killed. Consequently, if the human body was conceived as a mere inanimate object, lacking the value assigned to the human qua civilian, it would not be useful as a shield. A human body becomes a shield *by virtue of its vulnerability*,[4] whereby the vulnerability associated with civilianhood aims to produce moral deterrence on the part of the opponent.

The distinction between the two types of shields appears in an infographic that Israel circulated in 2014.[5] Providing an image of two kinds of shields ostensibly deployed by the two warring factions, 'Hamas Protects its Weapons with Human Shields" (see following page) has been used to lay claim to a civilizational divide – between Israelis and Palestinians, the coloniser and colonised – and to intimate that Palestinian civilians are killed in large numbers because they are used as shields. But the infographic also underscores the distinction between animate and inanimate shields. As opposed to the inanimate shield, which is ultimately conceived and produced in order to protect human vulnerability in war, in the case of human shields vulnerability itself becomes the means of protection.

Building on Banu Bargu's work, Perugini and I have drawn a link between the vulnerable body and the ethics of violence, claiming that when faced with vulnerable shields a certain moral obligation is meant to emerge, and this obligation is meant to dissuade or deter belligerents from attacking a target defended by such shields.[6] According to the infographic, Palestinians exploit this vulnerability and use civilians as shields to achieve military objectives, thus violating the laws of war. Regardless of whether this is the case or not, human shields are meant to defend a combatant or a military object, but they do so through their vulnerability. It is in this sense that human shielding is fundamentally a politics of vulnerability, a form of warfare in which the vulnerable body occupies a central position in determining whether the violence deployed by belligerents within the battlefield is ethical.[7]

Perugini and I have also claimed that the history of human shields is inextricable from the history of the human. We have shown, for example, how the racialisation of human shields has changed over the years, laying bare how, in the past, only white people could become human shields because only they were considered to be fully human and could be cast as civilians deserving protection and as people who could, at least ostensibly, generate moral deterrence. We tied this observation to claims made by Antony Anghie, Anne Orford, Frédéric Mégret and others, explaining that non-white civilians in the colonies could be killed during armed conflict without it being a crime.[8] Indeed, it was only after decolonisation, when the ex-colonised were admitted to the 'family of nations' and hence endowed with legal protections, that non-white civilians could become human shields.

Our empirical analysis shows, however, that following decolonisation and the allocation of legal protections to formerly colonised civilians, western militaries began casting non-white civilians whom it had killed as human shields regardless of whether they were actually used as shields. This became increasingly evident and widespread after the United States launched the War on Terror. Because the use of human shields is a war crime

source: IDF blog

according to IHL, western warring parties began invoking the legal clauses pertaining to shielding either before or immediately after killing civilians as a means of justifying their deaths. In short, these western warring parties frame their enemies – which today are mostly non-white non-state warring parties – as having used thousands of human shields. This allows them to accuse the non-state warring parties of being responsible for the deaths of civilians that the western warring parties themselves had killed.[9]

We went on to distinguish between three kinds of shields: involuntary, voluntary, and proximate.[10] Involuntary human shields are protected people – civilians or prisoners of war – who are 'used as shields' by a warring party. The legal provisions against the deployment of involuntary shields are informed by the presupposition of a passive civilian body that a warring party forces into becoming a shield.[11] Voluntary human shields are civilians who willingly stand between a warring party and a legitimate military target. They challenge the legal ascription of passivity assigned to civilians but also the very logic of war by actively resisting the whole economy of violence.[12] In the West, they tend to be white people, because security forces in the Global North often only recognise whites as having the capacity to be non-violent, while the moral cachet that comes with being white and having a western passport can, in some instances, serve as a deterrent. This also highlights Bargu's claim that voluntary shielding helps to reproduce existing social and political hierarchies and power relations even as it resists them.[13]

While in both cases the vulnerability of the civilian body is used to produce moral deterrence, the distinction between these two types of shields is related, on the one hand, to the location of agency, and, on the other hand, to shielding's relation to violence.[14] Voluntary shields are people who visibly assert their own agency, while involuntary shields are those whose body is exploited by an active warring party to advance its own goals. Agency, in other words, is located within the voluntary shield, while it acts upon the involuntary shield. Just as importantly, when it comes to the shield's relationship to violence, voluntary shields use their body in a non-violent way to prevent or stop violence, while involuntary shields reluctantly become part and parcel of the existing economy of violence.

Finally, the third kind of shields are the proximate ones: namely, civilian populations trapped near combatants in besieged cities or other war zones. Our analysis reveals that civilians are cast as proximate shields almost exclusively when they are trapped near non-state fighters, who are usually cast as terrorists, and not when they are located near state military forces. So when Israel bombs a Hamas rocket launchpad in Gaza and kills civilians who live nearby, the civilians are framed as human shields; by contrast, when Hamas bombs the IDF central command centre in Tel-Aviv, the civilians around it are never cast as human shields. Perugini and I have also demonstrated how this form of shielding has become by far the most prominent in battlespaces around the globe over time – from the Middle East to Southeast Asia.[15] Part of the reason clearly has to do with the War on Terror and the increasing involvement of non-state actors in both inter and intra state conflicts.[16] Moreover, one of the fallouts of the ubiquitous War on Terror – that frames multiple countries across different continents as terrorist bases harbouring 'terrorists' and hence legitimate sites of military intervention – is that entire civilian populations are continuously exposed to lethal violence due to their proximity to military targets.

While proximate human shields are mainly embodied by non-white people, they also tend to be gendered and defined by age.[17] Proximate human shields are almost always women, children and the elderly. By casting them as people who are illegally used as shields, a warring party that kills them can transfer responsibility for their deaths to the party that ostensibly used them as shields. Men who are killed in warzones are rarely cast as proximate human shields and tend instead to be framed as MAM or 'military aged men'. The acronym MAM was first introduced by the US in Vietnam and, not unlike human shields, the term is also a technology for justifying the killing of civilians. Whether they participate in hostilities or not, men between the age of 15 and 65 are *by default* characterised as fighters or terrorists, and therefore warring parties can claim that they were legitimately killed. Indeed, if one were to believe Israeli military spokespersons, there are no civilian men in Gaza since practically every single man whom the Israeli military has killed in the five cycles of violence since 2008 has been cast as 'terrorist' or 'participant in hostilities'.

Analysing 150 years of human shielding in different geographical locations, these are among the major claims Perugini and I made about human shields. However, in Israel's 2023–24 war on Gaza, we have witnessed three significant departures in relation to shields: the first is the dressing of involuntary shields in military uniforms, which inverses the very logic of vulnerability and moral deterrence informing the human shielding practice; second, the casting of practically all civilian structures as shielding structures; and third, the use of the shielding provisions in IHL to justify genocide.

The hunter's bait

Let's begin with dressing Palestinian civilians in IDF uniforms. While militaries have forced civilians to serve as human shields for centuries, Israel has introduced this new form of shielding in Gaza, one that appears unprecedented in the history of warfare. The practice was initially revealed by *Al Jazeera*[18] but, subsequently, *Haaretz* published an exposé about how Israeli troops have abducted Palestinian civilians, dressed them in military uniforms, attached a camera to their body, and sent them into underground tunnels as well as buildings in order to shield Israeli troops from enemy fire.[19] One IDF soldier noted that 'it's hard to recognize them. They're usually wearing Israeli army uniforms, many of them are in their 20s, and they're always with Israeli soldiers of various ranks'. But if you look more closely, *Haaretz*'s journalists proceeded to explain, 'you see that most of them are wearing sneakers, not army boots. And their hands are cuffed behind their backs and their faces are full of fear.'[20]

To be sure, Israel's use of shields is not new. Israeli troops have used robots and trained dogs with cameras on their collars as well as Palestinian civilians as shields primarily in urban warfare. However, Palestinians who were used as shields in previous rounds of violence always wore civilian clothes and could thus be identified as civilians. Again, the visibility of their civilian status is meant to deter Palestinian fighters from attacking or firing and is central to the constitutive logic of human shielding as traditionally understood: it is precisely the recognition of vulnerability, and that they are fellow Palestinians, which are key to the purported effectiveness of human shielding and for deterrence to have a chance of working.

By randomly detaining (that is, kidnapping) Palestinian civilians – including youth and the elderly – and then dressing them in military garb before forcing them to walk in front of soldiers, the Israeli troops violate not only the legal provision against the use of human shields but also the provision that deals with perfidy and prohibits warring parties from making use of military 'uniforms of adverse Parties while engaging in attacks or in order to shield, favour, protect or impede military operations'.[21] Here we have two war crimes in a single action.

Yet the perfidy dramatically alters the logic of human shielding. Instead of highlighting the vulnerability of Palestinian civilians, the Israeli military purposefully conceals their vulnerability. By forcing Palestinian civilians to wear IDF uniforms, they make them appear as if they were enemy combatants – people who can be killed without it being a crime – in the eyes of Palestinian fighters. Israeli troops deploy them as shields not to deter Palestinian fighters from striking the soldiers, but rather to draw fire and thus reveal these fighters' location, allowing the Israeli troops to launch a counterattack and kill the fighters. Thus, the moment these human shields are sent into the tunnels, they are transformed from vulnerable civilians into cannon fodder.

The treatment of Palestinian civilians in this manner might not come as a surprise given the genocidal violence that Israel has been deploying in Gaza. Yet, it does provide a clear indication of the relationship Aimé Césaire draws between colonialism and the 'thingification' of the colonised.[22] It also echoes Paulo Freire's claim that 'the more the oppressors control the oppressed, the more they change them into apparently inanimate "things"'.[23] Dressing Palestinians in IDF uniforms and sending them into tunnels is not only a paradigmatic example of how Israeli soldiers relate to colonised Palestinians, but also of how the thingification of Palestinian civilians plays out when they are used as shields in the battlefield. It reveals how the military operationalises ex-defence minister Yoav Gallant's racist assertion that 'we are fighting human animals', exposing how for the Israeli soldiers Palestinians are either prey or bait, animal or bare flesh.[24] Like hunters who use raw meat to lure animals they want to capture or kill, the Israeli troops use Palestinian civilians as if they were bare flesh whose function is to attract the hunter's prey.

Palestinian civilians become a 'thing' when they are transformed into bare flesh, but to be transformed into bare flesh they had to have already undergone processes of racialisation that constitute them as nonhuman. According to Alexander Weheliye's analysis in *Habeas Viscus*, such racialization explains why for Israeli Jews the Palestinian's expulsion from humanity 'appears both deserved and natural'.[25] Indeed, it is not only active-duty soldiers who support the practice, but also the majority of those who commented on the *Haaretz* article exposing the practice, on a news site that attracts primarily Israeli liberals. Settler colonial racism is central to this unprecedented way of using human shields. If in the past, Israeli racism cast Palestinians as not-quite-human, savages who are incapable of making the distinction between civilian and military objects, the condition of possibility of this new form of human shielding, which uses perfidy to present Palestinian civilians as if they are Israeli soldiers, is that the Palestinian civilian is completely evacuated of humanity and becomes a thing. Instead of using Palestinian civilians as *human* shields, Israel's new practice transforms them into inanimate or bare shields.

Function is everything

Before turning to the second difference that we have witnessed in Gaza – the casting of practically all civilian structures as shielding structures – we need to make a brief detour in order to discuss how IHL defines legitimate targets. When one speaks of human shields, most people think of humans who either volunteer or are forced into becoming shields. The International Committee of the Red Cross claims, for example, that the term human shields 'describes a method of warfare ... where the presence of civilians or the movement of the civilian population, whether voluntary or involuntary, is used in order to shield military objectives from attack, or to shield, favor or impede military operations'.[26] Notwithstanding this description, the notion of shielding in IHL is actually much broader and does not apply to humans alone. In our previous work, Perugini and I examined attacks on hospitals in war zones and described how they are both used and framed as shields.[27] However, even though we also mentioned charges of shielding levelled against schools and mosques, we failed to indicate and fully develop the significance of the fact that the shielding accusation can extend well beyond the human to include any legally protected (namely, civilian) inanimate object.[28]

IHL provides protection to civilian property and prohibits attacking and destroying civilian sites and structures where this is not justified by military necessity. The legal protections do not apply where a civilian site is used for military purposes and its destruction offers a warring party a definite military advantage. At such point, the civilian sites become a 'military object' which is a broad and fluid term that is difficult to define but casts that which it names as a legitimate military target.[29] Thus, civilian sites and structures can become a legitimate military target at any time depending on how they are used and the advantage offered by attacking them.[30] Some civilian sites, such as medical facilities and sites of cultural value, are entitled to special protections under IHL, rendering it, for example, illegal for armed forces to occupy them. Yet even these sites can be legally attacked if they are transformed into a 'military object'.[31]

In short, according to IHL, any structure that has a military function can be legitimately targeted while structures that have a civilian function cannot. Yet a structure that has a civilian function can assume a military function, and, once this occurs, that structure can be legitimately targeted provided certain principles such as proportionality, precaution and military necessity are taken into account. IHL, in other words, recognises that objects might have 'dual use' and that in addition to their civilian function they might also serve a military purpose, and that often they can be used for civilian and military purposes simultaneously.[32] A hospital that is treating patients might also have a military function. As a hospital, the building and the people within it are perceived as vulnerable and in need of protection, but once the hospital is charged with hiding an arms depot its signification changes and it becomes a 'military object'.[33] The process through which the hospital is transformed into a legitimate military target also alters the conception of the people within it: doctors, nurses, professional staff, as well as the sick and injured patients. They become potential 'collateral' damage, a phrase that subsumes under the same umbrella both civilians and civilian structures and in effect collapses the distinction between the human and nonhuman, an issue to which I return below.

It is important to underscore that within IHL the perception of the structure's function determines the signification ascribed to it, and if a structure takes on both civilian and military functions concurrently, then the military function usually trumps the civilian one, transforming the structure into a 'military object'. As Henry Shue and David Wippman point out, according to a 'permissive reading of Article 52(2) [of Additional Protocol I of the Geneva Conventions], if an object by virtue of its "nature, location, purpose or use make[s] an effective contribution to military action," and its destruction under the circumstances "offers a definite military advantage," then the object becomes a legitimate military objective. No attention need be paid to that object's contribution to civilian life'.[34] To be sure, a warring party is obliged to take into account the principles of proportionality, precaution and military necessity before launching an attack on such an object, but the object's military function can readily eclipse the civilian value ascribed to the structure and the people within it. Hence, the perception of the hospital's function shapes how it is imagined – as a vulnerable place that cares for the sick and wounded or, conversely, as a shield being used to hide weapons – and these conceptions shape, in turn, the kinds of protections IHL allocates. While civilian sites and structures can be transformed into 'military objects' in different ways, the most prevalent one is when they are framed as shields because combatants are allegedly hiding within the civilian site or are using the site to hide weapons. Civilian sites and structures can also be framed as shields and thus as a 'military object' when they are in proximity to a legitimate target.

The militarisation of civilian objects has become increasingly widespread due to the urbanisation of warfare – the transformation of urban spaces into battlefields – alongside the vast asymmetry of many current conflicts.[35] Michael Schmitt underscores the difficulty of distinguishing between civilians and combatants in contemporary wars, explaining how during the US invasion of Afghanistan guerrilla groups were scattered and 'wore no uniforms or other distinctive clothing that allowed immediate visual identification', and 'the mere position of a group, vehicle or other mobile target seldom served as a reliable indicator of its enemy character'.[36] Accordingly, new technologies have been developed that aim to analyse human activity within theatres of violence. Determining what a person *does* rather than how one looks is now considered vital for understanding who a person *is*, and, in a similar way, detecting how a structure is used determines whether to classify it as military or civilian. The increasing significance of detecting a person's and structure's function in battlespaces, particularly in urban settings, emphasizes the vital role currently played by the 'military gaze', which is manufactured and mediated through the interactions among different technologies and forms of intelligence, surveillance, and reconnaissance.[37]

This has implications for IHL and the politics of human shielding. In our previous research on the history of human shielding, Perugini and I discovered that in several theatres of political violence civilian sites and structures are repeatedly framed as shields in order to justify striking them. In Gaza, however, the shielding charge has been summoned to indict an unparalleled number of structures. Already in January 2024, just three months after Israel's attack began, the BBC reported that between 144,000 and 175,000 buildings across the whole Gaza Strip had been damaged or destroyed,[38] amounting to 60 percent of all civilian structures in Gaza.[39] Israel justified the destruction by repeatedly accusing Hamas of using civilian structures as shields. Shielding, in effect, had become a catch-all justification for Israel's transformation of Gaza into rubble. Crucially, the law effectively lends itself to these practices. Warring parties – in this case Israel – that wish to dramatically alter the signification of both civilians and civilian structures can invoke the shielding exceptions within IHL, namely that persons or structures are protected except when they serve as a shield.

My claim is not only that the perceived dual function of civilian structures has enabled Israel to interpret the shielding exceptions as the rule in Gaza (a claim I return to in the last section), but that through the 'shielding exception', IHL produces an analogy between the materiality of the animate civilian body and the inanimate civilian structure: both lose protections bestowed on them when they are used as shields. Rather than some ontological essence and thus distinction between flesh and blood and inorganic structures, it is the perceived function of bodies and objects – both animate and inanimate, human and nonhuman – that determines the legal protections allocated to them. The crux of the matter is that an analysis of human shielding reveals how international *human*itarian law has been constituted in a way that *enables* the *dislodging of the fundamental distinction between the human and nonhuman*, a distinction that has informed humanism since its inception and has been central to the very notion of rights and to the ethicality ostensibly informing IHL.[40] Instead of the human/nonhuman distinction, IHL accentuates the distinction between civilian and military, which is determined by function – or more accurately perceived function – and casts both the animate and inanimate as either vulnerable civilian objects deserving protection or as 'military objects' that can be legitimately targeted. This move, as Gaza teaches us, can readily lead to the disavowal of human inviolability.

Racialised buildings

The question remains, however, of what can happen to inanimate structures as a result of IHL's undermining of the age-old human/nonhuman distinction in a context like Gaza, where urban warfare operates under the broader logic of settler colonialism. We have already seen that when it comes to human shields, racism informs the transformation of the human into a thing. But the nonhuman, too, undergoes a major transformation. Even before a military function is attributed to a civilian structure and its signification is modified from a civilian to a 'dual use' structure that can be legitimately attacked, the structure itself undergoes a process of racialisation – which is vital for rendering the 'dual use' charge believable among certain publics. The point is that settler colonial racism shapes the way soldiers interpret not only the function of Palestinian civilians, but also of civilian structures.

For instance, an Israeli soldier uses a whole range of surveillance techniques to monitor a Palestinian civilian on a rooftop. The soldier must then decide what the civilian's function is – whether they are going to the roof to catch the cool breeze, hang wet laundry, clean a pigeon pen, or whether they are using the roof as a watchtower to identify the movements of the Israeli military. Both the civilian and the structure's function are determined by the military gaze, while the gaze is informed by a series of biases that shape the soldier's judgement. The conclusions the soldier reaches determine how the soldier will act.[41] Perugini and I have already shown how black and brown women and children trapped in war zones are much more likely to be perceived as human shields than their white counterparts who, even in similar situations, continue to be recognised as civilians.[42] The racialisation of civilians alters both how they are 'seen' and the value ascribed to them, and in the context of war can readily lead to their signification as shields which decreases the protections the law bestows on them.

While I cannot discuss the scholarly literature that analyses the embedded racial biases shaping surveillance technologies or the impact of pervasive social norms and racial biases on the way people see,[43] it is important to stress here that the processes of racialisation that inform the military gaze and help shape the perceived function of civilians within war zones are also pertinent to civilian structures. To be sure, the structures' racialisation is linked to the racialisation of the people with whom the viewer associates it, but ultimately the structure itself is ascribed a race that helps shape the value assigned to it and the way its function is perceived and signified. Moreover, the power to signify and to reinforce and circulate that which has been signified is unequal, with hi-tech states having considerable advantages. Ultimately, signification, in our case by the coloniser, helps determine the protections allotted to civilian structures.

The notion that space and the structures within it are racialised is not new to scholars of Israel/Palestine or to scholars of settler colonialism more generally, since inanimate structures are also subsumed under what Patrick Wolfe has called the 'organizing grammar of race'.[44] And indeed, a plethora of studies have shown that one of the prime objectives of every Israeli government since Israel's establishment in 1948 has been to Judaise the space it controls.[45] In reality, this meant the destruction of Palestinian space and its reproduction as Jewish.

During and after the 1948 war, for example, Zionist forces destroyed about five hundred Palestinian villages and most of their inhabitants were either expelled or fled across international borders, becoming refugees in neighbouring countries. In total, about 750,000 Palestinians were displaced in what Fayez Sayegh has called 'racial elimination'.[46] In an effort to Judaise the space that became Israel, 350 of the 370 new Jewish settlements established soon after 1948 were built on or in proximity to the 500 Palestinian villages that had been destroyed.[47] Ultimately, most Palestinian built-up space was destroyed and then reproduced as Jewish by planting forests, building kibbutzim, moshavim and so on.[48] Once both the land and structures upon it are considered Jewish, then Palestinians who enter this space can be cast as 'invaders'.[49] Elsewhere, Yinon Cohen and I have characterised these 'invaders' as biocriminals, since they become criminals simply due to the mismatch between the race ascribed to them – Palestinian – and the race ascribed to the space they occupy: Jewish.[50] All of this is crucial background for understanding that Israel thinks of space and structures in racial terms, which helps, in turn, to make sense of how the military perceives civilian structures in the Gaza Strip and its drive to completely or almost completely destroy Palestinian space.

Before providing an example of how structures in Gaza are racialised, it is important to emphasise that among the characteristics attributed to 'backward races' is their supposed inability to sustain the primary legal distinction between civilian and military objects and their inclination to adopt forms of perfidy.[51] These were the major claims levelled by fascist Italians against Ethiopians in the 1930s and Americans against the Vietnamese in the 1960s and 1970s, and they are now a central claim that Israelis level against Palestinians.[52] But Israel's claim is not only made about people but also structures.

Consider, for instance, the following assertion made by Israel's Ministry of Foreign Affairs. The ministry's spokesperson has maintained that 'the mere fact that seeming "civilians" or "civilian objects" have been targeted' does not mean 'that an attack was unlawful'.[53] The term 'seeming' is, of course, key here. The subtext is that Palestinian perfidy is all-pervasive and that the function of civilians and civilian objects – that the spokesperson puts in scare quotes – is not what it seems: namely, they are routinely used as shields or serve other military purposes. The argument is that Palestinian homes might *seem* to be homes, hospitals might *seem* to be hospitals, mosques might *seem* to be mosques, schools might *seem* to be schools, but Israel's military gaze reveals that in Gaza they are not what they seem because they have taken on a military function. Instead, the military gaze reveals that each home is actually a hideout, hospitals serve as arms depots, mosques conceal tunnel piers, and schools shield rocket launch platforms.[54]

To be sure, there may have been cases when civilians and civilian objects have been used in Gaza for military purposes, but Israel has used these cases to indict hundreds of thousands of civilian structures. Israel's accusations operate exactly like conspiracy theories that include a kernel of truth but advance inflated and bogus claims. The point here is that while the signification 'school shield' is circulated by the spokesperson, it is produced by the military gaze which, in turn, is informed by the interaction between an assemblage of surveillance apparatuses and racial biases. Not unlike civilians who are perceived as civilians when they are located near an Israeli military base in Tel Aviv but as human shields when they are located near a Hamas command post in Gaza, civilian structures are more likely to be cast as 'shielding structures' due to their prior racialisation as Palestinian structures.

The interplay between racialisation, the military gaze and the function the gaze identifies has led to the indictment of most school buildings in the Gaza Strip, casting at least 477 of 564, or 85 percent as legitimate targets.[55] Put differently, one cannot sever the ease with which Israel indicts so many schools as shielding structures from the way Palestinian space and buildings have been racialised and attributed a lesser value than that accorded to white or Jewish schools. Given that for many of those within the corridors of Israeli power the objective of this genocidal war is to destroy the Gaza Strip and regenerate it or parts of it as Jewish, killing and displacing Palestinians is not enough: the military must destroy and then reproduce the space and this necessitates the mass indictment and destruction of civilian structures.[56]

Mass killing and mass destruction

Since October 7, Israel has indicted most if not all hospitals, schools, universities, mosques, government and media structures and apartment buildings in Gaza, claiming that they function as shields. The sheer scale of the shielding accusation, whereby a whole area and every civilian and civilian structure within it is defined as a shield or potential shield, is unprecedented and has become part of the toolkit used by Israel to destroy the Gaza Strip and even erase it from the map.[57] I mentioned earlier that historically, the shielding accusation was limited, with warring parties charging specific people, groups or structures of being used as shields for a circumscribed period. However, since the War on Terror was launched over two decades ago, we have witnessed a pivotal shift.

In our book, *Human Shields,* Perugini and I identified the 2008–09 Sri Lankan Civil War as one of the key moments when this shift took place. We showed how prominent legal scholars framed tens of thousands of civilians as human shields being used by the militant group Tamil Tigers in order to justify the massacres carried out by Sri Lankan government forces.[58] During the 2016 war against ISIS in Mosul, the Iraqi coalition, United Nations agencies and even Amnesty International characterised 100,000 civilians trapped in proximity to the fighting as human shields.[59] These instances demonstrate that as part of the War on Terror, non-white civilians trapped near non-state fighters in war zones as well as the civilian structures surrounding them have become more and more likely to be framed as shields. Israel's ongoing war on Gaza has accelerated and broadened these dynamics and this trend.

Because Hamas has built what are believed to be hundreds of kilometres of underground tunnels beneath Gaza as part of its guerrilla tactics, the Israeli legal team has invoked international law to claim that all civilian objects – and every single civilian – situated on Gaza's land surface are potential human shields and thus are not immune from attack. Gaza's entire population and all its civilian structures can be framed as shields because they exist above the tunnels and their mere proximity seemingly serves as a shield. Significantly, proximate shielding plays a vital role in Israel's genocidal drive since these kinds of shields involve no agency. Their functionality as shields does not entail any act on the part of civilians or even on the part of Palestinian fighters, since they can be indicted simply due to their ostensible proximity to tunnels or fighters. And since Palestinian civilians and civilian infrastructures become shields due to their location above the tunnels or near fighters rather than an action they or Palestinian fighters carry out, they can be characterised as shields for as long as the fighting persists.

Indeed, this was the logic from the very beginning of Israel's onslaught. One week after its war on Gaza began, Israel ordered 1.1 million Palestinians in northern Gaza – about half of the enclave's population – to leave their homes. According to international humanitarian law, parties to an armed conflict cannot deport or forcibly transfer the civilian population of an occupied territory unless 'the security of the civilians involved or imperative military reasons so demand'.[60] In this case, Israel claimed that it was removing Palestinian civilians from their homes as a humanitarian precaution that would protect them from the epicentre of violence (namely, Israeli bombings). In effect, however, Israel transformed this humanitarian norm into a tool of mass expulsion. But more relevant to the argument presented here, Israel also used a similar strategy to undermine the legal protection of those Palestinians who were unable or unwilling to leave their homes as well as of all civilian structures in northern Gaza. Israel is legally required to treat such people, who numbered in the hundreds of thousands – alongside all civilian structures – as protected. But since it had dropped leaflets instructing people to evacuate, Israel claimed that it could designate all of northern Gaza as a legitimate military target, and that the Palestinian civilians who remained were putting themselves in the line of fire. When Israel launched its attack on the area a few days later, killing thousands of civilians, the military cast the civilians who remained in the north as either terrorist accomplices or human shields, and the civilian structures that were destroyed as shielding structures. The decision to stay at home and not be expelled like their parents and grandparents had been in 1948 is what transformed Palestinian civilians into shields.

Crucially, voluntary and involuntary human shielding are very different from proximate shielding, since these two kinds of shields are tied to an action that dramatically circumscribes the number of shields, the space they occupy, and length of time they can be deployed as shields.[61] The unprecedented nature of the proximate shielding charge would appear to strain credulity. However, as a US ally fighting non-white, non-state actors, Israel has found Western politicians and international press very amenable to the narrative that 'savage' Palestinian militants are using their own civilians and civilian structures as fodder. While Perugini and I have documented the particular ways in which the operations of IHL are problematic in and of themselves, it is hardly likely that Israel's legal justifications would have carried any weight had the victims been white Ukrainians. Indeed, large segments within the international political elite seem to believe Israel because they share similar racial biases.

In an article for *Jewish Currents*, Perugini and I argued that Israel's unprecedented broadening of the human shielding charge is now being applied to justify genocidal violence, including mass expulsions and killings.[62] Israel's wholesale indictment of civilians and civilian structures as shields is not being used to defeat the Palestinians but to destroy them. The stakes could not be higher.

Israel is aware that legal work is interpretive work, and that the laws of war are always open to interpretation and can be used both to justify the need to continuously protect humans and nonhumans by highlighting their vulnerability, or alternatively, to render them legitimate military targets. Tellingly, Israel's legal defence team at the International Court of Justice put the shielding idea front and centre. In his opening statement, the attorney representing Israel noted that Gaza's civilian infrastructure is actually 'the most sophisticated terrorist stronghold in the history of urban warfare', and argued that Hamas, not Israel, was responsible for the destruction of Gaza.[63] The Israeli legal team returned to these arguments again and again, marking the first time in history that shielding provisions have been used to carve out a justification for a colonial war of elimination. Indeed, if the international legal apparatus can be used to justify acts that can destroy a people, 'in whole or in part', then the rules-based order created in the aftermath of World War II to regulate war according to humanitarian principles becomes a tool for its own undoing. Israel's mobilisation of legal instruments created to guarantee

'Never Again' are now being used to legitimise a genocide.

I would like to thank Sandra Noeth and Lucia Ruprecht for inviting me to participate in the Body/Concepts seminar at HZT and FU Berlin where I first presented the ideas informing this article. I would also like to thank Eva Nanopoulos, Nicola Perugini, Rahul Rao and Catherine Rottenberg for comments on an earlier draft.

Neve Gordon is Professor of International Law and Human Rights at Queen Mary University of London.

Notes

1. ICRC, 'Rule 97. The use of human shields is prohibited,' accessed 29 November 2024, https://ihl-databases.icrc.org/en/customary-ihl/v1/Rule97. The prohibition of the use of human shields appears in 1949 Geneva Convention III, art. 23; 1949 Geneva Convention IV, arts. 28 and 49; 1977 Additional Protocol I, arts. 51(7) and 58; 1977 Additional Protocol II, arts. 5(2)(c) and 13.
2. Yoram Dinstein, *The Conduct of Hostilities under the Law of International Armed Conflict* (Cambridge, UK: Cambridge University Press, 2004).
3. Neve Gordon and Nicola Perugini, *Human Shields: A History of People in the Line of Fire* (Oakland, CA: University of California Press, 2020).
4. Neve Gordon and Nicola Perugini, 'The politics of human shielding: On the resignification of space and the constitution of civilians as shields in liberal wars', *Environment and Planning D: Society and Space* 34:1 (2016), 168–187.
5. Israel Defense Forces, 'Hamas Protects its Weapons with Human Shields', accessed 3 December 2024, https://x.com/IDF/status/490476864494788608.
6. Banu Bargu, 'Human shields', *Contemporary Political Theory* 12:4 (2013), 277–295.
7. Bargu, 'Human shields'; Judith Butler, 'Human shields', *London Review of International Law* 3:2 (2015), 223–243; Gordon and Perugini, 'The politics of human shielding'.
8. Antony Anghie, *Imperialism, Sovereignty and the Making of International Law* (Cambridge: Cambridge University Press, 2007); Anne Orford, ed., *International Law and Its Others* (Cambridge: Cambridge University Press, 2006); Frédéric Mégret, 'From "savages" to "unlawful combatants": a postcolonial look at international humanitarian law's "other"', in *International Law and Its Others*, ed. Anne Orford (Cambridge: Cambridge University Press, 2006).
9. Neve Gordon and Nicola Perugini, 'Human Shields, Sovereign Power, and the Evisceration of the Civilian', *AJIL Unbound* 110 (2016): 329–334.
10. To the best of my knowledge the first scholars to discuss the notion of proximate shields were W. Matthew Ezzo and Amos N. Guiora, 'A Critical Decision Point on the Battlefield – Friend, Foe, or Innocent Bystander', in *Security: A Multidisciplinary Normative Approach*, ed. Cecilia M. Bailliet (Leiden: Brill, 2009), 91–116.
11. Helen Kinsella, *The Image before the Weapon: A Critical History of the Distinction between Combatant and Civilian* (Ithaca, NY: Cornell University Press, 2017).
12. Gordon and Perugini, *Human Shields*; Nicola Perugini, 'Decolonising the Civilian in Third World National Liberation Wars', *Millennium* 52:2 (2024), 252–278.
13. Bargu, 'Human shields'.
14. Neve Gordon and Nicola Perugini in conversation with Ayça Çubukçu, Noura Erakat and John Reynolds, 'Human Shields and the Location of Agency', accessed 30 November 2024, https://twailr.com/wp-content/uploads/2021/02/TWAILR-Dialogue-Human-Shields-Gordon-Perugini-with-Cubukcu-Erakat-Reynolds.pdf.
15. Gordon and Perugini, *Human Shields*.
16. Colonial wars were also characterised by fighting between state and non-state actors, but prior to decolonisation states parties did not consider the laws of armed conflict applicable to those conflicts. Anghie, *Imperialism, Sovereignty and the Making of International Law*.
17. Helen Kinsella, 'Gender and Human Shielding', *AJIL Unbound* 110 (2016): 305–310.
18. Al Jazeera Arabic, 'Al Jazeera exclusive photos show the occupation using Palestinian prisoners as human shields', 30 June 2024.
19. Yaniv Kubovich and Michael Hauser Tov, 'Israeli Army Uses Palestinian Civilians to Inspect Potentially Booby-trapped Tunnels in Gaza', *Ha'aretz*, 13 August 2024, https://www.haaretz.com/israel-news/2024-08-13/ty-article-magazine/.premium/idf-uses-gazan-civilians-as-human-shields-to-inspect-potentially-booby-trapped-tunnels/00000191-4c84-d7fd-a7f5-7db6b99e0000.
20. Ibid.
21. 1977 Additional Protocol I, Article 39.
22. Aimé Césaire, *Discourse on Colonialism* (New York: NYU Press, 2000).
23. Paulo Freire, *Pedagogy of the Oppressed* (London: Routledge, 2020), 57.
24. Emanuel Fabian, 'Defense minister announces "complete siege" of Gaza: No power, food or fuel', *The Times of Israel*, 9 October 2023, https://www.timesofisrael.com/liveblog_entry/defense-minister-announces-complete-siege-of-gaza-no-power-food-or-fuel/.
25. Alexander Weheliye, *Habeas Viscus: Racializing Assemblages, Biopolitics, and Black Feminist Theories of the*

Human (Durham: Duke University Press, 2020), 5, 73; Ronit Lentin, *Traces of Racial Exception: Racializing Israeli Settler Colonialism* (London: Bloomsbury Books, 2018).

26. ICRC, 'Human Shields', accessed 30 November 2024, https://casebook.icrc.org/a_to_z/glossary/human-shields.

27. Neve Gordon and Nicola Perugini, '"Hospital Shields" and the Limits of International Law', *European Journal of International Law* 30:2 (2019), 439–463; Nicola Perugini and Neve Gordon, 'Medical Lawfare: The Nakba and Israel's Attacks on Palestinian Healthcare', *Journal of Palestine Studies* 53:1 (2024), 68–91.

28. 1977 Additional Protocol I largely distinguishes provisions relating to attacks upon persons from provisions relating to attacks upon objects. Articles 50 and 51 define and prohibit attacks upon 'civilians' and the 'civilian population'. Article 52(2) specifies which objects are 'military objectives'.

29. British Institute of International and Comparative Law, *Protecting Education in Insecurity and Armed Conflict An International Law Handbook Second Edition*, accessed 30 November 2024, https://www.biicl.org/documents/10245_peic_summary_2nd_edn.pdf, 32–33.

30. 1977 Additional Protocol Protocol I Article 52.

31. In addition to the regular protections, IHL provides special protections to medical units, vehicles, and other transport (AP I Arts. 12, 21; AP II Art. 11; Rules 28 and 29 of the customary IHL study); cultural objects and places of worship (AP I Art. 53, AP II Art. 16, and Rules 38–41); protection of objects indispensable to the survival of the civilian population (AP I Art. 54, AP II Art. 14, Rule 54); and natural environment (AP I Art. 55, Rules 43–45).

32. Henry Shue and David Wippman, 'Limiting Attacks on Dual-Use Facilities Performing Indispensable Civilian Functions', *Cornell International Law Journal* 35: 3 (Winter 2002), 559–580. The authors note that Protocol I does not use the term 'dual-use' or refer explicitly to dual purpose facilities or objects. However, the definition of military objective in the first part of Article 52(2) can be read to classify every dual-use facility as a potential military objective.

33. Gordon and Perugini, '"Hospital Shields"'.

34. Article 52(2) of Additional Protocol I of the Geneva Conventions reads as follows: 'Attacks shall be limited strictly to military objectives. In so far as objects are concerned, military objectives are limited to those objects which by their nature, location, purpose or use make an effective contribution to military action and whose total or partial destruction, capture or neutralization, in the circumstances ruling at the time, offers a definite military advantage'. Shue and Wippman, 'Limiting Attacks on Dual-Use Facilities', 562.

35. Stephen Graham, *Cities Under Siege: The New Military Urbanism* (London: Verso, 2011); Cécile Fabre, *Cosmopolitan War* (Oxford: Oxford University Press, 2012).

36. Michael N. Schmitt, 'Targeting and International Humanitarian Law in Afghanistan', *Israel Yearbook on Human Rights* 39 (2009), 99–132.

37. Antoine Bousquet, *The Eye of War: Military Perception from the Telescope to the Drone* (Minneapolis: University of Minnesota Press, 2018). During the 2021 war on Gaza and much more so following 7 October 2024, Israel's miliary gaze has also included machine learning algorithms that have identified thousands of targets. Yuval Abraham, '"A mass assassination factory": Inside Israel's calculated bombing of Gaza', *+972 Magazine*, 30 November 2023, https://www.972mag.com/mass-assassination-factory-israel-calculated-bombing-gaza/; Yuval Abraham, '"Lavender": The AI Machine Directing Israel's Bombing Spree in Gaza', *+972 Magazine*, 3 April 2024, https://www.972mag.com/lavender-ai-israeli-army-gaza/.

38. Daniele Palumbo, Abdelrahman Abutaleb, Paul Cusiac and Erwan Rivault, 'At least half of Gaza's buildings damaged or destroyed, new analysis shows', *BBC*, 30 January 2024, https://www.bbc.com/news/world-middle-east-68006607.

39. Al Jazeera, 'Israel's war on Gaza', accessed 15 December 2024, https://interactive.aljazeera.com/aje/2024/gaza-before-after-satellite-images/?utm_source=aljazeera.com&utm_medium=website&utm_campaign=ucms.

40. To be sure, there is ample criticism of the humanist and human rights traditions. For the former see Ayça Çubukçu, 'Thinking against humanity', *London Review of International Law* 5:2 (2017), 251–267; and for the latter see Jessica Whyte, *The Morals of the Market: Human Rights and the Rise of Neoliberalism* (London: Verso Books, 2019).

41. Complex surveillance and identification technologies have increasingly been adopted for gathering data about warring parties from mobile phones, emails, and social media, while also using satellite images, heat-seeking sensors, electronic signal detectors, thermal imaging, GPS, GIS, aerial photos and videos, and acoustic vector systems. To be sure, the function of these technologies is to alter ways of 'seeing' so as to expand what militaries can observe, but no less important from the perspective of this article is that dominant social norms have been coded into these surveillance technologies and shape the way militaries see. Louise Amoore, 'Cloud geographies: Computing, data, sovereignty', *Progress in Human Geography* 42:1 (2018), 4–24.

42. Gordon and Perugini, *Human Shields*, 185–190.

43. Saher Selod, *Forever Suspect: Racialized Surveillance of Muslim Americans in the War on Terror* (New Brunswick, NJ: Rutgers University Press, 2018); Safiya Umoja Noble,

Algorithms of Oppression: How Search Engines Reinforce Racism (New York: New York University Press, 2018); Ruha Benjamin, *Race After Technology: Abolitionist Tools for the New Jim Code* (New York: John Wiley & Sons, 2019).

44. Patrick Wolfe, 'Settler Colonialism and the Elimination of the Native', *Journal of Genocide Research* 8:4 (2006), 387–409.

45. Nadia Abu El-Haj, *Facts on the Ground: Archaeological Practice and Territorial Self-Fashioning in Israeli Society* (Chicago: University of Chicago Press, 2008); Ghazi-Walid Falah, 'Dynamics and patterns of the shrinking of Arab Lands in Palestine', *Political Geography* 22:2 (2003), 179–209; Rassem Khamaisi, 'Mechanism of Land Control and Territorial Judaization of Israel', in *In the Name of Security*, eds. Majid Al-Haj and Uri Ben-Eliezer (Haifa: Haifa University Press, 2003), 421–49; Geremy Forman and Alexandre Kedar, 'From Arab Land to "Israel Lands": The Legal Dispossession of the Palestinians Displaced by Israel in the Wake of 1948', *Environment and Planning D: Society and Space* 22:6 (2004), 809–30; David Sibley, 'Survey 13: Purification of Space', *Environment and Planning D: Society and Space* 6: 4 (1988): 409–21; Naama Blatman-Thomas, 'Commuting for rights: Circular mobilities and regional identities of Palestinians in a Jewish-Israeli town', *Geoforum* 78 (2017), 22–32.

46. Fayez A. Sayegh, *Zionist Colonialism in Palestine* (Beirut: Palestine Liberation Organization Research Center, 1965).

47. Alexander Kedar and Oren Yiftachel, 'Land Regime and Social Relations in Israel', in *Realizing Property Rights*, eds. Hernando de Soto and Francis Cheneval (Zurich: Rüffer and Rub, 2006), 129–46.

48. Mori Ram, 'White But Not Quite: Normalizing Colonial Conquests through Spatial Mimicry', *Antipode* 46:3 (2014), 736–753.

49. Nicola Perugini and Neve Gordon, *The Human Right to Dominate* (Oxford: Oxford University Press, 2015).

50. Yinon Cohen and Neve Gordon, 'Israel's Biospatial Politics: Territory, Demography, and Effective Control', *Public Culture* 30:2 (2018), 199–220.

51. Nicola Perugini and Neve Gordon, 'Between Sovereignty and Race: The Bombardment of Hospitals in the Italo-Ethiopian War and the Colonial Imprint of International Law', *State Crime Journal* 8:1 (2019), 104–125.

52. Gordon and Perugini, *Human Shields*.

53. Israel Ministry of Foreign Affairs, 'Hamas-Israel Conflict 2023: Key Legal Aspects', 2 November 2023, https://www.gov.il/en/pages/hamas-israel-conflict2023-key-legal-aspects.

54. Nicola Perugini and Neve Gordon, 'A Legal Justification of Genocide', *Jewish Currents*, 17 July 2024, https://jewishcurrents.org/human-shields-gaza-israel-a-legal-justification-for-genocide.

55. Barbara Plett Usher and Thomas Mackintosh, 'Israeli strike in Gaza kills more than 70, hospital head says', *BBC*, 10 August 2024, https://www.bbc.co.uk/news/articles/c8erk37yn2no.

56. On the social reproduction of space see Henri Lefebvre, *The Production of Space* (Oxford: Basil Backwell, 1991).

57. Israeli politicians who recently voiced such a wish are echoing the desire of Israeli leaders ever since 1967. In the months following the 1967 war, Israel contemplated plans to transfer Gaza's population to Al-Arish, to the West Bank, to Iraq, and to several countries in Latin America. Hadeel Assali, 'Diary: Palestinians in Paraguay', *London Review of Books* 45:10 (18 May 2023), https://www.lrb.co.uk/the-paper/v45/n10/hadeel-assali/diary. Prime Minister Levi Eshkol was clear: 'I want them all to go, even if they go to the moon'. Tom Segev, *1967: Israel, the War, and the Year That Transformed the Middle East*, trans. Jessica Cohen (New York: Metropolitan Books, 2007), 534. And in 1992, Prime Minister Yitzhak Rabin asserted: 'I wish I could wake up one day and find that Gaza has sunk into the sea'. 'Will Rabin's Dream of Gaza Being Swallowed by the Sea Come True?' *Middle East Monitor*, 21 September 2015, https://www.middleeastmonitor.com/20150921-will-rabins-dream-of-gaza-being-swallowed-by-the-sea-come-true/.

58. Neve Gordon and Nicola Perugini, 'Human Shields and Proportionality: How Legal Experts Defended War Crimes in Sri Lanka', *Just Security*, 12 November 2020, https://www.justsecurity.org/73079/human-shields-and-proportionality-how-legal-experts-defended-war-crimes-in-sri-lanka/.

59. Amnesty International, *At Any Cost: The Civilian Catastrophe in West Mosul, Iraq* (London: Amnesty International, 2017).

60. 1949 Geneva Convention IV, Article 49.

61. Gordon et al, 'Human Shields and the Location of Agency'.

62. Perugini and Gordon, 'A Legal Justification of Genocide'.

63. President Donoghue presiding, in the case concerning Application of the Convention on the Prevention and Punishment of the Crime of Genocide in the Gaza Strip (South Africa v. Israel), 12 January 2024, accessed 2 December 2024, https://www.icj-cij.org/sites/default/files/case-related/192/192-20240112-ora-01-00-bi.pdf.

Terrestrial uprisings and living alliances

Non-human resistance to work and its challenge to the models of social critique

Paul Guillibert

Critical animal studies literature has placed a growing emphasis on animals' resistance to capitalist domination.[1] This tendency reflects a renewed understanding of the logic of capitalism conceived through the lens of capital accumulation, achieved thanks to the exploitation of human labour (whether free, forced or waged) as well as the primitive capture of natural forces. Jason W. Moore and Alyssa Battistoni, for example, describe capitalism as a system that 'puts nature to work', that is, an economic system that reconfigures various metabolic and environmental relationships with the purpose of producing value.[2] This idea also applies to the ecological systems of colonial plantations and contemporary industrial agriculture. In all these cases, animal resistance no longer figures as an abstract reaction against the impersonal domination of a machine-like subject, but as a form of concrete opposition to capitalists' attempts to put nature to work for profit. The study of non-human resistance to work thus offers an alternative to the frequent appeals to an abstract and unsupported ideal of 'interspecies justice.'[3]

In this way, environmental politics can extend the emancipatory socialist project of abolishing exploitation to non-human workers. However, often the manner in which this abolitionist project is presented seems contradictory: on the one hand, it is presented as an attempt to abolish all *animal* labour and the specifically speciesist modes of domination and heteronomy that underpin it; on the other hand, it involves a refusal of all *capitalist* labour, thereby framing the exploitation, even the alienation, of non-humans as being the result of a broader system of private property geared towards the accumulation of capital.

In this article, I will examine the philosophical assumptions that underlie these two ways of thinking about the abolition of work. I will show that part of the environmental literature has inherited a tension specific to Marxist thought, derived from its conception of anthropological difference.[4] I will then suggest that the usefulness of the category of work for non-human beings is, in the first place, that it serves to underscore living beings' intrinsic capacity for resistance whenever they are subjected to a regime of work. I will conclude by showing that the stakes of this question are twofold: on the one hand, the notion of work or labour implies a definition of the fundamental differences between human and non-human beings; on the other, the activity of non-human beings calls for a rethinking of the very concept of work.[5]

Resistance to work by non-human workers

Two positions stand out within the environmental literature on animal labour. The first position consists in extending the category of labour to some non-humans in order to denounce the exploitation of nature via the categories of the critique of political economy.[6] The second position, by contrast, involves a rejection of this extension because it erodes the anthropological distinction between human labour and animal activity. In this sense, 'the essence of man' would reside in the difference between work that generates value and activities regarded as 'free gifts of nature.'[7] The study of animal resistance offers a new way of addressing this problem.

Resistance to work stems from the capacity of human workers to stop deploying their physical, psychological and cognitive capacities to carry out technical activities that create new realities in the service of those who control production. Any resistance to, or refusal of, work proves that all labour activity presupposes a capacity for self-discipline or self-constraint, one which guarantees the consent of workers – however provisionally or reluctantly – to being put to work. In short, any individual who resists work demonstrates their nature as a worker. Therefore, the argument goes, if one can show that certain non-human animals resist work, one will have demonstrated that some animals do work, without undertaking a general and abstract account of anthropological difference.

Behavioural ethology has provided multiple evidence of such non-human resistance to work. A well-known case can be found in Jocelyne Porcher and Typhaine Schmitt's article, 'Do Cows Collaborate at Work? A Sociological Question.'[8] The authors studied the relationship between cows and the milking machine in a mid-altitude dairy farm which kept 60 cows on zero-grazing. The farmer had established a set of rules that were followed by most of the cows. However, a few cows resisted by physically avoiding the farmer, hiding in a barn where they couldn't be milked, or, in another show of refusal, by walking extremely slowly until the farmer shouted at them. 'The implicit rules imposed by Christian [the farmer] are all known to the cows, but they sometimes still try to resist them.'[9] On the farm, there was no procedure for getting the cows to the milking machine: the animals had to manage this by themselves in the waiting area. Porcher and Schmitt show that this sort of self-adjustment was not based on any conditioning or hierarchy, but consisted of arrangements organised amongst the cows themselves. Against this, some rebellious cows would block the machine and stop it working completely; they would start it up again as soon as the farmer came back to the cowshed. The others were instead keen to ensure that the process ran smoothly. As in the case of a factory horse, the problem with cows is that they are independent creatures. This is what the designers of milking machines are trying to control by turning the cows' natural strength into a natural resource. Porcher and Schmitt conclude their article by claiming that agricultural engineers and machine designers are in fact 'seeking to prevent the cows from working.'[10] By reducing living beings to an object of labour rather than to their labour power or force, they limit their autonomy and thus also their capacities for resistance. Indeed, an animal's capacity to resist implies its ability to move freely and to cooperate with individuals of the same species. The transformation of living beings into machines that naturally produce commodities involves a reduction of their autonomy via various forms of technological control. Limited in their movement and in their relationships to each other, the capacity of certain animals to resist can thereby be reduced considerably.

Porcher explicitly refers to Marx's *Economic and Philosophical Manuscripts* of 1844 as a source of inspiration for her theory of animal labour. For her, the definition of work outlined in the *Manuscripts* represents an 'emancipatory relationship with nature, a transformative action on the world.'[11] Porcher interprets resistance to work as a struggle against alienation in favour of a freer type of collaborative work between humans and non-humans. Two lessons can be drawn from Porcher's work. On the one hand, there is no doubt that animals engage in work as part of human production. An obvious sign of this animal labour is animals' capacity for resistance, their refusal of work, something amply illustrated in Porcher's research. It should be pointed out that, unlike figures such as the philosopher Kendra Coulter, Porcher rejects the notion that wild animals engage in actual work or labour.[12] Work for Porcher presupposes a social division of labour, a separation between functions and of the people who carry these out. On the other hand, she views such resistance to work purely in terms of a struggle against certain forms of work performed by domesticated livestock. It is not therefore a matter of refusal of work as such, but of resistance to capitalist domination within the context of industrial agriculture. Many activists and researchers have criticised her for this reduction and not drawing what they see as the right political lessons from her framing of breeding practices as forms of domination. To be consistent, these critics argue, one should oppose not only all livestock farming but all forms of animal labour that are based on domination and thus relations of constraint and heteronomy. Such resistance should instead be viewed as the sign of a more radical rejection of work. What explains this difference in interpretation?

Dairy cattle going to milking. Royal Veterinary College. Source: Wellcome Collection.

Among the wide array of accounts of animal resistance three main models for critiquing eco-social pathologies stand out: a critique of *alienation* within the framework of a sociology of work extended to animals; a critique of the *exploitation* of nature within the framework of a Marxist political ecology; and a critique of the *domination* of animals within the framework of moral anti-speciesism. Each of these three models of social critique rests on a different definition of work.

Animal alienation and human-animal collaboration

The critique of animal labour as a form of alienation is founded on an understanding of traditional livestock farming in which domestication is considered a type of collaborative work between humans and non-humans. Porcher formulates such a general definition of work on the basis of Marx's anthropology. The purpose behind the anthropological definition of labour formulated in the 1844 *Manuscripts* had been to make it possible to both criticise alienated labour and defend the centrality of labour as an aspect of all human production and praxis.

In one of the best-known passages of his *Economic and Philosophical Manuscripts*, Marx defines the human being in terms of his 'species-being', that is, as a being that is determined via its transformation of nature by labour. But how does this sort of activity differ from the building of a hive by bees or that of a dam by beavers? Indeed, Marx explicitly notes in the same passage that 'animals also produce.'[13] Although he does not employ the category of 'labour' (he reserves this for alienated labour in the preceding paragraph and for the activity of species-being in the next paragraph), Marx here allows for a non-human type of 'production.' Production, in this general sense, can be grasped as the transformation of natural matter into an object adapted to the satisfaction of the vital needs of a particular species. A swarm of bees needs a hive to shelter its larvae and produce honey just as the human reproductive unit needs a habitat in which to carry out productive and reproductive tasks.

25

Marx, however, then moves to a series of differences between human and animal needs. Animal production is 'one-sided', necessary and driven by instinct. Its products are immediately incorporated into the organism or used for the survival of the species. Human labour by contrast is universal, free from immediate physical needs. Capable of reproducing the whole of nature, humans fashion objects that are not consumed straightaway and that are tailored to the needs of the species. Finally, humans also make things in accordance with the laws of beauty. This text's philosophical goal is not to delimit the specificity of non-human activities, but rather to identify the essence of human life and production. More precisely, it is to draw out a critique of alienation out of an anthropological theory of labour and a definition of species-being. In the chapter on the labour process in *Capital*, Marx develops a close analysis, albeit with a different bestiary. The project was different, however, since what was at stake was not so much to demonstrate the universality of human labour, as to emphasise its intentional dimension.

The activity of species-being consists in actualising its potentialities in a relationship to nature characterised by the transformation of natural matter. Labour or work is thus the activity through which unity with nature is maintained via a continuous process of interaction between an 'organic' and an 'inorganic body.'[14] The dispossession of the instruments and products of labour within alienated work thus brings about a separation from natural conditions that prevents humans from realising their natural objectivity. Deprived of the natural conditions of production and of the objective products of their labour, workers become pure subjects shorn of all objectivity, that is, robbed of their objective relationship to other living beings.

In this text, the essence to human [*le propre de l'homme*] is the achievement of species-being by means of work, that is, through the conscious modification of his environment as a species. The human being is species-being not just because he participates in the 'practical engendering of an objective world', but because, in doing so, he becomes conscious of being a member of a genus which transforms nature. The objects with which he is in relation, those of which he can have a sensible intuition, are already, or are potentially, the objects of a human transformation. The world of human experience is a world of objects. It is through contact with these objects that man can experience his species-being, knowing that is he a member of the genus that produces or reproduces them. Thus, a woodcutter from the national forestry department will recognise in the arrangement of trees a form of organised activity undertaken since Colbert's 1669 decree on 'the proper use of forests'. This is the mark of his shared belonging to a human race which is aware of its capacity to produce and plan.[15] In other words, although in this text non-human beings are said to produce, this production for Marx remains is oriented solely at satisfying immediate physical needs and the reproduction of the species, whereas human work satisfies the universality of needs. That is, human beings seek to fulfil needs that are universal and through work grasp their universal, that is, species-wide, character. It would be astonishing if in the Marxian text – including that of 1844 – the universality referred to the idea of needs that would be the same everywhere and always. How, then, are we to understand the universality of needs? Firstly, it implies that the satisfaction of needs always presupposes a set of social activities involving exchange, cooperation and organisation. Needs are therefore universal in a first sense: the individual act of satisfying needs always presupposes the human community within which this act unfolds. There is no satisfaction of needs without a social organisation of the labour process. But the universality of needs also points to a second dimension of human action: humankind is potentially in relation with the nature as a whole. As Marx puts it, the whole nature is an immediate mean of subsistence and a spiritual condition of his intellectual life. Human relationships with each other and with the world are always redoubled at the level of consciousness or ideality, captured in the element of thought. It is the consciousness of need and the social nature of its satisfaction that implies the idea of universality, i.e. of what can be grasped in thought by any mind, insofar as the structure of need is itself social.

Marx's 1844 text remains difficult to interpret because it employs a homogenous conception of the animal as a criterium for distinguishing the human, determining human's nature negatively. Yet there is something of an unresolved gap between Marx's bestiary of social animals – such as beavers, bees and ants, which impose significant transformations on their environment – and Marx's definition of animal production centred on individual and specific needs. The characteristics Marx attributes to non-human labour are only the remainder of a negation – or rather deprivation – of those he attributes to human labour. Rather than a gradualist theory of anthropological difference or a synthetic theory of the variation between the different modes of existence of living beings, Marx proposes a negative deduction of the properties of animal production from human production. Here, the function of animality is therefore to establish an anthropological difference and set up a critique of alienation on the basis of a distinction between 'species-being' and 'species life'.

> The animal is immediately one with its life activity. It does not distinguish itself from it. It is its life activity. Man makes his life activity itself the object of his will and of his consciousness. He has conscious life activity. It is not a determination with which he directly merges. Conscious life activity distinguishes man immediately from animal life activity. It is just because of his that he is a species-being [*Gattungswesen*].[16]

It is therefore through consciousness that humanity forms its relationship to the world, that is to say through the mediation of work which involves consciousness, that its 'species-being' is distinguished from the 'life activity' of animals.

Nevertheless, researchers in animal studies have extended this critique of human alienation to animals themselves. Barbara Noske for instance has shown that the fundamental aspects of alienation can be found within modern livestock farming. According to Noske, under the conditions of capitalist production, animals are (a) alienated from their own bodies and their offspring, (b) from their bodily functions, (c) from the wider community of their species, as well as from potential relations with humans and their natural environment, and (d) from their own species-being. For example, in industrial production, milk represents a sort of foreign and hostile force that completely dominates a cow's life.[17] Forced to produce as much milk as possible, the cow is subjected to a single-grain feed, growth hormones, milking machines and frequent rounds of artificial insemination. Not only is the cow thereby robbed of the products of her body, but these products are turned against her to the point where – her production capacity sometimes exceeding her capacity to metabolise food – her body begins to consume its own tissue in order to produce milk.[18]

But, as Omar Bachour has noted, a final dimension of the theory of alienation is the worker's separation from his 'human essence' or 'spiritual nature', which is therefore founded on a notion of anthropological difference. In this sense, the Marxian theory of alienation seems bound up with a philosophical anthropology. Despite this, a non-anthropocentric conception of species-being can still be defended.[19] Thus, the theory of alienation could apply to those animals that may be said to *experience a dispossession* of their species-being under capitalist production. One does not have to look too far to spot the signs of such a deprivation within certain forms of animal resistance. Marx himself mentions this in *Capital* in relation to the factory horse. As he puts it, 'a horse has a head of his own', and so these creatures represent the worst kind of labour force for capitalists.[20] When the factory horse resists work, it is because it experiences this work as an imposition, a constraint depriving it of its freedom to act as it likes. An important point emerges here. Alienation presupposes an *experience* of dispossession, that is, a type of conscious awareness – however minimal – of being deprived of one's autonomy. One sign of this awareness is resistance to work. The literature on animal revolts includes numerous cases of animals refusing to bow to the demands of economic rationality. From the sheepdog who abandons his shepherd owner because she 'won't stop harassing him', to horses who refuse to accomplish their assigned tasks, to cows who jam their milking machines or the zoo animals who refuse to appear in front of visitors, such examples of resistance speak of an intentional refusal to work – albeit to varying degrees.[21] It seems to me, then, that it is entirely possible to speak of alienation for living beings who experience the dispossession of their species-being under the conditions of capitalist labour. The direction followed by Porcher and Noske therefore seems like the right one, but their Marxian presupposition of a fundamental anthropological difference requires some revision.

Indeed, rather than an *absolute anthropological difference*, it would be better to speak of *interspecies relational differences*, namely, discontinuities particular to the specific historical contexts and relations in which a living being is situated. Thus, the categories of animality and humanity should not abstracted from these specific settings. For instance, a human who hunts caribou as part of a hunter-gatherer society is not exactly the same kind of being as an exploited worker on an industrial farm producing meat.²² Similarly, animals themselves possess relational identities that emerge from the various kinds of relationships in which they are engaged. A wild horse and a racehorse are not beings of the same nature.

Yet this model of animal alienation – like Marx's model of human alienation – presupposes a form of non-alienated labour, a model of the relations of domestication that is both critical and normative. In the context of a theory of human-animal relations, this implies that we can distinguish between forms of livestock farming that promote alienation and other, less brutal, forms of domestication which instead favour non-pathological relations. However, Hannah Fair and Matthew McCullen have warned against such a model – as represented by Porcher's critique of animal alienation – because it makes traditional livestock farming seem like a fulfilling kind of work. But domestication always involves forms of constraint, heteronomy and domination, which humans impose on nature through instrumental relations. We might therefore ask why all animal labour should not be abolished since it constitutes a form of heteronomy, an instance of the human power to dominate nature.

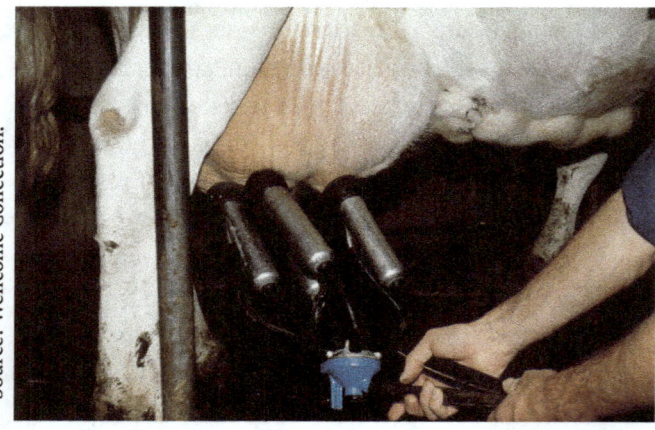

Source: Wellcome Collection.

Exploitation and emancipation

Unlike the critique of animal *alienation*, the anti-speciesist critique of animal *domination* does not envisage better working relationships between humans and animals. Animals' resistance is taken as the expression of their general refusal to being put to work, that is, to being subjected to relations of domination founded on a purely instrumental relationship to nature.

Some animal liberation theories have formulated the problem of exploitation in terms of an ethics, that is, in terms of behaviour conforming to abstract conceptions of good or evil.²³ In most of these works, animals appear as beings who suffer, as victims of human exploitation. But it should also be noted that their agency – their capacity to engage with or *resist*, to collaborate or *refuse work* – is completely denied here. Animals can teach us nothing. This is a kind of moral paternalism that is also echoed in the many analogies in such texts between animal liberation and moral anti-racism and liberal feminism. In short, the problem of work is reduced to a moral injunction 'to do no harm', not a desire to transform social relations based on the division of labour and private property. Finally, by focusing on animals defined by their individuality or species, these approaches tend to relay a specifically modern blindness to the richness of interspecies environmental relations. Léna Balaud and Antoine Chopot have thus sought to mark out a third way between, on the one hand, the critique of alienation (which assumes that a mode of fulfilling human-animal collaborative work is possible), and, on the other, the anti-speciesist critique of animal domination.

In *We Are Not Alone: The Politics of Terrestrial Uprisings*, Balaud and Chopot portray non-human resistance as a sign of living creatures' general refusal of work under the logic of capital.²⁴ Such resistances are not limited to those of a few charismatic animals endowed with intentionality, but include those of plants and, ultimately, broader ecosystemic relationships that resist profit-driven production. The amaranth crop in Argentina's struggle against monoculture provides a good example of this. In Malvinas, Argentina, a movement against genetically modified MON810 soya seeds was set up in 2016. The company Monsanto was planning to build the largest genetically modified maize production centre in the world (50,000 hectares). Three years of occupation led by the women of Malvinas resulted in the abandonment of the project. But, over the course of a struggle in which many tactics were developed, an 'interspecies faction' was born.

An interspecies faction refers to a 'heterogeneous, multifaceted grouping of living beings and sites whose combination of powers to do and feel, through joint actions, produces emancipatory political effects in a situation of domination and conflict.'²⁵ Unlike the notion of *alliance*, which emphasises the connections between living beings, the notion of *faction* emphasises the power of division and rupture which aims to defend one vision of the world against another. A 'network of interspecies acts' makes it possible to introduce a discontinuity and political rupture within a field of extractivist practices. In the Argentinian case, Monsanto was planning to develop a seed variety to be sold to farmers every year genetically modified to resist Round-Up. This total herbicide contains a glyphosate molecule that affects birds and insects and contaminates water, air and soil. It can eradicate all weeds except the desired crop.

Things changed, however, when an amaranth of the species *Amaranthus Palmeri* developed some resistance to Round-Up. Through random mutation and natural selection, amaranth had multiplied the number of copies of the gene that the herbicide was supposed to target and eradicate. Now immune to Round-Up, it would unwittingly select it and thus interfere with the extraction of Monsanto's crop. Resistant to all known herbicides, the plant invades plantations and prevents the cultivation and harvesting of corn and soybeans. An Argentinian collective then gathered and produced amaranth 'seed bombs' to combat the contamination which results from the spraying of glyphosate on farmland. These are small balls of clay mixed with amaranth seeds. The plant can thus be considered an ally in the terrestrial uprisings described by Balaud and Chopot: it resists what the activists are also fighting against. From this perspective, the amaranth's resistance can be seen as an initiative one can participate in. It has led to losses of up to 70% in crop yields in those farmlands where this tactic has been used. This amaranth population has thus mutated into a 'super weed'. Some of the farmers affected by these tactics have gone back to using old peasant seed varieties and traditional methods to guarantee food supply. This shows that a network of human and non-human interspecies acts exists, constituting an alliance against the damage caused by single-crop farming and the use of genetically modified plant varieties. It is a victory for the complexity of the living against the genetic simplification caused by extractivist capitalism.

Unlike theories of animal alienation, the political ecology of terrestrial uprisings does not presuppose a general theory of labour. On the contrary, as with Donna Haraway and Maan Barua, these approaches tend to adopt a limited definition of labour in which the labour process is equated with the process of capitalist valorisation.[26]

> Labour does not refer to all activities indiscriminately, but to any activity, human or non-human, enlisted in a value relation and contributing to the valorisation of money. It represents, therefore, any activity, whether commodified or not, which is essential for the generation of profit or for establishing the conditions that make the generation of profit possible.[27]

Porcher's general theory of labour therefore sees human and non-human resistances as calls to *improve working conditions*. In the thinking of Balaud and Chopot, on the other hand, the absence of a general theory of labour leads them to view such forms of resistance as the expression of a general refusal to work. For them, it is not so much a question of defending forms of collaborative work as of defending spaces of free evolution, not interfering in the wild part of the natural world which refuses to be subjected to capitalist work. We can see that whether one has a general theory of labour or not is crucial for determining the sort of relationship one can envisage between the human and non-human spheres: in the first case, this relationship is understood in terms of human interactions with non-humans following a model of domestication; in the second, this relationship is one of withdrawal or separation, in the sense of letting the living emerge and exist in its singularity. The purpose of reducing the category of labour to its alienated capitalist form thus becomes clear: by merging labour with the process of capitalist production, all human or non-human resistances to work become part of a struggle against capital, thereby opening up the possibility of interspecies alliances or factions. Yet such a definition of labour is clearly too historically limited. There exist forms of labour that do not contribute to 'the valorisation of money', for example, the work of a peasant under a mode of production not subjected to the market. Nevertheless, this limited definition serves to highlight the role all ecological relationships today play within the circuits of capitalist valorisation, and to interpret the resistances of the living as part of a broader refusal of capitalist work.

The reintroduction of beavers to some forests in the north of England in the mid-2000s provides a good example of how animal labour can be integrated into the process of capitalist valorisation. Underlying this 'rewilding' programme was a twin desire to preserve the natural wilderness and reduce public spending. Maintaining the wetland ecosystem and protecting biodiversity are necessary measures to ensure resilience against floods and droughts. These tasks have been delegated to beavers who are not just more effective but also cheaper than hiring professional forestry experts. The beavers harvest willows, clear up unwanted vegetation, place bundles of twigs in the rivers that provide a refuge for fish, dig canals in between the reeds and create open spaces in the water. As Jamie Lorrimer notes in *The Probiotic Planet: Using Life to Manage Life*, keystone species like beavers are reintroduced into certain ecosystems with the aim of replacing costly human labour with practically free animal labour.[28] But is it correct to suggest, as some of the environmental literature does, that such work produces value?

Donna Haraway, for instance, has argued that animal labour produces value. This is what she writes in *How Species Meet?*:

> Working dogs are *tools* that are part of the farm's capital stock, and they are *labourers* who produce surplus value by giving more than they get in a market-driven economic system.[29]

If value creation depends on the expenditure of energy by living labour, it is indeed at first sight difficult to see how animal labour really differs from human labour. Animal labour in fact still involves the expenditure of some labour power in order to produce a commodity that is sold on the market. This is as true of wild animals as of domestic animals: honey produced by bees, wool by sheep, even fruit which is grown by cultivated plants. In all these cases, a living individual uses up a certain amount of energy to produce something that can be sold on the market (honey, wool, fruit). In this sense, value as such may be thought of as consisting of the *naturally* necessary labour time required to make a particular commodity.

In fact, this argument lies behind a whole current of environmental thinking that defends the idea that organisms and living beings more generally can produce exchange value. Such is the case of the environmental economics of Theodore Odum, Nicholas Georgescu-Roegen and Alf Hornborg.[30] These authors all appeal to an energetic or thermodynamic theory of value. Measuring the amount of energy expended in the production of a commodity allows them to obtain a concrete measure of value. Value is thus measured in terms of the amount of energy expended in the production of a commodity. In line with this, for example, Odum and Hornborg have invented a new unit of measurement they call an 'EmJoule' (embodied energy) which measures the amount of solar energy synthesised by a crop to produce a particular agricultural commodity.[31] The notion of energy expenditure in non-human production is thereby no longer confined to animal production, but extended to all beings capable of caloric metabolism or photosynthesis. This would make it possible to speak not only of animal work but also of plant work.

However, to say that plants and animals produce value (both use value and exchange value) does not mean that they produce surplus value, as Haraway claims in the quotation above. The notion of surplus value presupposes wages, that is, the payment of the prevailing value of labour-time, i.e. the socially necessary labour time required for subsistence. This amount corresponds to a share of the value produced, that must correspond to less than the total value produced – otherwise there would be no surplus value. For Marxism, the concept of value is not a universal concept but a socially and historically determined concept that only becomes hegemonic under capitalism. To say that nature does not produce surplus value does not mean that nature is not valuable, since it is made up of beings, processes and relationships that are priceless because irreplaceable. But nature only contributes to the production of economic value when the labour it supplies is quantified via a monetary relation that is the function of the time required to co-produce a commodity. While solar energy or the activity of plants *contribute* to the generation of wealth – that is, to the production of a good adapted to social needs – only the exchange value – representing the socially necessary labour time for its production – is expressed in the price at which that commodity is sold on the market. Indeed, the production of value through wage labour presupposes a prior set of natural conditions, a certain expenditure of non-human labour power or natural energy, which supply the energy later expended by the wage labourer. In agriculture, the production of value depends not only on human labour but also on the economic use of land (which can be formalised by a differential theory of rent), on the biotic and microbiotic activity in the soil, on photosynthesis and therefore ultimately on solar energy. Social wealth, i.e. goods adapted to the satisfaction of social needs, is based on the natural forces that contribute to its formation. Exchange value, on the other hand, comes from the socially necessary labour time to produce a commodity. Nevertheless, capitalists' prices and margins can vary according to the ease of access to and use of natural resources. This then contributes to the formation of use value, without which the realisation of exchange value is impossible. What then is the difference between the appropriation of free unwaged labour (human or non-human) and the exploitation of wage labour?

Only salaried human labour produces surplus value because it is the only form of work that receives a wage in return for selling its labour power. The payment of a wage is the fulfilment of a contract whose purpose is the commodification of labour power. But the question then arises: why do some expenditures of energy (human ones) receive a wage while others do not (those that are non-human)? The aim of environmental economics has been to integrate precisely this expenditure of energy by non-human labour into the measurement of economic value so as to come up with a 'payment for ecosystemic services': for example, a water basin – legally constituted as a moral person through its proprietors – can receive money as compensation for the water purification service provided by the surrounding woodland canopy. But does this really count as a wage?

A wage is the monetary fulfilment of a contract designed to compensate the worker at the minimum level of reproduction of his or her labour power. 'The value of labour-power is determined, as in the case of every other commodity, by the labour-time necessary for the reproduction, and consequently also the reproduction, of this specific article. [...] For his maintenance', Marx goes on to explain, the living individual 'requires a certain quantity of the means of subsistence', and the wage must allow the worker to acquire this quantity.[32] Human needs are social and historical. They vary according to the conditions of existence and level of production that pertain in a particular time and place, but also in relation to moral judgements about the ultimate purpose of human actions and needs. The wage is thus a monetary variable corresponding to the social variation in human needs. We therefore see why only human beings can receive a wage.

A wage is the fulfilment of a contract for the sale of labour power, a contract which presupposes the participation of a formally free will. In this respect, the sort of transaction (monetary or in kind) defined by environmental economics is not a salary. In all such cases of 'payments for ecosystemic services', it is the legal owners or the moral person as represented by some humans who receive the payment. So, while there may indeed be forms of production that require the capitalist to maintain the conditions for the natural reproduction of a non-human worker, this does not involve the sale of labour power by its owner. But then, what is the difference between slave and animal labour?

Slaves, too, are commodities. It is not just their labour power that is bought, but their person as well. As Marx writes in *Capital*, Chapter 8 on the working day, 'The slave owner buys his worker in the same way as he buys his horse. If he loses his slave, he loses a piece of capital, which he must replace by fresh expenditure on the slave-market.'[33] Unlike machines, animals are living individuals with the capacity to produce more than they cost to reproduce their labour power. A sheep can produce a lot of wool with only a little pasture land, a bee a lot of honey with just some wild flowers and a hive. Contrary to a machine, which simply transmits its value without creating any additional value, a living individual (human or non-human) can produce goods worth more than the cost of reproduction. But unlike slaves, animals demand neither a wage nor freedom from bondage. It is therefore an interspecies relational difference – the capacity of practical reason to imagine a goal and to turn it into a law that the will can follow – that determines the possibility of a contract and thus of a wage.[34]

In this respect, the fundamental difference between human and non-human work lies in human beings' symbolic, moral and political capacity to suspend their own exploitation by negotiating a contract or by pursuing a politics of emancipation.

The fact that there exist forms of non-human work does not mean that all work should be regarded under a single lens (either from a philosophical standpoint or through the framework of political economy), because non-human work can never produce surplus value, despite it always contributing in a decisive way to the formation of wealth. The specificity of the wage form – the compensation for the sale of labour power by its holder – thus resides in the human discursive possibility of negotiating a contract or organising political struggle.

Interspecies alliances

Non-human resistances to capitalist labour seem to provide an alternative image of nature to that of 'the moderns'. The intensification of natural productive processes in the service of valorisation leads to a reduction of nature's passive modes of existence. Contrary to the idea – even if this idea is not entirely false – that modernity has reduced nature to a collection of completely passive objects, it could be argued that the environmental history of capitalism involves a pathological, disruptive and alienated intensification of nature's productivity with profit as its aim. As a result, living beings that do not produce value appear as superfluous beings, an ecological excess population with respect to a regime of accumulation. Under contemporary capitalism, therefore, nature no longer figures as a pure passivity. It is not a collection of inert objects that can simply be appropriated; on the contrary, it is a set of productive processes whose utility depends solely on their potential for valorisation.

Does this mean we need to rethink the composition of the proletariat from an ecological point of view? Three positions seem defensible: the first would be to assert the absurdity of any consideration of the interests of living beings as exploited subjects. This position is certainly the most widely shared, and not incomprehensible from the point of view of human physical, cognitive and psychic capacities for political commitment. But it leaves aside the real experience of forms of domination and alienation experienced by non-human living beings. The second option would be to rethink the ecological composition of the working class, i.e., to think of exploited living beings as part of a class itself fragmented by interspecific differences. Such an option has the advantage of emphasising the shared experience of capitalist domination of labour, but shifts the problem to the articulation of interspecific differences within the class. It will be humans who take the lead in organising the multispecific class. A final solution, on the contrary, aims to propose interspecific alliances, i.e., the consideration of non-human interests while acknowledging the possibility that human and non-human interests may diverge. But here again, two interpretations are possible: either the alliance has a tactical function in the effective overturning of relations of domination (as in the case of the Amaranth seed bombs in Argentina); or the alliance aims to name a moral, even theological-political pact, which would anticipate within contemporary practices the possibility of other relations between humans and non-humans, relations that spare divergent interests. These two interpretations are certainly not mutually exclusive, but the second invites us to relativise the importance of an anti-capitalist political strategy based on interspecies alliances, without denying its real interest in anticipating the world to come.

Paul Guillibert is the author of Terre et capital. Pour un communisme du vivant *(2021) and* Exploiter les vivants *(2023).*

Translated by Giovanni Menegalle

Notes

1. Fahim Amir, *Being and Swine: The End of Nature (As We Knew It)*, trans. Geoffrey C. Howes and Corvin Russell (Toronto: Between the Lines, 2020); Alex Blanchette, *Porkopolis: American Animality, Standardized Life, and the Factory Farm* (Durham, NC: Duke University Press, 2020); François Jarrige, *La Ronde des bêtes: le moteur animal et la fabrique de la modernité* (Paris: La Découverte, 2023).
2. Jason W. Moore, *Capitalism in the Web of Life: Ecology and the Accumulation of Capital* (London: Verso, 2015); Alyssa Battistoni, 'Ways of Making a Living: Revaluing the Work of Social and Ecological Reproduction', *Socialist Register 2020: Beyond Market Dystopia: New Ways of Living*, 182–198.
3. Charlotte E. Blattner, Will Kymlicka and Kendra Coulter, eds., *Animal Labour: A New Frontier of Interspecies Justice?* (Oxford: Oxford University Press, 2020).
4. Ted Benton, 'Humanism=Speciesism: Marx on Humans and Animals', *Radical Philosophy* 50 (1988), 4–18.
5. Maan Barua, 'Nonhuman Labour, Encounter Value, Spectacular Accumulation: The Geographies of a Lively Commodity', *Transactions of the Institute of British Geographers* 42:2 (June 2017), 274–288.
6. Jocelyne Porcher, *Vivre avec les animaux une utopie pour le XXIe siècle* (Paris: La Découverte, 2014).
7. An illustration of this can be found in the work of Paul Burkett, who distinguishes work and nature, taking for granted that work is an exclusively human activity and nature external to the entire labour process. Two funda-

mental aspects of work are thereby side-lined: the naturalness of one's own body within living labour, on the one hand, and the potential for nature to be put to work by capital, on the other. See Paul Burkett, *Marx and Nature: A Red and Green Perspective* (New York: St Martin's Press, 1999).

8. Jocelyne Porcher and Tiphaine Schmitt, 'Les Vaches collaborent-elles au travail ? Une question de sociologie', *Revue du MAUSS*, 35:1 (2010), 235–261.

9. Porcher and Schmitt, 235–261.

10. Porcher and Schmitt, 235–261.

11. Jocelyne Porcher, 'Les Vaches rêvent-elles du travail? Bien-être animal et souffrance au travail. Entretien avec Jocelyne Porcher et Lise Gaignard', ed. Romain André et al., Jefklak, April 2017, https://jefklak.org/wordpress/wp-content/uploads/2017/04/PorcherGaignard_SiteJK.pdf.

12. Jocelyne Porcher, Nicolas Lainé and Sébastien Mouret, 'Hommes et animaux domestiques. Le travail en partage', *Revue d'anthropologie des connaissances* 17:1 (2023), 8. See Kendra Coulter, *Animal, Work, and the Promise of Interspecies Solidarity* (New York: Palgrave Macmillan, 2016), 60.

13. Karl Marx, *Economic and Philosophic Manuscripts of 1844* (Moscow: Progress, 1977), 73.

14. Judith Butler has put forward a 'perspectivist' reading of this naturalist account of organic and inorganic bodies. See Judith Butler, 'The Inorganic Body in the Early Marx: A Limit-Concept of Anthropocentrism', *Radical Philosophy* 2.06 (Winter 2019), 3–17. For a critique of this perspectivist reading see Paul Guillibert, *Terre et capital. Pour un communisme du vivant* (Paris: Amsterdam, 2021), 74–77.

15. Catherine Larrère and Raphaël Larrère, *Du bon usage de la nature: pour une philosophie de l'environnement* (Paris: Flammarion, 2009).

16. Marx, *Manuscripts*, 73.

17. Barbara Noske, *Humans and Other Animals: Beyond the Boundaries of Anthropology* (London: Pluto Press, 1989).

18. See Astra and Sunaura Taylor, 'Our Animals, Ourselves: The Socialist Feminist Case for Animal Liberation', *Lux Magazine* 3 (2024), https://lux-magazine.com/article/our-animals-ourselves/.

19. Hannah Fair and Matthew McMullen, 'Toward a Theory of Nonhuman Species-Being', *Environmental Humanities* 15:2 (July 2023), 195–214.

20. Karl Marx, *Capital: A Critique of Political Economy, Volume One*, trans. Ben Fowkes (London: Penguin, 1982), 497.

21. Jocelyne Porcher, Nicolas Lainé and Sébastien Mouret, 'Hommes et animaux domestiques, Le travail en partage', *Revue d'anthropologie des connaissances* 17:1 (2023), 1.

22. Tim Ingold, *The Appropriation of Nature: Essays on Human Ecology and Social Relations* (Manchester: Manchester University Press, 1986).

23. See, for example, Tom Regan, *The Case for Animal Rights* (Berkeley: University of California Press, 2004); Peter Singer, *Animal Liberation* (New York: Harper Perennial, 2009).

24. Léna Balaud and Antoine Chopot, *Nous ne sommes pas seuls. Politique des soulèvements terrestres* (Paris: Éditions du Seuil, Anthropocène, 2021).

25. Balaud and Chopot, *Nous ne sommes pas seuls*, 326.

26. Donna Haraway, *When Species Meet* (Minneapolis: University of Minnesota Press, 2008); Barua, 'Nonhuman labour, encounter value, spectacular accumulation', *Transactions of the Institute of British Geographers* 42 (2017).

27. Balaud and Chopot, *Nous ne sommes pas seuls*, 143.

28. Jamie Lorimer, *The Probiotic Planet: Using Life to Manage Life* (Minneapolis: University of Minnesota Press, 2020).

29. Haraway, *When Species Meet*, 55 (my emphasis).

30. Howard T. Odum and Jan E. Arding, 'Emergy Analysis of Shrimp Mariculture in Ecuador', Working Paper, University of Rhode Island, Coastal Resources Center, 1991; Nicolas Georgescu-Roegen, *The Entropy Law and the Economic Process* (Cambridge, MA: Harvard University Press, 1971); Alf Hornborg, 'The Commodification of Human Life: Labour, Energy and Money in a Deteriorating Biosphere', *The Palgrave Handbook of Environmental Labour Studies*, eds. Nora Räthzel, Dimitris Stevis and David Uzzell (Cham: Springer International, 2021), 677–697.

31. Alf Hornborg, 'The Unequal Exchange of Time and Space: Toward a Non-Normative Ecological Theory of Exploitation', *Journal of Ecological Anthropology* 7 (2003), 4–10.

32. Marx, *Capital, Volume One*, 274.

33. Marx, *Capital, Volume One*, 377.

34. Marx, *Capital, Volume One*, 283-284.

By all means
On Heide Gerstenberger's *Market and Violence*
Peter Hallward

Heide Gerstenberger's sprawling 'analysis of capitalism as it has existed in history' is first and foremost a reminder of what we are dealing with.* In the terms implied by one of her underlying metaphors, to live in a world dominated by capital is to live at the mercy of a wild animal, a predator motivated by a single instinct – the drive to exploit labour and thus maximise profits by all available means. Wherever these means might include overt enslavement or the myriad forms of 'ersatz slavery' that came to replace it, capital will draw on them as much as circumstances allow. Left to itself, capital's exploitation of labour obeys one and only one imperative: accumulate as much as possible, as quickly as possible. To comply with this imperative, capital will simply do whatever it can get away with doing. There is then no 'inner rationality' or 'civilising tendency' internal to capital that might reign in its insatiable appetite for profits. From the sugar plantations of Saint-Domingue or Morelos to the forced labour camps of the Third Reich, wholly 'unbounded' or unrestricted exploitation [*entgrenzte Ausbeutung*] will suck all life and energy, as thoroughly as possible and as ruthlessly as necessary, from the people it uses or employs. The local imposition of political limits on its behaviour may temper its excesses, but no amount of social reform, economic development or historical 'progress' will ever tame capital as such.

The result of Gerstenberger's many years of inquiry into the historical functioning of capitalism, as she observed in 2018,

> can be summed up in a nutshell. It runs as follows: Exceptions apart, owners of capital make use of all the means to achieve profits which are open to them in a certain place and at a certain time. If direct violence is not one of the practices which are being made use of, this is not prevented by economic rationality but only by public critique and state activity.[1]

Given the nature of the beast, so to speak, Gerstenberger concludes that sovereign or state power alone has the binding force required to limit capital's recourse to violent exploitation. Everything then depends on the unstable balance of class forces that orients the use of state power in what plays out as an essentially zero-sum contest, a struggle to bend public priorities in favour of either labour on the one hand or capital on the other. In a 2014 article that distils the overall argument of her book, Gerstenberger boiled her main conclusions down to two points:

> Firstly: the domestication of capitalism hinges on the state safeguarding private and collective rights of labourers, and secondly: no level of economic development safeguards against the brutal use of direct violence against labourers. … Far from marking a certain epoch of capitalist development, violence is constantly hanging about in the wings of capitalist labour relations. It comes into the open when governments and societies refrain from decisive objection.[2]

Gerstenberger acknowledges, of course, that the objections made and sustained by organised labour in parts of Europe and then the rest of the imperialist core, from the mid-nineteenth through to the mid-twentieth centuries, did indeed succeed in limiting some workers' exposure to direct coercive force. In these places, as cap-

---

* Heide Gerstenberger, *Market and Violence: The Functioning of Capitalism in History*, trans. Niall Bond (Chicago: Haymarket Books, 2023), 109; hereafter abbreviated as MV.

ital's workforce become more organised and more assertive, chattel slavery and child labour were phased out, trade unions were legalised, labour contracts were upheld, limits were set to the working day, and so on. Such achievements, however, were secured not by following or enhancing capital's own immanent tendencies but by opposing them. 'The history of capitalism has not confirmed the notion that capitalist forms of exploitation generally tend to overcome the violence which was present in historically earlier forms. If, in some places and during some periods, violence has indeed been reduced, this has always been achieved by political measures, and these have usually been demanded by widespread critique and opposition.'[3] Slavery in Saint-Domingue or the American South, for instance, no less than in Nazi Germany, was overcome not as a result of economic progress or rationalisation but by political confrontation, culminating in military struggle (MV, 410). By the same token, wherever openly forced labour persists or returns it should be understood not as an anachronistic remnant of pre-capitalist relations of production, let alone as some extra-capitalist aberration, but rather as a regression to capital's less 'bounded' methods of exploitation. On this score Gerstenberger might well agree with Maria Mies and Sylvia Federici: when the conditions are right, 'violence itself becomes the most productive force.'[4]

The persistence of direct violence

Best known in anglophone circles for another substantial and acclaimed book on the *History and Theory of the Bourgeois State*,[5] Heide Gerstenberger is generally reluctant to position herself in relation to current philosophical trends. She doesn't see herself as 'theoretically affiliated to any school of interpretation' (least of all what she dismisses as 'orthodox Marxism'), and only accepts broad characterisation of her work as archive-based 'historical sociology'.[6] Published in German in 2017 and issued in a much-anticipated though rather rushed English translation as part of Brill's Historical Materialism series in 2023, the bulk of *Market and Violence* consists of dozens upon dozens of detailed and harrowing studies of capital's more unrestricted sites of exploitation, ranging from the Assam 'tea gardens' to the mines of Rhodesia. The fruit of a lifetime's work and winner of the 2023 Deutscher Prize, Gerstenberger's book is sure to become an influential and controversial point of reference in a good many contemporary debates, both empirical and theoretical, about capitalism and its history.

Before we try to summarise Gerstenberger's account of this history it's important to emphasise that she approaches her task very much as a historian. She isn't herself interested in many of the more abstract debates that have absorbed Marxist attention in recent years. You'll find no discussion in this book of falling rates of profit, of capitalism's propensity to crisis, of recent forms of mechanisation or automation, of the differences between monopoly capitalism and techno-feudalism, etc. The phrases 'commodity fetishism' and 'value theory' do not appear in the text, any more than do detailed discussions of money, credit or financialisation. Fernand Braudel and Immanuel Wallerstein are only mentioned in passing (with Braudel censured for over-estimating the importance of world trade and the merely 'psychological' factor of 'merchants' desire for profit' [MV, 34]). There are no references to Giovanni Arrighi or Moishe Postone, and only parenthetical notes on Robert Brenner or Ellen Meiksins Wood – if Gerstenberger agrees with the 'political Marxists'' emphasis on relations of power and domination, she clearly resists their characterisation of (fully developed) capitalism as a mode of production that, by comparison with ancient or feudal alternatives, is uniquely able to rely on merely 'economic' or non-coercive means of extracting surplus labour from its workforce.[7] Gerstenberger offers no systematic discussion of feudalism, and seems to treat many aspects of the transition from feudalism to capitalism, or from manufacturing to industrialisation, as self-evident. For all her emphasis on capitalist recourse to violence, she stops well short of William Robinson's recent analyses of 'capitalism's extermination impulse,' or of its growing reliance on 'militarized accumulation.'[8] She has plenty to say about the relation between capitalism and slavery (of which more later), but she doesn't engage in a systematic assessment of, for instance, the 'New History of Capitalism' associated with Sven Beckert and Walter Johnson's recent work on the role cotton production played in the early stages of US industrialisation: for a long time Gerstenberger has taken the 'slave economy [to be] an integrated and profitable part of the process of capitalist development' (MV, 83n.80), and generally interprets this too as self-evident. She is closer to Ellen Wood than e.g. Charles Post when she claims that, while capital will certainly make use of whatever means of discrimination might enhance its dominance over labour, 'it is not *constitutively* racist or sexist.'[9] As far as Gerstenberger is concerned, capitalism's inclusion of chattel slavery among its strategies of exploitation is a demonstrable and suggestive historical fact; theoretical arguments about whether capitalism *must* be racialised or gendered are secondary speculations.

In a recent discussion of her book and its initial reception, Gerstenberger confessed that when she wrote it she assumed she could take the general concept of capitalism for granted.[10] This assumption helps to explain why her first chapters don't include a succinct account of what makes capitalism distinct by comparison with previous modes of production. Her third chapter in particular, on the 'Historical Preconditions for Capitalist Accumulation', characterises the process in broadly familiar terms: these preconditions include the generalisation of commodity production, the 'pacification of transport routes' (i.e. military or political control over the principal avenues of domestic and international trade), the removal of feudal obstacles to the untrammelled exploitation of labour (e.g. restrictions posed by guilds and other corporate bodies, inherited privileges or exemptions, time-honoured traditions, etc.), the generalisation of market mechanisms and the consequent primacy of competitive pressures, and so on.

Gerstenberger has plenty to say about all these things, but her own particular focus is on *one* very specific question, and it's not a question that helps account for what makes capitalism different from previous modes of production – on the contrary. Her question is: what is the relation between capitalist relations of production and recourse to physical or direct violence against persons? Whether exercised or threatened by an employer, or by state agencies acting in support of an employer, as Gerstenberger defines it such violence includes all the means of causing bodily harm (or the threat thereof) that might compel people to accept limitations on their movement and their activities, including acceptance of abysmal working conditions, of wages paid at rates below the value of their work, and so on, as well as acceptance of their exposure to dangerous conditions and materials, acceptance of the expropriation of their lands or pos-

sessions, the theft of their collective resources, and so on (MV, 4-5). Gerstenberger is clear that she aims to limit the category to 'personal' and 'physical' forms of violence, thereby explicitly excluding both psychological and 'impersonal' forms of coercion. Framed negatively, Gerstenberger can thus say that 'direct violence consists in practices that theoreticians of capitalism regard as unnecessary if not indeed as harmful for developed societies' (3).

This then is the central argument that runs all through the book. From Adam Smith through Karl Marx and Max Weber to Pierre Bourdieu or Moishe Postone (to say nothing of Friedrich Hayek and any number of neoliberal ideologues), prevailing theoretical accounts of capitalism present it as 'a historically progressive countermodel to economies based upon the direct domination of labourers or upon predatory appropriation.' These accounts assume that older forms of 'personal' or direct coercion are made redundant by capital's reliance on less abrasive and more impersonal or market-mediated forms of exploitation. It is this that allows both critics and apologists of capitalism to celebrate it not only as more productive, innovative, efficient, and so on, but also as more 'civilised' and humane. Gerstenberger sets out to demolish this assumption. She aims to show that 'there is no developmental trend inherent to capitalism which is conducive to impersonal relations in economic dealings' (MV, xi).

In this sense, the whole of Gerstenberger's enormous work is 'limited to a single criticism: a criticism of the assumption that the practice of direct violence against persons occurs far less often in capitalism than in previous economic forms, because such violence is economically counterproductive' (MV, xii). Gerstenberger acknowledges, of course, that in many situations capital has no need to rely on direct violence, and that to threaten such violence might often be counterproductive. But this all depends on the situation, and on the way capitalists assess the prevailing balance of political forces. Gerstenberger's target is that widespread 'certainty concealed in mainstream opinion and economic analyses that the laws that dictate how capitalist economies themselves function are conducive to abstention from violence. To be more precise, my critique focuses on those aspects of a philosophy of history which have been passed down in both Marxist and liberal theories of capitalism' (xi-xii). Though she limits her critique to the past history and present operations of capitalism, it isn't hard to see how – not least in the increasingly authoritarian and militarised global context of 2024 – Gerstenberger's approach helps to anticipate aspects of its likely future as well.

If it's impossible to do justice here to even one of the many specific situations she investigates, the broad shape of Gerstenberger's alternative history of capitalism is easily sketched. After reviewing the legal measures that constrained the initial forms of waged labour in early modern Europe, she traces the prolonged transition from plantation slavery and debt peonage through to the global trade in nineteenth-century 'coolie' labour and its contemporary variants, illustrated as much by the Kafala system of the Gulf states as by the 'boundless exploitation of "foreigners"' in Europe and North America (MV, 438). The systematic use of prison labour in the post-Reconstruction (and then neoliberal) carceral system of the United States is another example among many more. If such open or unabashed assertions of private 'property rights over labour are rare today', at least in some societies, this is largely 'because the cost of obtaining replacements is very low.' The more disposable workers become, the more easily they can be harnessed and discarded in the machinery of 'just-in-time production', the less capital needs to respect rights won by previously-organised labour, or to rely on longer-term labour contracts. Although such hard-won contracts remain 'the historically legitimated justification of capitalist exploitation' (425), there is no trans-historical tendency, immanent to capitalist production itself, that compels it to respect the rights and 'freedom' of wage labour per se.

Sites most removed from public scrutiny and government oversight – for instance the export processing zones that dot the peripheries of the neoliberal world order (MV, 474), or the 'high seas' ploughed by international shipping and its 'flags of convenience' (466) – offer illuminating examples of what vulnerable workers may be subjected to when capital is fully let off the leash. Gerstenberger's earlier archival work on globalised and ultra-exploited maritime labour is re-deployed here to great effect – a recent lecture she gave on 'the political economy of seafaring labour' shows how, in recent decades, stripped of any meaningful means of organisation or self-defence, it has been wholly subsumed within 'capitalism at its purest.'[11] Though she doesn't discuss it in detail, another exemplary case would be the indescribable conditions that have long prevailed in the global meat industry (451). The most illuminating examples of all, however, remain those places where capital is not merely unencumbered by state regulations but actively enabled and enhanced by them – most obviously, these are the places colonised by European capitalists, and their neocolonial counterparts. For the British in India or the Germans in South West Africa, the colonies figure here as a sort of laboratory for exploring what untrammelled capitalist exploitation might be capable of, in circumstances that deprive workers of all significant political representation or rights. 'Nothing was as important for the political economy of colonial capitalism than the direct subordination of workers to state power', i.e. their exposure to 'radical extortion' without redress (207). By the same token, nothing remains more important to the political economy of neo-colonial capitalism, in the era opened up by the wars of national liberation in China and Vietnam, than the ongoing subordination of formerly colonised states to the power of international capital.[12]

The cumulative impact of Gerstenberger's lengthy inventory of capital's crimes and outrages is overwhelming, and her book is a devastating refutation of any residual attempts to portray capitalism as an essentially 'civilising' or progressive phase of human history. Although it is far more concerned with documenting specific labour practices than with engaging in abstract philosophical arguments, the book is also punctuated by ten parenthetical 'theoretical remarks', and intervenes in a number of important discussions that continue to divide Marxist circles. Three of these interventions are likely to generate particular interest among readers primed to agree with Gerstenberger's unequivocal condemnation of capitalist coercion, and perhaps the simplest way to introduce them is via her occasional and rather guarded references to Marx himself.

Command over labour

In the first place, Gerstenberger aligns herself with Marx by defining capital most fundamentally as a political relation of domination and command. Just as its natural i.e. unbridled economic tendency is towards consolidation and monopoly rather than 'free competition', capital's natural political form is autocracy rather than democracy; the more fully capital prevails, the more fully it imposes itself as a naked form of class dictatorship. What is most distinctive about capital as a social force, from this perspective, is then neither its alleged rationality nor an intrinsic orientation towards technological progress, but simply the depth and scope of its capacity to compel people to work for it. If the capitalist mode of production is indeed more profitable and innovative than earlier modes, this is primarily because capital has invented more far-reaching means of compelling its workforce. In particular, by comparison with its predecessors, capital has invented and exercised more compelling mechanisms of public or state power.

In his most concise and instructive definition, Marx characterises capital as 'essentially the command over unpaid labour.'[13] 'Capitalism essentially involves commanding the labour process' (MV, 208), echoes Gerstenberger, and 'while this is achieved in mechanised production by turning labour forces into "appendages of the machine" (Marx), in colonial production it was achieved predominantly through commands in the literal sense of the word and through discipline produced and maintained through coercion' (208). This is one of the several reasons why Gerstenberger pays special attention to the way the *colonial* state exercises its coercive power. 'Just as the state in Europe's Ancien Régime, the colonial state was an institution for the appropriation of property. And just as in the Ancien Régime, appropriation through armed violence was a central element of domination' in the colonies, as was reliance on caste-like privilege and 'factual legal inequality' between social groups (301-2).

What was most distinctive and symptomatic about the colonial state, by contrast with the (relatively) more law-bound machinations of the metropolitan states, is its relative freedom of manoeuvre. Capitalist colonies are places in which the dominant classes can do whatever they might want. In the face of popular resistances that might require inter-class negotiations back in Europe, colonial states could instead rely on expansive emergency provisions designed to crush them by all necessary means. Back in the days of Winston Churchill, Smedley Butler and other unabashed 'gangsters of capitalism', there was nothing subtle about such means.[14] Compared with its metropolitan counterpart, in other words, the colonial state is a closer approximation to the kind of modern state that is *utterly* devoted to its primary role as enabler and enforcer of capitalist accumulation. Even acts of repression so severe that they eventually resulted in public debate – Gerstenberger considers the examples of the great Indian Rebellion of 1857 (suppressed with the killing of hundreds of thousands of Indians) and the 1865 Morant Bay revolt in Jamaica (suppressed with many hundreds of floggings and 439 executions) – could readily be justified as necessary for the preservation of that balance of terror upon which minority white rule relied (MV, 307-310).

So long as such rule could safely ignore the needs and concerns of the indigenous majority, the colonial state could continue to fulfil its most essential function: the conversion of this majority into a largely powerless and disposable workforce. Trade unions and mass suffrage campaigns eventually obliged metropolitan campaigns to restrict if not renounce the use of direct violence against European workers, but such coercive 'labour relations in the colonies remained part and parcel of political power until the very end of the colonial era.' Not only did the state itself continue to employ forced labour for its infrastructure projects, it also justified coercion as a social benefit – 'because "natives" were considered by nature lazy, unwilling to work, and obtuse, it was for their own good that they were turned into willing workers by means of forced labour (*travail obligatoire*)' (MV, 312). In short, whereas in Europe trade unions and popular political pressure succeeded in establishing at least a degree of separation between the exercise of state power and the economic interests of the dominant class, in the colonies no separation of society and the state was allowed to take hold, for the simple reason that 'society, understood as a sphere in which autonomous individuals become aware of their common interests through public (or if needed secret) debates, could hardly develop.' In the absence of social constraints, the colonial states were free to use whatever kinds of force and discrimination the requirements of super-exploitation seemed to demand. 'Colonial states remained apparatuses of violence designed to further private appropriation', and 'any and all attempts to claim that their nature was theoretically more complex are misleading' (313-4).

Back in a metropolitan country like mid-nineteenth-century Britain, pending the rise of organised labour and mass suffrage, comparable though less dramatic results could still be achieved via the combined effects of punitive poor relief and capital's ability to draw on the state's judicial apparatus to prosecute workers who, in their eyes of their employers, broke their contracts by escaping their place of employment or failing to fulfil their obligations with sufficient zeal (MV, 406-7). Through to the 1870s, British 'labour relations continued to be a relationship of domination sanctioned by the state. As late as 1823, in the middle of the development of industrial capitalist production, certain penal provisions of the Master and Servant acts were even substantially exacerbated' and 'the punishment of workers who had not fulfilled their contractual obligations was considered a matter of course. They could be whipped or sentenced to prison or to forced labour or to a fine or to losing all rights to the wages they had previously earned' (60-2).

Throughout her book, Gerstenberger emphasises the role played by the state in both the emergence of capital and also its subsequent, partial and forever resisted 'domestication' – 'not only the historical constitution, but also the continuation of domesticated capitalism is based on state power' (MV, 408). More generally, and in contrast to approaches that prioritise the abstract 'logic' of capital's law of value,[15] one of the great virtues of Gerstenberger's emphasis on the state and its assertion of a monopoly on violence or coercive force is that it foregrounds specific class and institutional actors in ways that ordinary usage presumes – as she points out early on, 'violence (like the French term *violence* or the German term *Gewalt*) necessarily involves intent, and consequently actors who harbour this intent' (2). Even quasi-automated financial transactions, she reminds us, are still 'based on the decisions of concrete institutions and thus also real human individuals' (421). The relative and tenuous freedoms occasionally accorded to labour, in the capital-labour relation, were always won by specific groups of workers engaged in specific campaigns. 'Everywhere, political struggles had to be fought out and political decisions had to be taken to create the form of labour relations that now we have come to consider as being adequate for capitalist production' (110). In Britain, for instance, long-standing assumptions that employers could resort to state coercion in order to enforce labour contracts were only challenged and eventually overcome when large numbers of working people gained the right to vote after 1867.[16] In France workers won certain rights and freedoms long before their British counterparts, and indeed well before the local development of capitalism itself, precisely as a result of the political pressures unleashed in the years that followed 1789. In France, 'the political necessity to decree that the two parties of a contract were to be equal before the law was brought about by the political necessity of constituting state power after the revolutionary demise of nobility. It was a direct result of the Revolution, and had nothing to do with any economic rationality.'[17]

Ongoing accumulation

There is a second way in which Gerstenberger's history of capitalism builds on Marx's account, while also challenging some of its central distinctions. Although she mentions it only once (on her opening page), Gerstenberger certainly agrees with the broad outlines of Marx's famous reconstruction of the origins of capital, his demonstration of how capital 'comes into the world ... dripping from head to toe, from every pore, with blood and dirt' (C1, 926). Countering the 'idyllic' fantasies peddled by bourgeois political economists, the famous final part of *Capital, Volume 1* shows how the primitive or originary accumulation of capital was rooted in the expropriation of peasant farms, the conquest and enslavement of indigenous populations, and the theft of collective resources. Like some other readers of Marx, however, including Rosa Luxemburg, Sylvia Federici and David Harvey, Gerstenberger objects to the way that he tends to associate the role of violence ('conquest, enslavement, robbery, murder, in short, force [*Gewalt*]' [C1, 874]) with the originary *rather* than the subsequent or routine accumulation of capital. Gerstenberger's own priority, of course, is to show how recourse to violence remains characteristic of capital at every stage. No less than Federici, Gerstenberger refuses 'to see the advent of capitalism as a moment of historical progress.'[18] She rejects, then, any account of capitalism that associates its development with any necessary reduction in direct violence against persons, and thus any intrinsic preference for the use of 'free' or uncoerced labour. Insofar as Marx and his readers are themselves committed to such an account, she rejects this too.

Of course Gerstenberger admits the *possibility* that capital might, under certain circumstances (i.e. under sufficient pressure from organised labour or a state sympathetic to labour), chose to rely on the 'impersonal domination' of market forces, rather than on more direct and intentional, i.e. 'personal', means of compulsion. As Gerstenberger explained to Jasper Strange in an illuminating 2018 interview, by focusing on the general law of value,

> Marx did not have to make capital owners responsible for all the evils inherent in capitalism. Once the capacity to labour of many men, women (and children) was transformed into a commodity, the violence inherent in the anonymous forces of the market could replace the practice of direct violence against labourers. Marx's theory of value enabled him to explain that even if nobody cheats and everything is exchanged according to its value, the productive capacity of labour power reproduces the capital relation, i.e. the class difference.[19]

Gerstenberger accepts that this 'focus on capitalism as a system ... enabled Marx to explain that the reproduction of capitalism is possible without the use of direct violence against persons.' So far so good. However, 'whenever this historical possibility is mistakenly conceived of as historical necessity, the analysis of capitalism is transformed into a philosophical concept of history'.[20] This transformation subsumes empirical analysis in an unjustified teleological conception of historical development, one that orients capitalism towards the exploitation of free or uncoerced labour in the short term, and towards its own revolutionary self-destruction over the longer term. Faced with a choice between the analysis of 'actual history' and a dubious 'philosophical concept of history', Gerstenberger's preference is very clear.

So is her contribution to the ongoing debates regarding Marx and slavery, on the one hand, and the relation between plantation slavery and capitalism, on the other. As is well known, Marx recognised the fundamental role that plantation slavery played in the development of capitalism as a world system, most especially in the development of the industrial product par excellence, cotton. 'The veiled slavery of the wage-labourers in Europe needed the unqualified slavery of the New World as its pedestal' (C1, 925), just as 'the discovery of gold and silver in America, the extirpation, enslavement and entombment in mines of the indigenous population of that continent, the beginnings of the conquest and plunder of

India, and the conversion of Africa into a preserve for the commercial hunting of blackskins are all things which characterize the dawn of the era of capitalist production' (C1, 915). Marx also insists, however, that an essential part of capital's unprecedented ability to harness 'more colossal productive forces than have all preceding generations together' – its creation of 'wonders far surpassing Egyptian pyramids, Roman aqueducts, and Gothic cathedrals', etc.[21] – is its equally unprecedented ability to rely on economic and thus 'impersonal' rather than directly coercive forms of compulsion. Capital's distinctive reliance on market-mediated relations of production allow it to buy or rent labour-power as a commodity, rather than simply compel labourers to work by force. Capital's unique relations of production thus pit free capital against labour that is 'free' in a double sense – workers who have both been 'freed' of any ownership of their own means of production, and who are now free to be employed by one of several possible employers (C1, 271-3).

On this condition, Marx argues, 'as an agent in producing the activity of others, as an extractor of surplus labour and an exploiter of labour-power, [capital] surpasses all earlier systems of production, which were based on directly compulsory labour, in its energy and its quality of unbounded and ruthless activity' (C1, 425). Direct compulsion and repressive legislation against 'vagabonds' and 'idlers' was and is certainly required in order to establish these 'free' relations of production, and to drive workers into that dependence upon capital that will oblige them, eventually and reluctantly, to accept its new forms of subordination. But the key point about capitalist development, according to Marx, is that its consolidation generates means of commanding labour that are both more imperious and more insidious than those available to any previous mode of production.

> The advance of capitalist production develops a working class which by education, tradition and habit looks upon the requirements of that mode of production as self-evident natural laws. The organization of the capitalist process of production, once it is fully developed, breaks down all resistance. ... The silent compulsion of economic relations sets the seal on the domination of the capitalist over the worker. Direct extra-economic force is still of course used, but only in exceptional cases (C1, 899).

However much capital's production processes 'distort the worker into a fragment of a man', however much they 'degrade', 'torment' and 'alienate' him, however much they 'subject him during the labour process to a despotism the more hateful for its meanness' (C1, 798), capital nevertheless confronts, over time, a working class that is more and more 'willing' to work for capital.

Gerstenberger accepts that the idea of 'free wage labour', based in apparently voluntary contracts and upheld by apparently neutral state and judicial institutions, is indeed an essential aspect of capital's 'magnificent legitimacy' (MV, 108). She argues, however, that Marx was too quick to treat this merely *ideological* dimension of capital's self-conception as a tendency of actually-existing capitalist exploitation. He was too quick to interpret the rise of 'free labour' as an economic rather than *politico*-economic tendency. It's true that 'there were economic prerequisites for creating conditions of production the constitution and maintenance of which was due to the coercion of conditions rather than direct private violence and state coercion', namely a sufficient supply of destitute would-be workers, and technological developments that made these workers easier to replace and discard. But drawing in particular on the work of Robert Steinfeld and Marcel van der Linden,[22] Gerstenberger insists that 'nowhere has it been a purely economic process for free wage labour to became dominant in a society. Everywhere, political struggles had to be fought out and political decisions had to be taken to create the form of labour relations that now we have come to consider as being adequate for capitalist production.'[23] Such decisions may be reversed. Capital needs compliant workers who can be exploited for a profit, this is non-negotiable – whether their work is formally 'free', or not, is an optional extra.

Marx recognised that the exploitation of slave labour might be *compatible* with capitalism. He admits for instance that once the export of cotton was integrated into capitalist supply chains so then formerly 'patriarchal' relations between master and slave were replaced by a more 'calculated and calculating system. It was no longer a question of obtaining from him a certain quantity of useful products, but rather of the production of surplus-value itself.' (C1, 345).[24] Nevertheless, Marx clearly considered the direct exploitation of chattel slaves to be less efficient and less profitable than the exploitation of more willing and less threatening 'wage slaves', and some recent analysts of plantation slavery have likewise stressed the ways its labour practices (by replacing the purchase of waged labour-power with the purchase of bonded labourers themselves) remain pre- or non-capitalist.[25] Gerstenberger disagrees, firmly aligning herself with Robin Blackburn's 'irrefutable' conclusion that 'slavery was not overthrown for economic reasons but where it became politically untenable.'[26] Not only can it be shown (drawing among other things on Rebecca Scott's work on sugar production in Cuba) that 'slaves could be just as easily introduced and subjugated to mechanised production as free wage workers';[27] the widespread but mistaken 'conviction that slavery and capitalism are not compatible' is most directly refuted by recalling the practices of former slave owners who, in the wake of the Confederacy's defeat in 1865, 'developed all sorts of "Ersatz- slavery".' Even more than the harsh labour codes mandated by Toussaint Louverture and André Rigaud in the last years of colonial Saint-Domingue, the various 'Black Codes' that were passed in the South immediately after the end of the Civil War were intended to preserve plantation slavery in all but name. If these soon had to be abandoned in the face of strong Republican political pressure, 'vagrancy laws, the widespread use of peonage and the renting out of convicts more or less achieved the same goal. All of these forms bound labour to a certain employment. None of these forms hindered the development of capitalism'.[28] Once the temporary pressure from the Republican North eased off, over the 1870s, the spirit if not the letter of the Black Codes could be restored in full, and imposed by the combined force of the Ku Klux Klan, on the one hand, and Jim Crow legal rulings, on the other.

Likewise, once political and moral pressure finally made chattel slavery indefensible in Europe, capital in the Caribbean and then across much of the colonised world 'immediately invented and exploited legal forms of surrogate slavery. Amongst these was the extensive trade in labour contracts which bound Asian coolies to their places of work for a number of years and very often for much longer.' Once again, what eventually ended this trade was not its inadequate rate of profit but the domestic political reactions its abuses provoked.[29] In each case the key thing to understand, Gerstenberger argues, is that 'free wage labour is not the irrefutable and thus almost automatic result of economic development, but the result of specific state regulation' (MV, 109), itself invariably 'the result of long and fierce struggles' (426).[30]

In other words, the difference we have grown used to, between free and forced labour, 'is not virtually "natural" and a matter of course; this distinction was and remains defined over the course of history through conventions and laws.'[31] Capital's reluctant acceptance of such conventions, in the form of concessions to the growing political power of organised labour in the metropolitan countries, may have resulted in the partial 'domestication' of capitalism in those privileged places, complete with state-enforced minimum wage limits and legal protections for workers – but this, too, did not hinder the development of capitalism itself, nor limit its capacity to challenge or *reverse* these conventions wherever and whenever the balance of class power might allow it. Germany's National Socialist regime is only the most extreme case of what capital may be prepared to do if no political force is available to stop it. As Gerstenberger shows in compelling detail, Hitler's Third Reich 'was not a relapse into a pre-bourgeois epoch', but its labour regime certainly 'constituted a relapse into pre-domesticated capitalism. Consequently, strategies of appropriation that had hardly been conceivable a few years earlier became possible, and even commonplace' (MV, 409). In the absence of any political (or moral) restrictions, liberated from even the most minimal requirements of social reproduction, Nazi managers were free to exploit their workers as an emphatically disposable resource.

If the aggressive strategies of appropriation developed more recently by neoliberal regimes have so far refrained from such extremities this is again best explained, Gerstenberger suggests, simply through reference to the evolving balance of class forces, rather than by appealing to any intrinsic tendencies or limitations inherent in the capital-labour relation per se. Gerstenberger hardly needs to stress just how lopsided this balance has become in recent years, as ever more authoritarian and neo-fascistic forms of capitalism compete with each other in situations of more or less open conflict.

Gerstenberger summarises the lessons of her empirical analyses in her last couple of pages. Since capital prioritises profits for the privileged few rather than 'a better future for all', it's a mistake to subscribe to any version of the old myth that a 'rising tide lifts all boats.'

> In metropolitan capitalist countries, the 'thirty glorious years' after the Second World War once again nurtured the expectation that it was possible to prevent crises through economic policy. The real development of globalised capitalism has not only disproved this expectation, but also laid to rest the hope for a general improvement in living conditions through continuous economic growth. It has also refuted the assumption that social upgrading of working conditions is an inevitable consequence of introducing technically sophisticated production processes. On the other hand, it has become emphatically clear that direct violence as a means of appropriation was not only used in the early days of capitalist development, but is still in use today. It is true that after the historical establishment of capitalist conditions in some countries, this practice was initially marginalised, both geographically and socially. However, this was only the result of economically rational calculation insofar as the need for a growing number of workers for industrialised production within the limits of the labour markets of the time gave clout to the demands of organised labour. Since the globalisation of capitalism has done away with previously existing boundaries of labour markets, direct violence has again become present within the spaces of established capitalism. This is not inevitable. If a closer look at historically existing capitalism confirms the hypothesis that owners of capital tend to use every means to achieve profit, which they are not being prevented to employ, it has also become clear that public opinion and governments can indeed prevent such practices (MV, 663-4).

The limits of class struggle

Gerstenberger's concluding appeal to 'public opinion and governments' points to the most obvious and far-reaching difference that separates her account of capital from that of Marx. However much Marx's later economic writings might focus on the intricate machinations of capital and its general 'laws of motion', his priorities remain, of course, political and revolutionary. If after 1850 Marx pays such close attention to capitalism's development, the main goal remains to illuminate the tasks confronting the class that is destined to challenge and overcome it. Like Luxemburg and Lenin after him, Marx remains confident that capital cannot avoid preparing and enabling the people it exploits to dig its own grave, and thereby 'begets, with the inexorability of a natural process, its own negation.' In the notoriously compressed lines that conclude the main argument of *Capital, Volume 1*, Marx reiterates his belief that, together with the consolidation and centralisation of capital, 'there also grows the revolt of the working class, a class constantly increasing in numbers, and trained, united and organized by the very mechanism of the capitalist process of production.' Eventually 'the centralization of the means of production and the socialization of labour reach a point at which they become incompatible with their capitalist integument. This integument is burst asunder. The knell of capitalist private property sounds. The expropriators are expropriated' (C1, 929).

Nothing about Gerstenberger's analysis of actually-existing capitalism leads her to embrace Marx's anticipation of its revolutionary overthrow. This applies to both the 'objective' and 'subjective' aspects of the question. Given her single-minded focus on the question of direct or physical violence, Gerstenberger's objective history doesn't do full justice to those corrosive and thus at least *partly* emancipatory social developments regularly associated with the eclipse of feudalism and the rise of capitalism – the growth of cities, of trade, of literacy, of less constrained forms of labour, and so on. Gerstenberger is surely right that capitalist employers would rather employ diligent but submissive and disposable servants than genuinely 'free' workers, but the sociological gap (and with it the space for new forms of association, new forms of institution-building, new forms of political organisation) between ancien-régime service and the emergence of waged labour seems wider than Gerstenberger allows.[32]

Regarding the subjective side of things, Gerstenberger has even less sympathy for that heroic proletarian mission that Marx embraced as an article of faith in the 1840s, and that would later inform every stage of Luxemburg's or Lenin's political lives. Gerstenberger understands why the *Communist Manifesto* still appeals to anti-capitalist activists, but considers it 'historically more wrong than correct.'[33] Gerstenberger finds no evidence to support the idea that the working class, the class of all those people who are employed and exploited by capital, can be understood as a 'social actor' in the proper sense of that word, i.e. an actor motivated by a common purpose and equipped with a shared capacity to act on it. If the term class remains an essential category for understanding 'the fundamentally contradictory interests which are present in any labour relation', Gerstenberger insists that 'to talk of a global working class amalgamates description with the theory of revolution.' While such amalgamation may offer political encouragement (or consolation), 'its theoretical foundation is not tenable'.[34]

Following Geoff Eley and Keith Nield, Gerstenberger argues that 'class analysis arose out of the fact that at the turn from the nineteenth to the twentieth century there were proletarian milieus which favoured the development of solidarities which then in turn allowed the development of a socialist and communist programmatic.' Even in those circumstances, however, "'class" was a fictive entity in so far as it was conceived as a social group which would act in a certain way. These milieus hardly exist in present day capitalist societies. If conflicts over the appropriation of the results of labour are present in any labour relation, this does not make them into parts and parcel of class struggle. In order to perceive a global conflict between classes we would have to assume that solidarity could overcome competition on a global scale'[35] – and today this assumption, Gerstenberger suggests, remains nothing more than wishful thinking.[36] 'Today, the working-class milieus that had once made class analysis plausible have largely disappeared', and while 'struggles over the appropriation of the fruits of people's labour exist in all capitalist societies, class struggles do not' (MV, 521-2). Organised and politically consequential forms of class struggle, Gerstenberger implies, exist even less.

Another standard term in the Marxist lexicon that doesn't appear in Gerstenberger's book is 'class consciousness'. According to her account of our situation as it stands, the conditions that might encourage the emergence of global proletariat, as a tendentially united and 'conscious' or purposeful political actor, simply haven't materialised. In these circumstances

> it is impossible to justify the theoretical construct of a global proletariat. If a child knocking stones in an Indian quarry, a worker constantly handling poison in a rose plantation in Ecuador, or a captive sailor on an Indonesian fishing boat are all indiscriminately assigned to the theoretical construct of a global proletariat, whose rage about their conditions can be heard in a 'cry', they are then not only being exploited by capital owners and oppressed or 'overlooked' by politicians, but they are also being disregarded by theoreticians. For although the very diverse forms of labour existing in globalised capitalism all share one aspect – that men, women and children have to employ their labour under conditions defined by cap-

ital owners – the alternatives available to them on labour markets and the possibilities of resistance available to them differ so fundamentally that theoretical analysis cannot be allowed to simply lump them together under the heading of a globally existing social group of 'proletarians' (MV, 522-3).

The rebranding of 'proletarians' as 'the multitude,' she adds, in a sharp dig at Hardt and Negri, only adds another layer of obfuscation. Again, as she put it in a 2018 article,

> If the class relation exists in any form of capitalism, and if it is present in most social struggles of our time, the classes which Marx assumed would organize and teach themselves, thereby getting ready for revolution, are not present in globalized capitalism. There is then no social force which will induce capital owners to overcome short sighted practices of exploitation by creating labour conditions which, according to Marx, embody the historical progress inherent in capitalist social forms of production because they obliterated the brute force of exploitation characteristic of historically earlier forms of production and also because they bring about the preconditions for social revolution. The continuing presence of direct violence in capitalist social forms of production contradicts Marx's expectations of the history of capitalism. It thereby also contradicts his theory of revolution.[37]

Where Marx or Lenin sought to combine partisan commitment together with scientific investigation in a single revolutionary-scientific project, Gerstenberger insists that we should keep these two dimensions strictly apart. As social analysts, she says, 'we should look at the facts without being overwhelmed by hopes for a better future.'[38] Gerstenberger's sustained analysis of seafaring labour, for instance, leads her to accept what she calls, with a degree of understatement, a rather 'sober' judgement of its future. Asked about what the workers currently recruited by international crewing agencies might be able to do to resist their exploitation and fight for better conditions of work on the high seas, Gerstenberger's answer is stark: 'nothing'.[39]

Given her scepticism about the emergence of anything resembling a class actor that might be able to challenge let alone overthrow global capital, the terse and deflating tone of the concluding lines to Gerstenberger's long book is perhaps less surprising than a first reading might suggest. After reminding her readers that suitably informed 'public opinion and governments can indeed prevent' abusive labour practices and condemn 'unbearable conditions', Gerstenberger ends her empirical analysis with an insistence that what's at stake can only be a matter of relatively modest reforms. Nothing more. As things stand, our horizon of political possibility seems to be limited to campaigning for measures like appropriate taxes on financial transactions and on multinational corporations, and the enforcement of 'legal liability of enterprises for the working conditions of their labourers regardless of the location of their firms.' Such measures, Gerstenberger continues, 'clearly focus on the reform of capitalism. I do not know of any convincing strategic concept for the transition from capitalism to socialism nor do I know of any clear conception of the society to be built after the end of capitalism. But I do think that reform of capitalism is possible. And if such reforms will change the life of children, women and men for the better, then I think that they are worth fighting for'.[40]

The whole of Gerstenberger's final paragraph reads as follows: 'This study cannot serve as a starting point for discussions about reforms that would transcend the limitations of capitalism. Such discussions would have to address the fundamental structures of capitalism. What I have discussed here are excrescences of capitalism. They can be reformed. The political prospects such reforms might lead to are necessarily limited' (MV, 665). Nothing more. In case anyone should miss the point, Gerstenberger also adds a final and revealing footnote:

> The words I have chosen are also an appeal to abandon the optimistic view that capitalist production produces its own negation with the necessity of a process of nature [referring to C1, 929]. ... Such optimism is not uncalled for because it is based upon delusions as to human nature, but rather because it is a teleological construct of human history, assuming that it necessarily aims at a certain goal. But if we dispense with a meaning of history under, over or in whatever sense outside the actual course of history, it is only consistent to dispense with a human nature outside history. What we in fact know about the potential and abysses of which humans are capable we know from history (MV, 665n.22).

Three questions

Readers who (like the author of this review) might be more impressed by Gerstenberger's general history of capital than by her reformist conclusions are entitled to raise at least three questions of their own. The first concerns the limits of an historical approach per se. The sub-title of her book is important: this is very much a study of 'the functioning of capitalism *in history*.' As Gerstenberger would be the first to admit, indeed emphasise, such a study is very different from a 'critique of political economy', let alone a theoretical and strategic framework for transforming that economy. Gerstenberger's approach is also very different to the sort of histories written for instance by E.P. Thompson or Georges Lefebvre (to say nothing of Jean Jaurès or C.L.R. James), whose accounts of the making of a class capacity combine an analysis of its emergence with an avowedly 'engaged' or partisan investment in its political future.[41]

It should go without saying that any political confrontation with slavery, colonialism or colonial capitalism needs to be informed by the best available historical accounts of their origins and development. Nonetheless, no merely historical account of slavery, however lucid or thorough it might be, could ever have predicted let alone guided the actual political steps that were improvised and taken by the slaves who, over the long and bloody course of Haiti's revolution, rose up and overthrew it. No merely historical account of what Gerstenberger herself pointedly calls 'Ancien Régime' states could ever have predicted that abrupt and far-reaching break with such regimes that began in France in the spring of 1789. Similar points could be made about the revolutions that transformed Mexico, Russia or Cuba. In the same way, no merely historical account of what capital has done and has proved capable of doing can suffice to answer the questions future political actors might and indeed must one day ask themselves, about what in turn *we* should do about capital.

A second question concerns a limit to Gerstenberger's own particular history of capitalism, as a history that foregrounds its reliance on violence or coercive force. Recognition that 'capitalism essentially involves commanding the labour process' (MV, 208) certainly helps to show what it has in common with earlier modes of production, but Gerstenberger pays remarkably little attention to what might be called the distinctive 'psychopolitical' dimensions of capitalist command. These dimensions are fundamental to what makes capitalism both unique in comparison to earlier labour regimes and so difficult to challenge. Precisely because Marx is interested less in the past than in the future of capitalism, his analysis of these dimensions has lost none of its pertinence.

Marx retained the term 'wage slavery' in order to remind his readers of what it meant for workers to be 'dragged beneath the wheels of the juggernaut of capital' (C1, 799).[42] His account of capitalist command abounds in military metaphors and references to its 'despotism' and 'autocracy'. Marx knew perfectly well that originary accumulation is a prolonged process, and that 'centuries are required before the "free" worker, owing to the greater development of the capitalist mode of production, makes a voluntary agreement, i.e. is compelled by social conditions to sell the whole of his active life, his very capacity for labour, in return for the price of his customary means of subsistence' (C1, 382). But Marx was also careful to distinguish between the heavy and blatant chains of chattel slavery and the equally constraining but more 'invisible threads' that bind wage labourers to their owner (C1, 719). As we have seen, once thoroughly established, 'the silent compulsion of economic relations sets the seal on the domination of the capitalist over the worker'(C1, 899). In the factory system, 'the capitalist formulates his autocracy over his workers like a private legislator and purely as an emanation of his own will', unchecked by that 'separation of powers' which serves to limit the scope of popular participation in politics (C1, 550). The workers used by capital experience their work and time as determined by 'the powerful will of a being outside them, who subjects their activity to his purpose' (C1, 450). As Marx understood perfectly well back in 1844, in capitalism 'man regards his will, his activity and his relation to other men as a power independent of him and them. His slavery therefore reaches its peak.'[43]

What's unusual about capital, in short, precisely *as* a form of slavery, is its capacity to compel its workforce not merely through violent coercion but also at the level of the *will*. A well-run capitalist economy can afford to replace the whips and chains of plantation slavery with less abrasive incentives, and trust the 'bony hand of hunger' to do the rest. Wherever capital is firmly in charge it can rely, to evoke Frederic Lordon's phrase, on an inexhaustible supply of 'willing slaves'.[44] Needless to say, the more willing and enthusiastic these slaves become, the easier it is to exploit them; the more they can be trusted to defer to their governments and pay their taxes, the more capital can build up those networks of credit upon which it relies to fund its wars and investments. By focusing so much of her attention on coercive force Gerstenberger rightly foreground the stark brutality of capitalist exploitation, but as a result she (quite deliberately) pays much less attention to the psycho-political dimensions of the subjection that accompany it. Gerstenberger has little to say, in other words, in response to the question variously posed by La Boétie, Spinoza and Rousseau, and then rediscovered in different ways by Horkheimer, Adorno, Reich, Deleuze and Guattari – why might people submit to 'voluntary' forms of servitude, and collude in their own oppression? As Deleuze and Guattari put it in a much-cited page of their *Anti-Oedipus*, 'after centuries of exploitation, why do people still tolerate being humiliated and enslaved, to such a point, indeed, that they actually want humiliation and slavery not only for others but for themselves?'[45]

To confront a mode of production that operates at the level of people's wants, needs and desires must include, one way or another, a strategy for winning that political 'battle of wills' upon which our future depends. As Gerstenberger's own emphasis on the primacy of politics makes clear, arguments about what we should do about capital can hardly begin, let alone be resolved, before a sufficient mass of people come to *want* to do something about it, and then organise themselves into a force that is willing and able to act on what it wants.

Building on this basic point, my third and final question to Gerstenberger concerns her refusal to treat class as a 'social' let alone 'political' actor, i.e. as a collective actor that might come to share common desires or goals and organise common means of pursuing them. In the absence of a political account of class composition and class capacities, when Gerstenberger discusses the social forces that might induce the state to pass reforms limiting capital's excesses she refers instead to the shapeless pressures of 'public opinion' and of 'human beings' who stubbornly assert their dignity in the face of the most degrading abuses. 'Throughout the world', Gerstenberger tells us, 'there are more and more people who transcend their working conditions every day' (MV, 427) – and though this may well be true, it's one of the few declarations in her book that is backed up more by anecdote than by evidence.

As we've seen, Gerstenberger asks what an agrarian worker handling toxic chemicals in Ecuador might have in common with 'a captive sailor on an Indonesian fishing boat' (MV, 522). From a sociological perspective perhaps it's easy to answer: nothing at all. Despite obvious quantitative differences in distance and scale, however, there is no qualitative difference between such questions and the similar sorts of questions that could be asked, and were indeed pointedly asked, of the disparate occupational groups that contributed to the *political* making of a working class in England, Russia or China, or any place you like. As is well known, the French Revolution was in large part responsible for making the country that gives the sequence its name – but before they combined in enthusiastic defence of 'liberty, equality and fraternity', before they began to participate in local revolutionary organisations, before they enlisted in their new National Guard or citizens' army, what did Breton peasants really have in common with artisans in Rouen or labourers in Paris? On the eve of their own revolution in 1917, what did a landless day labourer in the Tambov countryside have in common with a textile worker on the outskirts of Moscow or a skilled metal worker in inner-city Petrograd?[46] Any attempt to answer such questions on the basis of 'historical sociology', however well-documented it might be, may not get very far in explaining the outbreak and course of the Russian Revolution – a sequence which allowed the diverse mass of groups demanding a transfer of 'all power to the Soviets' to find, in practice, that they actually had enough in common to turn their world upside down. Nor might such an approach make proper sense of those national liberation and internationalist projects that, in the wake of Russia's revolution, sometimes succeeded in organising widely divergent groups into a transformative political force.

Working as a historical sociologist, Gerstenberger may be entitled to *see* nothing in common between the objective situations of a captive sailor and a plantation labourer. To limit the category of class to observable sociological factors, however, is to remain blind to its political status and significance. Understood as one term in an asymmetrical relation of production, 'class' is not merely an expanded concept of occupation or livelihood, let alone a marker of social identity. The great and abiding value of the term 'working class' is precisely its explicit indifference to matters of occupation, geography or status. Nurses, coal miners, teachers and retail staff obviously lead very different lives, but if they choose to do so they can all make common cause as exploited and precarious workers.

One of the virtues of putting things this way is that it helps to foreground the literally causal power such a class actor might acquire, should it succeed in organising itself as a political force. 'An adequate theory of agency must be a theory of the causal *powers* persons have', as Alex Callinicos notes, and 'intentional explanations of human action, invoking beliefs and desires as reasons for acting, are necessary because of the peculiar kind of living organisms human beings are.' If all actor- or action-oriented explanations of people's behaviour, furthermore, 'contain a hidden premiss referring to the agent's power to perform the action in question', the actual scope of such power varies with what Callinicos calls an actor's 'structural capacities.'[47] These capacities are themselves very largely shaped, of course, as Gerstenberger knows as well as anyone, by the way relations of production are structured under capital's command, and by the way such command is in turn resisted or challenged.

Despite its discouraging historical record, the enduring argument in favour of the working class – understood here in its original Marxian and inclusive sense, as the grouping together of all those who find themselves compelled to sell (or to try to sell) their capacity for work to employers who use and exploit them – as the only mass actor potentially powerful, determined and organised enough to challenge capital's grip over society is well summarised by Ellen Wood. Despite all attempts to co-opt, divide or distract it, the exploited or

> working class is the only social group possessing not only an immediate interest in resisting capitalist exploitation but also a collective power adequate to end it .... However difficult it may be to construct socialist practice out of popular consciousness, there is, according to this view, no other material out of which it can be constructed and no other socialism that is consistent with both political realism and democratic values. Perhaps the point is simply that socialism will come about either in this way or not at all.[48]

Gerstenberger concludes her book with a suggestion that, since no revolutionary actor is available to replace capitalism with socialism, so we should limit our political ambitions to legislative measures that might reform capitalism and reign in its tendencies to abuse its power.

But Gerstenberger's argument in favour of reform today no more follows from 'the facts of *history*' than did Luxemburg's argument, more than a century ago, in favour of revolution.[49] How we want to live depends in the first place on what we *want* for the future, precisely, not on what has prevailed in the past.

Gerstenberger herself shows that even the most 'domesticated' forms of capital are not only liable but eager to regress into untamed predation whenever and wherever the opportunity might arise. The more we learn about capital's past and present the more reasons we have to conclude that our future requires something rather more forceful and transformative than new taxes and reforms. Nothing in Gerstenberger's account of actually-existing capitalism suggests that our most basic political choice has changed since it was first distilled by Kautsky and Luxemburg: if not socialism, then barbarism. The time to make up our minds about this is running out fast, and it's a mistake today, as it was yesterday, to believe that there will ever be a third option.

Notes

1. Gerstenberger, 'Markt und Gewalt', *Historical Materialism* blog, 5 May 2018, https://www.historicalmaterialism.org/markt-und-gewalt-market-and-violence/.
2. Gerstenberger, 'The Political Economy of Capitalist Labour', *Viewpoint Magazine*, 2 September 2014, https://viewpointmag.com/2014/09/02/the-political-economy-of-capitalist-labor/.
3. Gerstenberger, 'Heide Gerstenberger, Interviewed by Jasper Strange', *Historical Materialism* blog, 17 October 2018, https://www.historicalmaterialism.org/heide-gerstenberger/
4. Silvia Federici, *Caliban and the Witch: Women, the Body and Primitive Accumulation* (New York: Autonomedia, 2004), 16; cf. Maria Mies, *Patriarchy and Accumulation on a World Scale: Women in the International Division of Labour* (London: Zed, 1986), ch. 5.
5. Gerstenberger, *Impersonal Power: History and Theory of the Bourgeois State* (Chicago: Haymarket Books, 2009).
6. Gerstenberger, 'Heide Gerstenberger, Interviewed by Jasper Strange'.
7. See for instance Ellen Meiksins Wood, *Democracy Against Capitalism: Renewing Historical Materialism* (London: Verso Books, 1995), 20–21, 28–29.
8. William I. Robinson, 'Global Capitalism's Extermination Impulse,' *Philosophical Salon*, 19 August 2024, https://thephilosophicalsalon.com/global-capitalisms-extermination-impulse/ Cf. Robinson, *Global Civil War: Capitalism Post-*

Pandemic (Oakland: PM Press, 2022); Robinson, *The Global Police State* (London: Pluto, 2020).

9. Gerstenberger, 'On *Market and Violence*,' presentation at the twenty-first *Historical Materialism* conference, London, 9 November 2024; cf. Charles Post, 'Racism and Capitalism: A Contingent or Necessary Relationship?' *Historical Materialism* 32:2-3 (2023), 78–103.

10. Gerstenberger, 'On *Market and Violence*,' presentation at *Historical Materialism* conference, London 9 November 2024.

11. Gerstenberger, 'The Political Economy of Seafaring Labour', Deutscher Lecture, *Historical Materialism* conference, London, 8 November 2024; cf. MV ch. 8, which draws in part on Gerstenberger and Ulrich Welke, *Arbeit auf See: Zur Ökonomie und Ethnologie der Globalisierung* (2008), along with their earlier collaboration, *Vom Wind zum Dampf* (1996).

12. A more detailed summary of some of the book's contents can be found in a helpful review of the German edition by Christian Lotz for *Marx & Philosophy Review of Books* (31 July 2018), https://marxandphilosophy.org.uk/reviews/16027_markt-und-gewalt-die-funktionsweise-des-historischen-kapitalismus-by-heide-gerstenberger-reviewed-by-christian-lotz/

13. Karl Marx, *Capital: Critique of Political Economy*, vol. 1 [1867], trans. Ben Fowkes (London: Penguin and New Left Review, 1990), 672; hereafter abbreviated as C1.

14. See Jonathan M. Katz, *Gangsters of Capitalism: Smedley Butler, The Marines, and the Making and Breaking of America's Empire* (New York: St. Martin's Press, 2022).

15. See for instance e.g. Moishe Postone, *Time, Labor, and Social Domination: A Reinterpretation of Marx's Critical Theory* (Cambridge: Cambridge University Press, 2008); Søren Mau, *Mute Compulsion: A Marxist Theory of the Economic Power of Capital* (London: Verso, 2023).

16. MV, 64-5, drawing on Steinfeld, *Coercion, Contract, and Free Labor*, 239ff.

17. Gerstenberger, 'The Political Economy of Capitalist Labour', *Viewpoint Magazine*, 2 September 2014; cf. MV, 58–59.

18. 'On the contrary', Federici continues, 'capitalism has created more brutal and insidious forms of enslavement, as it has planted into the body of the proletariat deep divisions that have served to intensify and conceal exploitation. It is in great part because of these imposed divisions – especially those between women and men – that capitalist accumulation continues to devastate life in every corner of the planet' (Federici, *Caliban*, 64).

19. Gerstenberger, 'Heide Gerstenberger, Interviewed by Jasper Strange'.

20. Ibid.

21. Marx and Engels, *The Communist Manifesto*, in Marx, *Selected Writings*, ed. David McLellan (Oxford: Oxford University Press, 2000), 248.

22. Robert Steinfeld, *Coercion, Contract and Free Labor in the Nineteenth Century* (Cambridge: Cambridge University Press, 2001); Marcel van der Linden and Magaly Rodríguez García, eds., *On Coerced Labor: Work and Compulsion After Chattel Slavery* (Leiden: Brill, 2016); van der Linden, *Workers of the World: Essays Toward a Global History of Labor* (Leiden: Brill, 2008).

23. MV, 110. Gerstenberger knows, of course, that 'in capitalist production, labour is used under conditions of competition. This became more possible on a larger scale in the first European countries to become capitalist when many people were forced to procure provisions for themselves and their families through wage labour. If they were legally free, they were able to offer their labour power to employers (in German, "'givers of work"', *Arbeitgeber*). However, contrary to widespread assumption, this did not immediately mean that labour was detached from control by authorities. That liberation had to be won through political struggle. It is not one of the founding characteristics of capitalism' (MV, 50).

24. David McNally, who is currently completing a book about Marx and slavery, raised some objections to Gerstenberger's account of slavery in his contribution to the online book launch for *Market and Violence*, hosted by HM on 30 Jan 2024, https://www.youtube.com/watch?v=6iwZEJ7HAP0.

25. See for instance Charles Post, *The American Road to Capitalism: Studies in Class-Structure, Economic Development and Political Conflict, 1620-1877* (Leiden: Brill, 2011); Dale W. Tomich, *Slavery in the Circuit of Sugar: Martinique and the World-Economy, 1830-1848* (NY: SUNY Press, 2016); Nick Nesbitt, *The Price of Slavery: Capitalism and Revolution in the Caribbean* (Charlottesville: University of Virginia Press, 2022).

26. Gerstenberger, 'The Political Economy of Capitalist Labour' (2014), citing Robin Blackburn, *The Overthrow of Colonial Slavery 1776-1848* (London: Verso, 1988), 520.

27. MV, 109; cf. Rebecca J. Scott, *Slave Emancipation in Cuba* (Princeton: Princeton University Press, 1985).

28. Gerstenberger, 'Heide Gerstenberger, Interviewed by Jasper Strange'.

29. Gerstenberger, 'Markt und Gewalt', *Historical Materialism* blog, 5 May 2018.

30. According to Gerstenberger, what prevents Marx and his more orthodox followers from understanding the basic continuity of waged and enslaved labour is their dogmatic investment in a teleological concept of history, one that includes both capitalism and socialism as necessary stages of a single sequence. No less than the bourgeois political economists they attack, Marx and his followers 'conceive of capitalism as a progressive stage in the history of mankind, not only because it was progressive in relation to pre-capitalist forms of economy and society but also because, according to Marx, the inherent dynamics of capitalism prepare the historical possibility of socialism.' Overall, Gerstenberger remains 'quite sure that it was [Marx's] concept of revolution which led to his refusal to accept that capitalism did not always and everywhere rely on the double freedom of labourers. Since he expected that labourers would organize and educate themselves in order to achieve the revolutionary transformation to socialism, he could not very well accept that slavery was a capitalist form of labour' (Gerstenberger, 'Heide Gerstenberger, Interviewed by Jasper Strange').

31. MV, 61, drawing on Steinfeld, *Coercion, Contract and Free Labor*, 14, 315.
32. David Cunningham developed some aspects of this critique in his response to a first draft of this essay, in June 2024.
33. Gerstenberger, discussion with the author, London 9 November 2024.
34. Gerstenberger, 'Heide Gerstenberger, Interviewed by Jasper Strange'.
35. Ibid.
36. Cf. Geoff Eley and Keith Nield, *The Future of Class in History: What's Left of the Social?* (Ann Arbor: University of Michigan Press, 2007). Gerstenberger made a similar argument in response to questions posed by David McNally at the online book launch for *Market and Violence*, 31 January 2024, https://www.youtube.com/live/6iwZEJ7HAP0?si=-di4wW-wXiD85jHH.
37. Gerstenberger, 'Markt und Gewalt', *Historical Materialism* blog, 5 May 2018.
38. Gerstenberger, discussion with the author, London 9 November 2024.
39. Gerstenberger, 'The Political Economy of Seafaring Labour,' discussion with the audience, 8 November 2024.
40. Gerstenberger, 'Heide Gerstenberger, Interviewed by Jasper Strange'.
41. I'm thinking here of E.P. Thompson's *Making of the English Working Class* (1963), Georges Lefebvre's *Les Paysans du Nord pendant la Révolution française* (1924), Jean Jaurès's *Histoire socialiste de la Révolution française* (1901-07) and C.L.R. James's *The Black Jacobins: Toussaint L'Ouverture and the San Domingo Revolution* (1938).
42. Cf. Bruno Leipold, 'Chains and Invisible Threads: Liberty and Domination in Marx's Account of Wage-Slavery', in *Rethinking Liberty before Liberalism*, ed. Hannah Dawson and Annelien de Dijn (Cambridge: Cambridge University Press, 2022), 194–214.
43. Marx, 'Comments on James Mill, *Elements of Political Economy*' [1844], in Marx and Engels, *Complete Works*, vol. 3 (NY: International Publishers, 1975), 212.
44. Frederic Lordon, *Willing Slaves of Capital: Spinoza and Marx on Desire* (London: Verso, 2014). Cf. Byung-Chul Han, *Psychopolitics: Neoliberalism and New Technologies of Power* (London: Verso, 2017); Peter Hallward, 'The Will of the People and the Struggle for Mass Sovereignty: A Preliminary Outline', *Crisis and Critique* 9:2 (November 2022): 143–219, https://www.crisiscritique.org/storage/app/media/nov-25/peter-hallward.pdf
45. Gilles Deleuze and Felix Guattari, *Anti-Oedipus: Capitalism and Schizophrenia* (Minneapolis: University of Minnesota Press, 1983), 29.
46. See in particular David Mandel, *The Petrograd Workers in the Russian Revolution: February 1917-June 1918* (Leiden: Brill, 2017); Stephen A. Smith, *Red Petrograd: Revolution in the Factories, 1917-1918* (Chicago: Haymarket Books, 2017); Diane P. Koenker, *Moscow Workers and the 1917 Revolution* (NY: Columbia University Press, 1981).
47. Alex Callinicos, *Making History: Agency, Structure and Change in Social Theory* (Ithaca: Cornell University Press, 1988), 274–77.
48. Wood, *Democracy Against Capitalism*, 103.
49. Rosa Luxemburg, *Reform or Revolution* [1900], in *The Essential Rosa Luxemburg*, ed. Helen Scott (Chicago: Haymarket, 2008).

The transformation of everyday life

Interview with Kristin Ross

Kristin Ross is a leading theorist of French cultural history and politics, and Professor Emeritus of Comparative Literature at New York University. She is the author of several widely-translated books including The Emergence of Social Space: Rimbaud and the Paris Commune *(1988),* Fast Cars Clean Bodies: Decolonization and the Reordering of French Culture *(1995),* May 68 and its Afterlives *(2002), and* Communal Luxury: The Political Imaginary of the Paris Commune *(2015). Kristin was interviewed for RP by Patrick Lyons to mark the publication of a career-spanning collection of essays,* The Poetics and Politics of Everyday Life *(2022) and the English translation of her latest book,* The Commune-Form: The Transformation of Everyday Life *(2024).*

Patrick Lyons: In your introduction to *The Politics and Poetics of Everyday Life* you describe beginning your academic career in a field dominated by post-structuralism, deconstruction and a general retreat from politics. How did this affect your trajectory as a scholar and your own method of working?

Kristin Ross: My thinking about literature, history and historical processes is very much a product of the 1970s: the post-'68 moment of 'history from below'. This was an era filled with experiments in historiography, some of which I wrote about later in *May 68 and its Afterlives*. One of the major afterlives of '68 was, precisely, this host of interventions into the field of who was entitled to write history and in what way. As an undergraduate, I was lucky to attend the 'experimental' campus of the University of California at Santa Cruz, built during the late 1960s. We students grew the vegetables we ate in the cafeteria and there were no grades. And, at that time – Vietnam, the bombing of Cambodia – many of us were caught up in various forms of street militancy. Because of its innovative practices, Santa Cruz, then, drew an amazing array of faculty across the disciplines who were my teachers: the Freudo-Marxian classicist, Norman O. Brown, and, occasionally, his friend and rival Herbert Marcuse; the theorist of schizophrenia, Gregory Bateson; the urban theorist Reyner Banham. Jonathan Beecher, who wrote intellectual biographies of Fourier and Considérant, taught French history. The most interesting faculty by far, in other words, were, if not Marxist, at least in some sense materialists fully conversant in Marxist theory. And each of these scholars had no trouble at all venturing far afield of their given disciplinary constraints, creating between them and making available a kind of 'interdisciplinary unconscious' to students and colleagues. Especially now, when we compare what they created to the shackles of today's academic conventions – little more than a breeding ground for specialisation and opportunism – this was an extraordinarily lively group. Brown, in particular, impressed upon me the importance of keeping the question of desire at the forefront of any Marxist analysis, and introduced me to the thinkers – Walter Benjamin, Ernst Bloch, William Morris, and an array of poets like Blake, Sappho and Charles Olsen – to help light up that path.

Graduate school, though, was a different story. My own case could be viewed as an example of both the fragility and strength of political transmission, especially during counter-revolutionary times, of which the late 1970s were certainly the dawning. Deconstruction had reached a quasi-liturgical status, at least at Yale where I was, and though it shrouded itself in layers of gravitas, it was hard for me to take such a hyper-intellectualised textual formalism very seriously. Political action was reduced to the romantic 'politics' of textuality and was limited to the thrill produced by the free play of the signifier; political struggle took the form of the battle between competing jargons; and political revolution transpired in the ruptures internal to the semiotics of a text. Fortunately, Fredric Jameson joined the faculty and helped me reestablish continuities with my earlier training. I found a way to start working against the grain of the theoretical hegemony, beginning with my first book on Rimbaud and social space.

PL: The essays in parts one and two of *The Politics and Poetics of Everyday Life* demonstrate an ongoing theoretical dialogue with Henri Lefebvre and Jacques Rancière respectively. In what way did the work of Jacques Rancière, whose *Le maître ignorant* (1987) you translated, influence your thinking? And how would you describe the contribution of Henri Lefebvre to your writing?

KR: As I was writing the book on Rimbaud, *The Emergence of Social Space: Rimbaud and the Paris Commune,* a fellow-traveller in the archives of the Paris Commune, Adrian Rifkin, introduced me to the early work of Jacques Rancière and the *Révoltes Logiques* collective. Rifkin had translated some of the early essays from *Révoltes Logiques* and submitted them to *History Workshop* where they were rejected on the grounds that they were insulting to the working class! Apparently, what had excited Adrian and myself about the particular kind of cultural history the collective at *Révoltes Logiques* was undertaking – their dismantling of Marxist literal-mindedness and sociological determinism, their unravelling of all the stereotypical representations that congeal in the writing of even the most progressive social scientists or political activists when it comes to workers – was exactly what made it anathema to the folks at *History Workshop*. In *Révoltes Logiques*, base and superstructure never quite lined up in any obvious way, edifying narratives about good workers were few and far between, and the terrain of class relations was shot through with fantasy, denial and misrecognitions. I decided to translate *Le Maître ignorant* – what for me remains Rancière's most interesting and innovative book.

As for my method, Rimbaud's famous response to his mother's question, 'But what does it mean?', that he wished to be understood 'literally and in all possible ways', did become a method of sorts for me. In my books on the political memory of major upheavals like the Paris Commune or May '68, I was trying to document a moment in an oppositional culture that cannot be detected as long as one approaches cultural production uniquely from the perspective of the relentless 'it couldn't have been otherwise' logic of the commodity. The Paris Commune and 1968 were moments of the social appropriation of space and the transformation of everyday life it implies. They were moments when the state recedes, its political temporality broken or interrupted, during which we can begin to detect the existence of forms of the organisation of material life that escape from the logic of profits. During these moments, discussions of collective interests occur outside of the realm of experts. But it's only by reconstructing the particular phenomenology of the event, gathering the voices of actors of the past and lingering with them for a good bit of time that one can arrive at an event's more centrifugal and far-reaching effects. It is only by respecting an event's singularity – what the people who made the Commune, for example, did and said, what they thought and said about what they were doing, the words they used, borrowed, imported, disputed, abandoned and all the many significations they gave to those words and the desires that informed them – that the event or struggle enters into the figurability of our day-to-day concerns and imagination and presents itself to us as a possible future.

I think a literary formation is helpful for this kind of attentiveness to language in that it places an emphasis on the scene of subjectivisation, on the importance of beginning with subjectivity, say, over beginning with concepts. There's a Benvenistian element to all of this that I share, I think, with Rancière – the idea that subjectivity is created literally when one says 'I', the profound equality enabled by the fact that we all share the pronoun 'I', the fact that everyone who speaks that pronoun appropriates to him or herself when they say it an entire language. I owe this kind of attention or listening to the *énoncé* to Rancière's conviction that workers' voices from the past are entitled to the same degree of attention we pay to the voices of those who make up theories about them later on. Provided, that is, that their setting, their conditions be de-naturalised, so to speak – so that people of the past, and particularly workers, may appear to us now as subjects, and not as mere data. To free them from the task of being nothing but the representation of their conditions, I sometimes have to stage unexpected encounters, paratactical rearrangements that open up their present, or reconstruct the phenomenology of the event using oblique transversals – and then listen to the dynamics that result from those encounters.

So, on the one hand there is the attempt on my part to document past capacities set in motion. This means mobilising several 'scales' of analysis at once, both the lived and the conceived, the biographical and the textual. On the other, though, I think no new politics can be constructed or reconstructed unless one disengages actively and polemically from the legends and thefts that surround the representation of such moments – the idea that May '68 was something benign for the state, for example. It's often necessary to remove all sorts of clutter from the stage, just as the Communards themselves did when they blew up what William Morris called 'that base piece of Napoleonic upholstery', the Vendome Column, in order to transform their city – however briefly – into a space of pure potentiality.[1]

The goal here for me has always been to destabilise our sense of unchanging conditions or what Barthes called the 'petit-bourgeois distribution of roles and places': that whole massive appearance of permanence that restricts not only the emergence of individual and collective subjectivities and political energies but even the mobility of ideas and the spontaneity and provocation of artistic invention.[2]

My books are always interventions into particular situations. *Fast Cars, Clean Bodies,* for example, was written at the high point of celebratory modernisation ideology. American social scientists had successfully promulgated the idea of value-free social science and the inevitability of the American model, and all sorts of scholars who claimed the objective 'neutrality' of the social scientist, historians like Richard Kuisel and many of the French frequenters of the Fondation Saint-Simon, were in fact busy doing the bidding of American capitalist interests. One of the ways they did so was to completely separate two post-war narratives about France: the story of the end of the empire and the residues of colonialism, on the one hand, and the story of shopping and modern appliances, on the other. Thinking the two narratives together, as I tried to do in my book, was an attempt not only to break through the consensus surrounding American neo-liberal inevitability, but to take seriously the enactment of a kind of 'colonisation of everyday life' in France in those years, to think that phrase literally and in all possible ways to arrive at an economic, non-culturalist theory of racism.

The idea of a 'colonisation of everyday life' is, of course, Henri Lefebvre's. The interdisciplinary reach of his thought – a reach that allowed him to conceive of the 'quotidian' in the first place and to elevate it to the status of a critical theory – was once much less unusual in France than it is now.[3] His idea that any history must be written beginning with, and in view of, the present (the 'progressive-regressive method'); the iconoclasm of his anti-structuralist stance in the era of high-Althusserianism (one of the few dimensions he shares with Rancière); his insistence on taking seriously women's magazines, horoscopes and youth culture at a moment when Second International macro-histories were still the fashion; his abiding relationship with literature; his fascination with moments when cities and urban space are transformed into theaters of strategic operations – all these aspects of his multidimensional thought have been rich resources for me. As with any theorist the question is always: what does his or her work allow one to do? In my case, when I returned to the Paris Commune to write *Communal Luxury,* I had in mind not Lefebvre's own book about the Commune but rather his 'dialectique du vécu et du conçu'. The conceptual, when it is in constant relation to the lived, does not resemble a finely philosophical abstract elaboration but is rather constructive, built in view of the lived, after it, in response to it, towards a political goal. For Lefebvre, revolutionary thought and action, while different, are obliged to return to each other periodically and regularly for renewal. His own life exemplified the idea. For me it opened up the structure of my book and pointed me towards thinking through the theoretical breakthroughs unleashed by the experience of the Commune as they were occurring and immediately afterwards, as though in a laboratory.

In the end you might say I borrowed from Rancière a way of thinking about emancipation and the resistance to work, an attentiveness to the desires that arise on the borders of the artisanal world, and the centrality of the division between intellectual and manual labour. From Lefebvre I owe the projection of that division onto the uneven levels that are city and countryside, including the level of everyday life. From the first, then, I owe the right to thought; from the second, the right to the city. And more lately – the right to the countryside.

PL: The middle section of the volume moves away from philosophy and theory *per se* to study a series of cultural texts – Zola's *The Ladies Paradise*, Genet's screenplay for Tony Richardson's *Mademoiselle*, the films of Jacques Tati, Matisse's *Odalisques,* and detective fiction on both sides of the Atlantic. Anglophone readers of French literature will likely be more familiar with Zola and Genet than with *polar* writers like Didier Daeninckx or Jean-François Villar. Yet as you frame things in 'Parisian Noir', the post-68 French detective novel inherits the political thrust of May, transposed into narratives which reveal crimes committed and suppressed by the French state. How do these crime novels, in your reading, function as political works?

KR: My work for some time has taken up the problem of the contingencies of political memory – the sometimes circuitous and unscheduled ways that incidents or moments from the collective past succeed in entering forcefully, sometimes jarringly, into our present consciousness. How do past emancipatory processes attain figurability for us today? When I was working on my book about the way May '68 in France has been remembered, forgotten, trivialised, celebrated and banalised in France,[4] I could not avoid confronting the whole, very French phenomenon of 'the commemoration' – '68 as pictured in the media ten years, twenty years after, and so forth. I remember the first time I came across the phrase 'commemoration industry' was in a text from 1978 written by detective writer, militant and surrealist, Jean-François Vilar.[5] He was complaining about the hijacking of the political memory of '68 already getting underway by the 'official', or rather the then-making-themselves-official memory custodians of the sixties – namely, those former student 'leaders' eager to capitalise on and publicly repudiate, in one breath, their militant past as they began to climb the career ladder to success in the media and culture industries. Of course, Vilar, and people like him, were not invited to the commemoration. Like all state-sponsored commemorations, this one would do nothing more than summon forth the past in order to consecrate the present and the status quo. Instead, as I discovered once I had immersed myself in the *noir* fiction produced in the 1970s and 80s by Vilar and his fellow travelers – Didier Daeninckx, Thierry Jonquet, Francis Zamponi, Gérard Delteil, Frédéric Fajardie and others – they were busy producing a whole repository of alternative political memory about not only the events of '68, but the Algerian War, the extermination of European Jews, and other significant events from recent history. And they were doing it using a genre that took as its principal task the representation of ordinary people and their entanglements with their (mostly urban) surroundings. Writers who took up detective fiction, in other words, were fully conscious of the struggle over the collective memory of the 1960s and 70s, and they were intent on producing a different kind of history of the postwar years – one that was neither commemorative, abject, nor nostalgic like the extravaganza shows televised in 1978 about May '68, and, particularly, in 1988 when the commemoration industry was doing double duty trying to hijack the memory of the French Revolution during the latter's Bicentennial celebration. A more belletristic novel form, it seems, could not be made to suit the purposes of writers like Vilar and Daeninckx – instead, the readily available, mass-market, 'pulp' medium of crime fiction, with its affinity with the streets and what goes on there, worked better for recovering the 'structure of feeling' that accompanied the transformation of everyday life, the conviviality and sense of possibility so many people recalled about those times: the experience of creating together a culture not as an institution but as a way of life.[6]

In the confusing and sometimes disheartening years of the decomposition of the movement, as groups, friendships, and political opportunities and vistas dissolved, and new agendas hovered only vaguely on the horizon, it is not too surprising that detective-writing should prove to be a refuge of sorts for militants unwilling, so to speak, to 'settle', to get back in the harness and return to the daily grind. Polar writing, often for series editors who were themselves former comrades, and often with an overt political thematic, was a way of maintaining a solidarity with the aspirations of the recent political past, a way of continuing a form of subversive work and sociability that had been opened up and made possible by the events of '68.

The choice of the detective genre was overdetermined as well by the way in which it could be adapted to the kind of inductive reasoning and critique of specialisation that were both hallmarks of '68 practice, conducted in any number of exercises in 'writing history from below' such as the workers' *enquête* (enquiry). Militants in search of workers' experience unfiltered through the mouthpieces of union leaders or militants themselves – the unmediated voice of the worker – performed *enquêtes* or investigations in workers' *foyers*,[7] in an attempt to gain knowledge of workers' experience inductively – from the particular, that is, as opposed to drawing deductive consequences from an abstract general principle, an a priori theory or a social profile. Documentary film and alternative journalism were also characterised by an inductive mode of reasoning that could easily be transposed onto a noir format. The post-68 years saw a considerable overlap as well between the *métiers* (professions) and the figures of journalist, photographer and detective (writer): Daeninckx, for example, was an investigative reporter for years (in the process gaining, as he put it, a taste for the terrain) before turning to detective fiction; Vilar's main character, an ex-68'er turned street photographer, drifts ineluctably into crime investigation.

Using a technique best summed up as 'the imbrication of eras',[8] French noir shows the disquiet, decomposition and devolution of the present social world to be intimately linked to the unresolved or actively covered-up residues of past political action, usually on the part of the state. Forgotten incidents from France's colonial past, for example, thread their way into the present and re-emerge as recurrent fascist comportments. A random street murder cannot be explained without ultimately revealing a state crime perpetrated decades past, buried under layers of artful bureaucratic obfuscation.

In the essays in *The Politics and Poetics of Everyday Life* that deal with detective fiction, I see the figure of the detective in the French case functioning as a kind of historical consciousness at the moment of a sweeping eradication of historical depth. The counter-revolution that set in in the late 1970s not only tried to re-write the '68 years as the birth of narcissistic individualism and neo-liberal consumerism. It also presided over massive urban renewal projects, especially in Paris, transformations on a scale comparable to the Haussmanian upheavals of a century earlier. Such widespread demolition and reconstruction resulted in the production of a prevailing consumer blandness in the city centre, a centre newly rid of its poorer inhabitants, destined to finish their days in the shoddy, hastily constructed high-rises now ringing the periphery of the city. The revolutionary memory embedded in the urban texture of a city like Paris was considerably eradicated in the process. The specificity of the French case, however, cannot be made without a significant detour through the urban imaginary and social geography of that other great noir city, namely the Los Angeles of Raymond Chandler and Ross Macdonald, Fredric Jameson and Mike Davis.

PL: Your previous books have focused largely on urban spaces and struggle – modernising France, May '68, the Commune – why the turn to the rural in the concluding essays in the volume? Can you describe how you came into contact with the ZADistes (Zone to Defend activists) at Notre-Dame-des-Landes, what your time with them was like, and how it has informed your most recent (and ongoing) work?

KR: In France at least, in recent years, zones of experimentation and pragmatic intervention into actually living differently – living, that is, in semi-secession from state and market – have flourished far more readily in the countryside than in the big cities, those centres of capitalist exchange and state decision-making. This is not too surprising, given the overlap between contemporary experimentations with what I call the commune-form and the overwhelming ecological imperative to defend the living against capitalist expropriation and destruction. Some of these rural communities are in areas that the market forgot or couldn't monetise sufficiently, while others, like Notre-Dame-des-Landes during the airport struggle, or, in the United States, the occupations in Cop City in the forests outside of Atlanta or Standing Rock in the Dakotas, are in areas fiercely contested by the state.[9] In the countryside, it is easier to reinvent forms of life in regions that have conserved, at least in part, residual pre-capitalist usages and practices. At the same time, the choices available to young people in the cities – no work, badly paid work, precarious work, meaningless work, or work that actively and directly facilitates the capitalist destruction of the lived environment – don't exactly inspire great enthusiasm. When I went to Notre-Dame-des-Landes for the first time in 2016, I saw the way that being off the radar, so to speak, even for just a while, two or three years, enabled the building of alternative, semi-autonomous communities. Remember that in the case of Notre-Dame-des-Landes, the state took a long nap during its project to build the airport – it forgot about its own intention for a number of years, and during those years a kind of wonderful political intelligence and solidarity developed between the very different individuals and groups on the site bent on sharing together, in a by no means conflict-free way, a movement and a territory.

PL: Your study of the 'Commune-Form' grounds the third section of *The Politics and Poetics of Everyday Life*. This is a flexible form with the potential to gather together disparate autonomous experiments across time and space, but your insistence upon historical specificity prevents it from floating off into abstraction. What do you see as the political potential of the commune-form, and how does it continue to shape your current work?

KR: I wrote *Communal Luxury* because the Movement of the Squares in 2011 had reawakened an almost worldwide communal unconscious and in so doing had brought the Paris Commune once again prominently and forcefully into the figurability of the present. At NDDL the following year, some of the occupiers had read the book and initiated discussions with me about the continuities and discontinuities between the urban nineteenth-century Communards and what they themselves were then living. These discussions made me think more generally about the commune-form – not, as you say, as an abstraction or a concept, but rather as a constantly changing and improvisational formation or set of processes that is nevertheless recognisable. The examples I use in the book are primarily, but not entirely, French and modern, but I am in no way claiming the form to be particularly French or that it is a new, novel invention. After all, the same term, 'commune' has been used to denote bourgeois town formations in the European Middle Ages, the most radically democratic aspects of the French Revolution, agrarian peasant communities throughout the world, the desires for a society built on association and cooperation that flourished in workers' clubs in Paris at the end of the Second Empire, and the alternative communities founded by mostly young people in exodus from establishment ways of life, particularly after '68. It is in fact a quite archaic form, reworked according to the specific needs, histories and emancipatory desires of those engaged in living it and the region they are defending and transforming. The form is inseparable from its different incarnations, from the individuals and non-human life-forms participating in each situation, all of whom confront the conditions and avail themselves of the resources of the present moment. A struggle that is at the same time a way of life, the commune-form implies taking creative responsibility for the management of everyday life in common – what Marxists call social reproduction – in an immediate and pragmatic way. As such, it's a struggle that already contains elements of a life beyond capitalist society.

So, if the early essays in the book tend to highlight the alienated dimensions of an everyday given over to the violence of economic logic, in the later essays it is the capacity of the everyday to harbour and unleash forms of social creativity that moves to the forefront. Lefebvre thought that changing society was meaningless without the production of an appropriated space – what I call the commune-form. Individuals and groups cannot constitute themselves as political subjects unless they appropriate a space – both social and physical – for themselves. Not in the sense of a possession, but rather as a social creation. Certainly the ZAD (Zone of Defence) at Notre-Dame-des-Landes was such a creation.

PL: In an interview with *Mediapart* from May 2023, you discuss your experiences with the *Soulevements de la terre* movement in France.[10] Can you say a bit about the group and your involvement?

KR: Something like a distinctively combative rural life is emerging in France – opposed to agribusiness, to the stockpiling and privatisation of resources, and engaged in defending and resuscitating a kind of agriculture associated with small farms and *paysans*. In recent years, I've been involved with the movement issuing from the ZAD at NDDL known as *Soulèvements de la terre,* whose defense of agricultural land against developers, unnecessary infrastructural constructions, polluters, agribusiness, the FNSEA and other destructive agricultural organisations, has the strongest political potential of anything I've seen in the cities or the countryside. The movement is still very much in its youthful stage. But it has elicited a terrifying degree of violence on the part of the state – some of which I've observed personally – a state that seems bent on nothing less than exterminating the movement and any traces of it. In a book I published recently in France that pursues some of my reflections on the commune-form, I argue that *Soulèvements de la terre*, which bases its actions on concrete living situations, regional particularities and the specific needs of the humans and other life forms living there, is the commune-mode for our time. The movement's ability to create and maintain solidarity across extreme diversity, as well as its ability to draw the gaze of city-dwellers onto the crimes being committed in the countryside, is in my opinion why it has given rise to the high degree of panic among the elites we were witness to in March 2023, in Sainte Soline and its afterlives.

PL: The figure of the peasant – and the subsistence farmer in particular – is central to the story you recount in *La Forme-commune,* rather than the urban student or worker. This requires you to confront all manner of stereotypes projected onto the peasantry, often from the left. Can you say a bit about the pejorative figuration you're working against and why it's important to confront it today?

KR: In the wake of the demonstration at Sainte Soline, where the government launched over 4000 military grenades in a few hours at its own citizens, injuring hundreds and putting two people into a coma, it's quite clear that there is a war between two different worlds transpiring in the French countryside.[11] On the one side, we have intensive, productivist agro-business, which deems itself justified in privatising and stockpiling a resource held in common like water (for the use of only 7% of the farmers in the region – those that grow water-intensive crops like corn destined to feed industrially-raised livestock.) And, on the other, a kind of agriculture associated with small holdings and *paysans*. It's important to understand that in my discussion of *paysans* I am not talking about *paysans* empirically, in the sense of the numerically ever-dwindling sociological entity – a population whose members can be counted – but rather about the *paysan* as a *figure*. In the same way that the *forme-commune* cannot be given a hard and fast definition because of the history of its ever-evolving specific manifestations throughout the world, so the name *paysan* has been given over time to large landowners, small subsistence farmers, and landless agricultural labourers alike. And even to non-city dwellers in general! For my purposes, though, the figure of the *paysan* is associated with a rootedness in the land, the cyclic nature of agricultural labour and activities, a way of reasoning that is basically social rather than economic, and, most importantly, with a subsistence economy that is not entirely subordinated to market relations. It is the situation of the *paysan* – physically, of course, but also temporally – that interests me. *Paysans* are regularly castigated for being out of step with modernity – they are seen as forces of tradition, even conservatism. But that conservatism is double-edged, and is frequently a mark of the stubbornness and resilience it takes to defend, at all costs, a way of life that is constantly under threat by the forces of capitalist modernisation. The anachronistic dimension of the *paysan,* as Erag Ramizi and others have pointed out, is what constitutes the force of the figure – out of step with their own time, *paysans* are not only figurations of a past but also, potentially, of a possible future. All this acts to make the *paysan* – again like the *forme-commune* – a kind of valuable repository of archaic, pre-capitalist ways of living that are well worth reviving and attending to as we begin to build a post-productivist world.

Patrick Lyons is Assistant Professor of French and Francophone Studies in the Department of Modern Languages and Literatures at Case Western Reserve University. He is currently completing a book manuscript on the literary history of North African immigrant labour in twentieth century France.

Notes

1. William Morris, *Political Writings: Contributions to 'Justice' and 'Commonweal', 1883-1890*, ed. Nicholas Salmon (Bristol:Thoemmes Press, 1994).
2. Roland Barthes, *Mythologies* (New York: Farrar, Straus and Giroux, 1972).
3. Henri Lefebvre, *The Critique of Everyday Life: The One Volume Edition* (London: Verso, 2014).
4. Kristin Ross, *May '68 and its Afterlives* (Chicago: 2002).
5. Jean-François Vilar, 'Le temps des fossoyeurs', *Rouge*, May 11, 1978.
6. Raymond Williams, 'Structures of Feeling', in *Marxism and Literature* (Oxford University Press, 1977), 128–135.
7. State and business-run dormitories.
8. Elfriede Müller and Alexander Ruoff, *Le Polar français: crime et histoire* (Paris: La Fabrique, 2002), 47.
9. On Notre-Dame-des-Landes and the ZAD, see Jade Lindgaard, ed., *Éloge des mauvaise herbes: ce que nous devons à la ZAD* (Paris: Les liens qui libèrent, 2018); and Mauvaise Troupe, *The ZAD and NoTAV: Territorial Struggles and the Making of a New Political Intelligence*, trans. Kristin Ross (London and New York: Verso, 2018).
10. Kristin Ross, 'Les Soulèvements de la Terre have succeeded in reorienting the gaze of city dwellers towards the countryside', Verso Blog, 23 May 2023, https://www.versobooks.com/en-gb/blogs/news/les-soulevements-de-la-terre-have-succeeded-in-reorienting-the-gaze-of-city-dwellers-towards-the-countryside. On Soulèvements de la Terre, see Les Soulèvements de la Terre, *Premières secousses* (Paris: La Fabrique, 2024).
11. See Kristin Ross, 'The War of the Worlds in France', *New York Review of Books* (August 23, 2023).

Exchange: Apathy and the neoliberal university

The irony of neoliberal higher education

Justin Cruickshank

In a recent article in *Radical Philosophy* (*RP* 215), Alan Bradshaw and Mikael Andehn argue that:

> The *Chronicle of Higher Education* reported that we are now amid a 'stunning level of student disconnection' … Despite enormous investment in the 'student experience' – ranging from campus architecture that looks like airport terminals … to the requirement for all university teachers to be certified by professional associations – the reality is that lecture theatres today are increasingly dysfunctional spaces in which teaching and learning does not, and often cannot, take place. Ironically, despite the chorus of indignation lamenting the rise of the student as consumer, today the student is all too often precisely the person who refuses to consume their education.[1]

They go on to propose that students experience 'flat affect' in the face of the attempt to manage their affective relationship to education:

> Implicit in the all-important UK National Student Survey, for example, is the idea that the 'student experience' must be constantly measured and responded to as the engine that will drive university reform towards its predetermined neoliberal endpoint. Student affect, therefore, becomes a form of capital that a university seeks to build. In this regard, the students' affective response is not just pre-determined ('the students want more employability content') but also the key point of legitimation and the primary alibi for the neoliberal reterritorialisation of the university. The student subjectivity they are expected to inhabit, therefore, is one that is not just pre-determined but also overdetermined, making excessive affective demands. In this context, the withdrawal into flat affect jams the juggernaut, leaving an excruciating absent centre.[2]

Rather than define such students as passive, Bradshaw and Andehn (drawing on Robert Pfaller), suggest that they are engaging in the strategy of interpassivity, which is the strategy of displacement. Students will go through the motions of studying but not engage in the process of learning. They note that Pfaller's examples of interpassive behaviour

> include a student who purposefully spends hours in a library photocopying course literature that they will never read. Or a person recording movies but never watching them. Or a person who watches a comedy show yet never laughs. In each case the pleasure is delegated onto an external object, as though it is the photocopier that studies the texts, the Tivo box that watches the movies and the canned laughter that is amused by the comedy.[3]

However, while this is a refusal to be co-opted affectively by neoliberalism, 'flat affect is the final recourse of the profoundly disempowered that carries the risk of self-negation'.[4] They conclude that:

> Interpassive withdrawal is ambivalent because, as Berlant argues, flat affect is the final recourse of the profoundly disempowered that carries the risk of self-negation. As educators, our role must be to comprehend how we might positively respond to student disengagement, accepting its radical potential as a form of anti-ideological behaviour and not just lamenting its destructiveness. We must learn how this can be done because the alternative is to exhaust ourselves reproducing the interactive fetish, or, worse, to allow this ambivalent strategy of interpassivity to lead to mutual self-negation.[5]

The reality of teaching is that of profound disengagement, yet UK universities continue to intensify their commitment to enhancing the student experience and journey based on the management's bureaucratic fiction of committed, engaged student-customer.

The problem, though, is becoming worse than the condition of interpassivity, with student disengagement now often leading to mass chronic non-attendance in lectures and seminars. Rather than go through the motions of learning, many students simply do not bother to go through the motions, except to submit essays and often that is done with the assistance of AI. While lectures may also be recorded, the viewing data suggests most are not watched or watched fully, and while the cost of living crisis forces more students into more paid work, universities which recruit many students from affluent backgrounds still experience chronic non-attendance. In response, some UK universities have decided not to force students to attend, fearing making students attend lectures and seminars may reduce the NSS (National Student Survey) scores, by undermining students' experience and journey. This creates the absurd situation that one method to increase student satisfaction with their teaching entails students not turning up to be taught. It would seem as if, on this topic at least, university management were themselves becoming interpassive, by going through the bureaucratic motions and letting the scores concerning teaching satisfaction take the place of actual teaching.

Against the notion that students are customers who need to be satisfied, Collini argued, writing in response to the fee increase to £9000, that unlike a consumption experience, the experience of being a student in higher education should be dissatisfying.[6] What Collini meant was that the experience of studying at university should produce an unsettling experience of having one's views challenged through immersion into a range of new ideas and values. This would be an uncomfortable experience but one that was positive because of the greater ability it produced to understand and engage meaningfully with new ideas. As students do not have a deep knowledge of a subject before starting their university education, and as that education is one that ought to produce dissatisfaction, the notion of assessing it in terms of student-customers being satisfied with a product they knew about fully beforehand was meaningless. With Collini's vision, a dissatisfying education would be one that helped students become knowledgeable and critically-minded citizens able fully to participate in democratic life, as well as being effective problem-solvers in employment.

However, this conception has for the most part become a normative fiction just as detached from the reality of teaching as the management's bureaucratic fiction of the engaged student. It is argued here that such disengagement is largely a consequence of university management's bureaucratic fiction creating the conditions for its fictional status. In search of increased customer satisfaction, university managers positioned students as consumers of a pleasurable experience and journey. In place of seeking to develop students as independent learners who value dissatisfaction, university management seek to position students as passive *homo economicus* customers who want to be given an emotionally satisfying experience along their journey. Students become positioned as both all-powerful knowlegeable customers who know not so much what a degree ought to entail in terms of dissatisfaction, but rather know what a good experience feels like, whilst at the same time being positioned not just as passive consumers of an experience 'delivered' to them, but as always being vulnerable to a decline in well-being.

Following the publicity around student suicides, universities rightly responded by seeking ways to improve their handling of mental health problems, but mental health became redefined as well-being, which is a far more vague and elastic concept. Under the heading of improving well-being, university managers have sought to increase not just academics' labour in terms of personal tutoring and pastoral time but increase their emotional labour. While the neoliberal approach to managing a population's health redefined 'healthy' as 'pre-illness' and sought to responsibilise individuals to manage their state of 'pre-illness' so they would be more efficient workers,[7] academics have become responsibilised to manage the well-being of all-powerful but always-vulnerable student-customers, by ensuring their student experience and student journey were always emotionally positive and marked by ubiquitous 'support'. If not the sole cause of disengagement amongst students, this positioning of students has arguably compounded the problem significantly. Students are continually told by universities they are consumers of an experience and a journey whilst the experience itself becomes hollowed out and meaningless.

The problems outlined above are a direct consequence of government policies over the last fourteen years. From the Browne Review on, English universities have been subject to a plethora of policies designed to marketise higher education. Political contingencies disrupted such policies, with the two main examples being the Conservative-Liberal Democrat coalition setting what became a fee-norm of £9000 rather than allowing a free market in fees, and the House of Lords breaking the connection between fee increases and the TEF (Teaching Excellence Framework) level a university or subject was awarded. Yet the most significant disruption to the neoliberal objectives sought came from the policies themselves being implemented as intended. This is because there was no foresight that the policies imposing marketisation would, ironically, create *homo economicus* behaviours which were predictable but not only antithetical to the objectives sought by government, but detrimental to students, academics, employers and the notion of developing a critically-minded engaged citizenry. Ironically the implementation of neoliberal policies to marketise higher education has resulted in market behaviour, but with managers acting as *homo economicus* agents in ways not anticipated by governments, and students acting as customers passively expecting an experience and journey to be delivered and managed by academics.

Critics argued that the fee increase would successfully nudge students into becoming *homo economicus* consumers to the detriment of appreciating education as a good in itself, developing a critically-engaged democratic citizenry, and the social sciences and humanities.[8] However when Student Number Controls were lifted university managers acted as *homo economicus* actors increasing recruitment to the cheap-to-teach humanities and social science courses. The £9000 fee created a problem with the RAB charge and increased public debt, meaning that any fee increase would meet hostility not only from students and parents but also the Treasury.[9] So when inflation massively outpaced the value to universities of the domestic fee, universities further increased recruitment to the cheap-to-teach courses. As universities were in brutal competition for students, they further intensified the focus on the student experience and journey, to ensure they had happy customers, successfully managed through their time at university. Many students responded to this environment in the way people socialised as consumers would respond, which was to expect a university campus reminiscent of a shopping mall or airport terminal but with no or limited expectation to engage with becoming independent learners benefitting from dissatisfaction in Collini's terms.

The Green and White Papers paving the way for the TEF held that student-customers should serve the market, rather than the market serve customers, and that they were failing to do this, by failing to purchase the right human capital investments.[10] Yet neoliberal governments created policies that nudged managers to provide more courses the government wanted reduced and to provide a consumption experience over an enabling-dissatisfying higher education experience. The irony of neoliberal higher education is that top-down marketisation created *homo economicus* behaviours that led to the higher education market creating outcomes that have benefitted no-one.

Justin Cruickshank is a Senior Lecturer in social theory at the University of Birmingham, with research interests in social and political theory and critical university studies.

Notes

1. Bradshaw and Andehn, 'Interpassive students in interactive classrooms', *Radical Philosophy* 215 (2023), 16.
2. Ibid., 21.
3. Ibid., 21.
4. 'Interpassive Students', 21.
5. Ibid., 21–22.
6. Stefan Collini, *What Are Universities For?* (London: Penguin, 2012).
7. David Armstrong, 'The Rise of Surveillance Medicine', *Sociology of Health and Illness* 17:3 (1995), 393–404.
8. See, for instance, John Holmwood, ed., *A Manifesto for the Public University* (London: Bloomsbury, 2011).
9. Andrew McGettigan, *The Great University Gamble: Money, Markets and the Future of Higher Education* (London: Pluto, 2013).
10. Justin Cruickshank, 'Economic Freedom and the Harm of Adaptation: On Gadamer, Authoritarian Technocracy and the Re-Engineering of English Higher Education', in Cruickshank and Ross Abbinnett eds., *The Social Production of Knowledge in a Neoliberal Age: Debating the Challenges Facing Higher Education* (London: Rowman and Littlefield, 2022), 271–298.

The racket university
Nathaniel Barron

> The world is so possessed by the power of what is and the efforts of adjustment to it, that the adolescent's rebellion, which once fought the father because his practices contradicted his own ideology, can no longer crop up.
>
> Max Horkheimer, 'The End of Reason'[11]

Of all the crises gripping UK higher education (HE), the learning spaces certainly abound with all the hallmarks of apathy. This withering of interest in learning routinely on display by large numbers of degree students is not the fault of those students themselves, however.[12] Neither is it explicable solely by a new generational attention economy nor by the expansion of customer sovereignty. One might be tempted to paint this reticence as an equivocal sign of resistance in a conjuncture where HE learning spaces are subjected to injunctions of technological interactivity and pedagogic optimisation. In a refrain of Bartleby's 'I'd prefer not to', the refusal to engage would arise from an ambiguous resistance hedging its bets on a strange passivity, as in Alan Bradshaw and Mikael Andehn's analysis in *RP* 215. If the student revolt at Milbank in 2010 'challenged the stereotype of apathetic youth',[13] then well over a decade later, apathetic passivity returns with a disobedient sheen.

But given the objectively pessimistic terrain of today's university, this framing seems much too sanguine. Can this reticence to actively participate in learning really be a student 'escape' from, and a potential 'antidote' to, the neoliberal capture of higher education?[14] Could it not be instead that this 'mass phenomenon of disengagement' speaks to an increasing erasure of student individuality ('self-negation') which has already travelled a fair distance within the contemporary university?[15] Instead of 'anti-ideological behaviour' resisting attempts to interpellate students into a techno-paradigm of hyper-interactivity,[16] one could explore student disengagement as an expression of a sector whose logic is more like a racket.

The Frankfurt School's fragmentary theory of the racket – an 'unfinished torso' – began during its American exile and principally at Horkheimer's instigation.[17] The members of the Institute for Social Research were attempting to come to terms theoretically with capitalism's 'monopoly-fascist phase' and were obligated to discard Marxist economism.[18] A debate ensued within the Institute concerning the state-capital relation during this classical stage of European fascism which was generally premised on the growing primacy of the political, as nineteenth-century *laissez faire* capitalism gave way to giant monopolies.[19] Importantly, the debate extended beyond the German context and was seen to be reflective of the American society that had welcomed the exiled Institute. The racket theory therefore identified a movement from private to state capitalism among 'very different political forms'.[20] Insofar as the theory named the return of political domination in light of capitalism's internal tendencies towards monopolism, it signalled the restoration of protection as domination's archetypical expression, domination's 'true nature'.[21] For a racket is the means by which protecting clients allows for their very exploitation. The 'political era' of monopolies,[22] or political capitalism, of which fascism was the most worthy example, is notably back on the agenda today.[23]

In Horkheimer's estimation, the racket model, as he sometimes called it, had indeed come to define all modern societal organisation: 'The racket … as was typical for the relationship of rulers and ruled', Horkheimer wrote, 'is now representative of all human relationships'.[24] Horkheimer's desire was thus to extensively apply the theory, since a 'study of such border phenomena as racketeering may offer useful parallels for understanding certain developmental tendencies in modern society.'[25] Although wide-ranging applications of the racket theory never took place, Horkheimer commented on education from its general spirit:

> With the decline of the ego and its reflective reason, human relationships tend to a point wherein the rule of economy over all personal relationships, the universal control of commodities over the totality of life, turns into a new and naked form of command and obedience.

No longer buttressed by small scale property, the school and the home are losing their educational function of preparing men [sic] for life in society.[26]

The suggestion that the contemporary university is one institution in which 'the practices and mores of the Mob have permeated'[27] is not, of course, to directly compare it and German fascism, nor to suggest that (the threat of) violence is an organising logic of the university. Defining the racket society just by reference to the use of violence to vouchsafe political domination discounts Otto Kirchheimer's more generalised notion of the racket, which

> ... expresses the idea that within the organizational framework of our society attainment of a given position is out of proportion to abilities and efforts which have gone into that endeavor. It infers that a person's status in society is conditional upon the presence or absence of a combination of luck, chance, and good connections, a combination systematically exploited and fortified with all available expedients inherent in the notion of private property.[28]

The mass student disengagement within HE is explicable by the atrophy of universality within society that the racket university reflects and compounds. Capitalism's monopoly phase ensures the death of classical liberalism's purported universalist rule of law, as well as the work ethic that was said to be required to fully reap the fruits of the marketplace. In the racket society those who command maintain the allegiance of those who obey not by ideology but simply 'by trading protection for obedience, abandoning any pretense to represent general interests or universal principles'.[29] This is why within a racket society, alongside 'the weakening of mediating universal ideologies went the erosion of an autonomous self who is capable of surviving outside the protective

cocoon of the racket.'[30] The student's ability to resist the 'father' is severely curtailed if, despite their evident cloaking of classed, gendered and racialised oppression and exploitation, the universalist principles which allowed a critical subject to emerge to take the measure of the social landscape have absconded, such as they are doing today. The dialectical traction of such universals has concretely expressed itself in previous conjunctures of the university's pre-neoliberal phase,[31] but this traction is eroding, stalling the process of resistance. Even a work like Pierre Bourdieu and Jean Claude Passeron's *Reproduction* acknowledged that despite the university being a key node through which 'cultural capital across generations' is transmitted, its institutional role of stamping 'pre-existing differences in inherited cultural capital' still relied on 'a meritocratic seal of academic consecration by virtue of the special symbolic potency of the *title* (credential).'[32] Although a 'fetish of ability',[33] the universal of meritocracy could be levelled as a contradiction against the continuing importance of group affiliation.[34] However, in a racket society

> Privileges that depend on distinctions in individual ability become increasingly rare. In acquiring and maintaining social positions it is not so much special skill that matters; what matters is that one gets the chance to find access to, and be accepted by, one of the organizations that dispose of the technical apparatus to which the individual has scant possibility of access.[35]

Society in its current state has rendered it reasonable on the students' part not to participate in the learning spaces, for that is no longer the name of the game to conform to.[36] In the social sciences, at least, it is increasingly difficult for students to fail, and the successful deregulation of assessment processes at the eleventh hour by university management in order to bypass the University and College Union's grassroots Marking and Assessment Boycott (MAB) compounds this trend, and is an indication that being merely enrolled on a degree is becoming increasingly more definitive than substantive participation itself. The university stakes much on 'student experience' but it sucks the life out of them by its very logic of being a 'naked clique system' that the students must learn to resemble.[37] The deformation of even illusory or unfulfilled universals like meritocracy thus ensures the increasing impossibility of fashioning critical subjectivity within the learning spaces of a racket university. As Adorno wrote, such universals 'have become so attenuated that they declare themselves to be lies in order to show those who believe them how impotent they really are.'[38]

The reticent student, then, is not to be understood as a subject that rejects alienation even by leaning on a vague notion of a better-universal such as meritocracy. Rather they suspect that they are beholden to a racket in which 'ultimately, every reference to universality ... is lost.'[39] It is but an expression of the 'association by sufferance' that a university degree is becoming.[40] The majority of students begin to suspect that the contemporary university protects them from the very thing that the university helps to create – a radical disenchantment stacking shelves.[41] Indeed, 'the archetypal form of racket is ... the protection racket in which the racketeers extort payment for protection from a threat which they themselves pose.'[42] The university is thereby increasingly coming to resemble a 'forced community', 'a modern *Vergemeinschaftung*.'[43] As Kirchheimer wrote:

> The term *racket* ... reflects on a society in which social position has increasingly come to depend on a relation of participation, on the primordial effect of whether an individual succeeded or failed to 'arrive'. Racket connotes a society in which individuals have lost the belief that compensation for their individual efforts will result from the mere functioning of impersonal market agencies. ... It is the experience of an associational practice which implies that neither the individual's choice of an association nor the aims that the latter pursues are the result of conscious acts belonging to the realm of human freedom.[44]

We are in a worse world than that painted by students' reticence being an ambiguous counter-offensive against alienation, which the educator can partner and shape towards better ends. More than good teaching practice will be required to turn the tide.[45] The untruth and internal tendencies of the market mechanism have produced a racket university in which students' participation is reduced to being merely present, to having 'arrived' at that place, to being on the 'inside'. Any attempt to ideologically bind students to a particularist interest that represents itself as universal is itself jettisoned in the racket university and replaced with increasingly unmediated compulsion that knows its own name. The idea that the contemporary university remains a potential space of liberation, despite, or precisely because of, the alienation it exudes, might then itself be vain hope.

Nathaniel Barron teaches social theory at the University of Birmingham.

Notes

11. Max Horkheimer, 'The End of Reason', *Studies in Philosophy and Social Science* 9:3 (1941), 381.
12. Alan Bradshaw and Mikael Andehn, 'Interpassive students in interactive classrooms', *Radical Philosophy* 215 (2023), 16–22.
13. Matt Myers, *Student Revolt: Voices of the Austerity Generation* (London: Pluto Press, 2017), 30, cf. 152–3.
14. 'Interpassive students', 19–21.
15. Ibid., 16, 21.
16. Ibid., 22.
17. Rolf Wiggershaus, *The Frankfurt School: Its Theories, History and Political Significance*, trans. Michael Robertson (Cambridge, MA.: MIT Press, 1994), 319; see Gerhard Scheit, 'Rackets', trans. Lars Fischer, in *The SAGE Handbook of Frankfurt School Critical Theory*, eds. Beverly Best et al. (London: Sage, 2018), 1551–66.
18. Wiggershaus, *The Frankfurt School*, 318.
19. Gerhard Scheit, 'Rackets', 1560.
20. Thorsten Fuchshuber, 'Saving Mediation: The Topicality of Max Horkheimer's Post-Liberal Concept of the Political', accessed 19 February 2024, https://www.telospress.com/saving-mediation-the-topicality-of-max-horkheimers-post-liberal-concept-of-the-political/
21. Max Horkheimer, 'The End of Reason', 374.
22. Frederick Pollock, 'State Capitalism: Its Possibilities and Limitations', in *The Essential Frankfurt School Reader*, eds. Andrew Arato and Eike Gebhardt (New York: Continuum, 1985), 78.
23. Dylan Riley and Robert Brenner, 'Seven Theses on American Politics', *New Left Review*, 138 (Nov/Dec 2022).
24. Horkheimer quoted in Martin Jay, 'The Age of Rackets? Trump, Scorsese and the Frankfurt School', in *Immanent Critiques: The Frankfurt School Under Pressure* (London: Verso, 2023), 122.
25. Horkheimer, 'The End of Reason', 375. Jay suggests that 'college admissions offices' are an instance in which the racket model realises itself in the contemporary university, but this is not elaborated upon. Jay, 'Rackets?', p. 127.
26. Horkheimer, 'The End of Reason', 379.
27. Jay, 'Rackets?', 115–133.
28. Otto Kirchheimer, 'In Quest of Sovereignty', *The Journal of Politics*, 6:2 (May 1944), 160.
29. Jay, 'Rackets?', 122–3.
30. Ibid., 123.
31. Alberto Toscano, 'The University as a Political Space', in Michael Bailey and Des Freedman, eds., *The Assault on Universities: A Manifesto for Resistance* (London: Pluto Press, 2011), 61.
32. Pierre Bourdieu and Jean Claude Passeron, *Reproduction in Education, Society and Culture*, trans. Richard Nice (London: Sage Publications, 1990), ix–x.
33. Theodor W. Adorno and Hellmut Becker, 'Education for maturity and responsibility', trans. Robert French et al., *History of Human Sciences*, 12:3 (1999), 23.
34. John Holmwood, 'Race and the Neoliberal University: Lessons From the Public University', in Gurminder K. Bhambra et al., eds., *Decolonising the University* (London: Pluto Press, 2018), 44.
35. Kirchheimer, 'Sovereignty', 161.
36. Theodor W. Adorno, 'Reflections on Class Theory', in *Can One Live After Auschwitz: A Philosophical Reader*, ed. Rolf Tiedemann, trans. Rodney Livingstone (Stanford: Stanford University Press, 2003), 97.
37. Adorno, 'Reflections', 102.
38. Adorno, 'Reflections', 96.
39. Thorsten Fuchshuber, 'Saving Mediation'. On the significance of overseas students for understanding a shift in meritocracy's conception within higher education, see Holmwood, 'Race', 47.
40. Kirchheimer, 'Sovereignty', 139–176.
41. Mark Fisher, *Capitalist Realism: Is There No Alternative?* (Ropley: Zero Books, 2009), 21–6.
42. Peter M. R. Stirk, *Max Horkheimer: A New Interpretation* (Hemel Hempstead: Harvester & Wheatsheaf, 1992), 209.
43. Fuchshuber, 'Saving Mediation'.
44. Kirchheimer, 'Sovereignty', 161.
45. See Andrew McGettigan, *The Great University Gamble: Money, Markets, and the Future of Higher Education* (London: Pluto Press, 2013).

Reviews

Fascist ships of Theseus

Alberto Toscano, *Late Fascism: Race, Capitalism and the Politics of Crisis* (London: Verso, 2023). 224pp., £17.99 pb., 978 1 83976 020 4

In most journalistic writing, the power of the contemporary far right to do hurt is nonreflexively theorised in the language of absurdist children's fiction. The metaphor of the looking glass, the metaphor of the 'mirror-world', the metaphor of the maze-like and uterine 'rabbit hole' – all are forms of description through which contemporary fascism is stripped of its menacing alterity and presented in the style of a storybook. The frequency with which the term is associated with 'nonsense literature' in turn seems to increase as the political authority and social acceptability of the 'far right' grows more undeniable.

Clarity of sense; possession of political authority. The concepts do not now seem to be intimately or deeply related, although they may well be deeply or intimately *non*related, in a world in which, like in *Through the Looking Glass*, 'everything is reversed, including logic'.

Recently, in her unusual semi-autofictional work on left-right 'diagonalism', *Doppelganger: A Trip into the Mirror World*, Naomi Klein appears to make a similar observation, when she argues that that the right-wing 'mirror world' tracks a decline in the 'meaning' of language in general. Power, which concedes nothing without a demand, also increasingly demands without a nothing concede. The nonsense of the second statement warps and seems to extend backwards, into the specific meaning of the first, to the point that it becomes increasingly hard to believe with lucid conviction (per Klein) in the integrity and significance of either. This has something to do with the internet, she suggests. For her part, Klein is clearly embarrassed to talk about herself at such length. Fascism in popular usage is widely understood as direct violence against political opponents utilised to enforce social hierarchy, including the structural social hierarchy of capital. It *seems* like it should feel extremely clear. So why doesn't it? The introduction to this review was drafted a day after the 2024 presidential debate between Donald Trump and Joe Biden, in which Biden said of Trump that 'he is … responsible for doing what is being that was done'. This scrambling or blurring of words into one another, the misuse of words that makes meaning feel obtainable and at the same time fugitive or nonsensical, or just pointless, seems somehow reflective of the present, as though speech when it is 'political' *were always like this*: a blurring and a scrambling that appears strangely only really to come into focus when the most powerful man in the world is unable to conjugate his sentences. There *is* a tradition of anti-fascist analysis that takes this experience seriously, by asking *how* instead of *what* fascism means, and which recognises that loss of clarity, confusion, directionless, but also deliberate violation of meaning, are important political instruments. But it remains a underground tendency. Sartre's statement 'Never believe that anti-Semites are completely unaware of the absurdity of their replies' provides a programmatic starting point, but the problem is how to link this intuition to larger historical developments. If Guy Debord was right that capital has arrived at 'such a degree of accumulation that it becomes an image', then the question remains, why the image of a rabbit hole? And why *images* in the first place?

Alberto Toscano's book *Late Fascism* is not another entry in the now voluminous literature on the periodisation of fascism (post-fascism, crypto-fascism, para-fascism), nor is it an attempt to decide whether current developments in US state politics can or cannot be classified as 'fascist'. The endless intellectual and biographical ornithology of minor contemporary trends on the political far right (a kind of left-liberal collector's mania) is fundamentally alien to Toscano's intellectual and political purposes. *Late Fascism* can more usefully be read as an essay in the meaning of political categories, or, more accurately, of the ways in which such categories are usefully or harmfully degraded, through the interaction of language and social activity. *Late Fascism* is thus not a history (or even really a 'mosaic') of heterodox anti-fascist theories – though Toscano modestly suggests that it can read in this way – so much as an essay in *how* to analyse a political moving target (one that shoots back). It can also be thought of as a kind of performative method of description, oriented towards an enormous organic object in which some parts 'contradict' or annul others and where the whole is constantly shedding and acquiring new elements, making a pugilistic virtue of its own complex and 'structured incoherence' – a tendency that many orthodox Marxist theories struggle to comprehend. At some more abstract level, it can be read as an exercise in prophylaxis against the tendency for 'the left' to make alliances with, or drift towards, or imperceptibly metamorphose into, the right, usually by dissolving its idea of class into some kind of ethnic or socially conservative majoritarianism.

Distinctively, *Late Fascism* achieves this prophylaxis without simply tailing alliances with bourgeois liberalism, whether of the 'elite progressive' or the 'economic-institutional' variety. Its basic contribution is to establish a way of opposing both liberalism and fascism at the level of *method*, without splitting conceptual hairs or by summarily dissolving the two tendencies into one another (as per varieties of ultra-leftism from the Stalinist Third Positionism of the 1920s through to the French Holocaust denying ultra-left of the 1970s). It is unusual in doing this *without* presenting a 'theory' of anti-fascism or of its correct, watertight and definitive practice. Readers will search the book in vain for a definition of anti-fascism that definitively distinguishes it from bourgeois liberal 'anti-fascism' and 'populist' diagonalism or red-brownism; there is none. But the distinction is nevertheless there. It exists in a specific angle of approach, or, as a form of relation.

How to justify such an indirect and 'meta-theoretical' method? Fascism as Toscano presents it is not so much a political philosophy as a 'scavenging' or mimetic *tradition*. The tradition is capable of mimicking aspects of revolutionary leftism as well as aspects of the liberal bourgeois order. Its core, articulated in the book's subtitle ('Race, Capitalism and the Politics of Crisis') is self-dissembling and fugitive, since, as Toscano shows, it is constantly dissolving or fusing its primary preoccupation – crudely defined, defence of existing hierarchy – into lexicons and forms of political address that seem (at least at first glance) to be alien to it. This may make the book's object of analysis sound too much like a hall of mirrors. But theories of fascism that are hostile to the question of representation (mimicry, ventriloquy, resemblance, appearance, likeness) are perpetually susceptible to being outflanked by fascism in the very effort to depict it. Recently this mimetic aspect of fascism discourse has become so blatantly obvious that it has been addressed even in the social democratic mainstream: this is the significance of Klein's recent turn towards 'fiction', as a way of dealing with online political experience. Fascism reveals itself everywhere as a system of will and representation. Even its 'concepts' are structures of likeness, mimicry and camouflage; the structured incoherences of its ideas are *systems* of maximum disruptive contrast. The motivating event for Toscano's book – the first election of Donald Trump in 2016 and the wave of explanations for this development in terms of his appeal to the 'white working class' – was perhaps the first great mimetic shock of recent political history, the discovery of a 'likeness' between fascist and leftist speech that much of 'the left' itself was unable or unprepared to understand, inaugurating years of theoretical bewilderment in which many socialists and communists made a pact with liberal constitutionalism and identity progressivism while others, as per the standard red-brown synthesis, boiled class and gender liberation down to its undifferentiated component parts of skin pigmentation and sex difference.

In many ways we are still wandering in this wilderness. One of the most useful ways to think of *Late Fascism* is as a demonstration that it is impossible to theorise fascism unless we understand that fascist theory is itself a system of appearance – a mirage. Toscano's own non-theory, with its distinctive ensemble of structured incoherences, can be understood among other things as a method of theoretical seeing. In this sense, it dovetails with other recent writings coming from a more literary-critical background that understand that fascism as a system of aesthetics, in particular a recent work by the poet William Rowe titled *Seeing Against Fascism*.

The opening chapter of *Late Fascism* sets out in more detail the context I have sketched in above. Originally published as a late intervention in the by then long-running debate on the usefulness of the term 'fascism' to describe the then recently elected first Trump government, the chapter is centrally about the supposed

neglect of the 'white working class' by 'the left', as well as, relatedly, the role of 'untimeliness' in different periods of fascist thought.

The trajectory of argument here is slightly different from that which emerges in the later chapters, and so it is worth setting down its basic movements step by step. Toscano begins by invoking two dissident Marxist authors for whom temporal and logical disjunction were explicit and central themes: Ernst Bloch and Georges Bataille. He dismisses the contemporary relevance of more orthodox theories of fascism from the 1930s whose central claim was that fascism was 'functional' for capital.

Three interesting and potentially contrary claims – what Toscano describes as 'disanalogies' between the past and the present – are introduced here, the tension between which will form one of the book's central points of interest:

(1) Early, 'orthodox' Marxist theories of the functionality of fascism to capital (as a form of state terrorism useful for overcoming 'economic' crisis) are inadequate to the present, when capital 'is not rushing en masse towards an exceptional state to counter existential threats to its reproduction': this argument is a brusque dismissal of much of the current 'Marxist' literature.

(2) Heterodox Marxists opened up a more complex understanding of the relation of the past to the present by trying to understand the role of pre-capitalist 'survivals' in the consciousness and the aesthetics of fascist movements (and by arguing these 'remained off-limits to a communism whose rational principles risked generating irrational strategies').

(3) *However*, these 'survivals' in the present are no longer clearly recognisable.

The opening chapter then begins to develop in a manner that is, with a few important differences, characteristic of the rest of the book. In reflecting on the possible termination of Blochian nonsimultaneity in contemporary society, Toscano turns to Pasolini's late reflections on consumer society as 'fascism', responsible for the 'genocide' of cultural difference. Leaning on Pasolini's claims – themselves intentionally 'exaggerated' or 'inflated' – he suggests that the form of nonsimultaneity specific to fascism in the late 2010s is a form of 'nostalgia for the present'; a desire not for 'lifeways' of a nonurban society that persist as fragments and yearning into industrial modernity, but for industrial modernity itself, in the form of the 'post-war affluence of the *trente glorieuses*'. The political motivations for this argument emerge into view in the following pages. Both Bloch and Bataille, introduced to help us to think more subtly 'the contemporary nexus of politics and history', are to be 'recalibrated' or 'corrected' to account for the loss of distorted utopian drives in the fascism of the present. This loss or denaturing is itself politically explicable in terms of 'the absence of one of the key determinants of fascism, namely the revolutionary threat to capitalist order'. A final series of leaps and transitions then carries us via Adorno's account of an anti-utopian 'phoniness' in the fascist follower and Jairus Banaji's Sartrean account of fascist 'serial groups' back to the chapter's point of political and conceptual origin: to the claim that the loss of a revolutionary horizon feeds through into contemporary fascism in the form of the essentially barren character of its groups, that is, into its conception of class as group, that is, into the processed pseudo-concept of 'the *white* working class'. This of course is the group whom authors of the most varied political tendencies reflexively declared in 2016–17 to have been 'abandoned' and placed as an intellectual and political totem at the centre of their accounts of the rise of the Trumpian right.

The chapter is a brilliant polemical intervention, disguised as a work of genealogy. But its complicated assessment of 'nonsynchronicity' also sheds light on the adjective in the book's title – 'late'. This has a peculiar status in Toscano's thinking. The phrase from which *Late Fascism* is derived, 'late capitalism', was originally proposed by the Fourth International Trotskyist Ernest Mandel to describe the post-war structure of capitalist society, before later (and perhaps more famously) being taken up by Fredric Jameson in his attempt to define its purported 'cultural logic'. Mandel's use of the term suggests capitalist continuity *within discontinuity*, the most significant and theoretically inconvenient form of which was the Second World War and the Nazi Holocaust itself. 'Late capitalism', Mandel writes in his book of that title, 'is ... merely a further development of the imperialist, monopoly-capitalist epoch'. Toscano's use of the term could hardly be more different. His *Late Fascism* is not an account of the qualified continuity of the past and the present so much as a work of *anti*-periodisation that systematically demolishes the borders between periods, categories, and traditions of analysis. It exists in a kind of 'nexus' (another favourite term) with the vocabulary of *salvage*, an approach to the theory of fascism that is invoked and then put to one side in the opening intervention on class – where it clashes with the deflationary and polemical tenor of Toscano's reading of the racialised 'working class' – only itself to be salvaged several chapters later, where an apparently contrary project is outlined: 'Among fascism's scavenged treasures was also utopia. And fascist scavenging was to be countered by communist salvage'.

As the book progresses, and the periodising and polemical aims of the opening chapter recede in importance, this topos of salvage becomes more and more central. The shifting emphasis can already be made out in the second chapter on race, where Toscano mainly draws on George Jackson's account of fascism, set out in his exchange of letters with his lawyer and Angela Davis, and other writings collected in *Blood in My Eye* (1972). Jackson's thinking, developed and written out in his cell in San Quentin, intersects closely with a Third Position approach to fascism, which defines it as one political guise taken by social democracy: this is the root of Jackson's well-known formulation of fascism as economic reform.

Toscano adopts a different approach to this theory than the one that defined his analysis of Bloch and Bataille. He does not 'correct' or 'recalibrate' it; instead, he quotes Jackson's own comments on fascism *as they are embodied by the material infrastructure of his prison*: 'the concrete and steel, the tiny electronic listening device concealed in the vent, the phalanx of goons peeping in at us, his barely functional plastic tape recorder that cost him a week's labour'. The method of reading has subtly but fundamentally changed. 'Concepts' that are 'degraded', exaggerated or merely mouthed as insults are to be treated with a 'great effort of imagination' (Jean Genet, as cited by Toscano). This isn't about Toscano condescending to Jackson, or even simply about making allowances, because it then becomes the method of reading for each of the book's subsequent chapters. *Late Fascism* increasingly treats theoretical concepts as both (to use a phrase later lifted from Adorno) 'tool and scar'. Toscano's own sensitive remark on Jackson and Angela Davis' correspondence, that it is 'marked by differences of interpretation interwoven by a profound comradeship', becomes the leitmotif of his own practice as a reader of the archive of communist theorisations of fascist politics, fascist psychology and fascist theory. The analysis of fascism ceases to be the struggle for a correct 'definition' and becomes instead (once again using a phrase repurposed from Adorno) something like the description of a 'psychological area'. The ability to establish profound comradeship between the apparently contradictory ideas and claims that inhabit this 'area' then becomes the measure of a meta-commentary's intellectual and political adroitness – its ability to prefigure 'coalitional possibilities'.

Here the work overlaps with some other important recent thinking on fascism. In 2023, the poet and critic William Rowe published a pamphlet on the poetry of the British poet Verity Spott titled *Seeing Against Fascism*. In Rowe's programmatic intervention, fascism is a property of vision, not of concepts. Any category can exist in its own way within what we can call the fascist 'area', as well as outside of or in opposition to it. The point here is not just to make the conventional argument that 'reification' is bad and 'relations' are good, but to explain why the attempt to define fascism by means of basic conceptual traits leads inevitably to circular reasoning and (perhaps more importantly) to a particular psycho-social sensation: something like intellectual and political claustrophobia. Just as the best response to the existence of a fascist 'way of seeing' is not to force long gold pins into your eyes *but to see differently*, the existence of fascism within the 'space' of our own categories of political understanding requires us to find different ways of orienting ourselves towards them. Rowe's approach, in which fascism is a mode of perception for which concepts possess only a secondary role, corresponds in some ways with Toscano's, for example when the latter writes about the 'differential *visibility* and experience of both fascism and democracy', in connection with Davis' argument that 'The dangerous and indeed fascistic trend toward greater numbers of hidden, incarcerated human populations is itself rendered *invisible*'; or when he insists on the centrality of 'differential experience of domination' in assessments of the 'correctness' of theoretical categories. Experience includes vision. The phalanx of goons peeping in on us experience with their eyes.

A productive way of approaching Toscano's chapters is to see them not only as about 'areas' of fascist thinking (a way of escaping additive 'definitions'), but also as areas within which communist thinking is superimposed. There are places in the book where this approach is made very explicit, for example in the programmatic declaration already quoted, where 'fascist 'scavenging' is contrasted with communist 'salvage'. But the issue is implicit elsewhere, in the way that Toscano's 'archive' is assembled. The fascist conceptual-thematic 'areas' that are introduced are always ways of thinking about communism too, present within the 'areas' of fascist thinking as

> an actual reality that has been denied ... a thing that's not supposed to be there manifesting in the imaginary ... A strong force that has no image' but which has 'convulsed space and removed the possibility of grounding this thing'.

This happens to be Rowe again, but the passage reads as a description of Toscano's method transposed into a different key.

Organic metaphors acquire a significant role here. Toscano often uses the figure of 'metastasis' to describe fascist thinking – an organicism gone wrong, a cancered Romanticism. His approach to the 'lateness' of 'fascism' often returns probingly to the vocabulary of 'malaise', defined in a different context in the art historian Georges Didi-Huberman's *The Surviving Image: Phantoms of Time and Time of Phantoms, Aby Warburg's History of Art*:

> The archaeological model occupied Freud throughout his life. His thoughts about time – that is to say, about the paradoxes and disorders [*malaises*] in evolution – were often indebted to it, for example when he linked the question of *stages* or of *stases* to the question of strata, i.e., of material depths.

Here both of Toscano's core metaphors are anticipated. The 'stages' or 'stases' cannot be thought without the *meta*-stases, the processes of anarchic transition. What Toscano speaks about in his first chapter on 'untimeliness' as the synchronicity of fascism in the twenty-first century, a 'nostalgia for the present', develops over the course of his book into the 'geologically displaced and piled up strata' of the twentieth-century histories of fascism, liberalism and communism *as theory and as practice*, in relation to which the present is defined. 'Synchronicity' becomes just one stratum within a system of modern political history defined as an – admittedly desecrated and despoiled – archaeological site, organised, to use Didi-Huberman's terms, by 'anachronisms, phase displacements, latencies, delays, [and] aftershocks'. The temporal malaise epitomised *not as impasse but as disorder* leads to an archaeology of uncontrollable growths.

This generalisation to the level of historical process of what we could call psychoanalytic time then joins up with Toscano's pursuit of a kind of fascist death drive (though Toscano avoids this Freudian concept): fascism's enjoyment of destruction and violence. This takes multiple forms in the book: the heroic death as national fate ontologised by Heidegger; the 'religion of death' of fascist esotericism; and the ideal of the 'useless task' or 'gratuitous brutality' that Toscano identifies in esoteric far-right cults and diffidently associates with fascist lone wolf shooters. A coda to the chapter on Furio Jesi connects this 'void' to the unspoken and mythic idea of race, but the image of a deep-seated desire for masochist gratuitousness *as void* provides Toscano with an unusual way of thinking about how fascism and anti-fascism relate to the same ideas, traditions, vocabularies and concepts. It also indicates something about how they both emerge and undergo metamorphosis in what I'm calling the same area – that is, about what it means to deal with problem of adjacency or overlap that is essential to the experience of political identity in the 'late' fascist period or antiperiod for which Toscano's book attempts to find means of expression, or experience. What Didi-Huberman describes as the 'geologically displaced and piled up strata', the 'geological stratification, temporal inversion, concentric stratification around a centre, a broken line that takes roundabout paths, the zizag line of the knight's move', etc., *define areas that are endlessly available*, both to the scavenging 'void' of fascist impulses and to the salvaging instincts of a communism that tries, by building unexpected connections between both concepts and people, to create new conditions for life. 'Anti-fascist theory', writes Toscano at the end of his chapter on time, 'cannot operate at the level of the commodity form and its time alone'. By the same token, anti-fascism cannot be 'defined', it can only be described. Like George Jackson thinking about all of capitalist history in his cell in San Quentin, it is 'an actual reality that has been denied ... a thing that's not supposed to be there'. To evaluate the *products* of Jackson's theory independently of the circumstances of its production (which, as Toscano points out, appear explicitly and pointedly in the texts themselves) is itself a form of denial, and is in this sense adjacent to fascist seeing as William Rowe defines it: blood in my eye.

The 'areas' that Toscano's book covers include fascist thinking about time, race, freedom, abstraction, history, myth and desire, i.e., all areas where communists might equally be expected to develop positions. Some claims essential to the account I am developing here can be set out schematically. First, that fascism has its own 'ideas' about freedom – in particular in relation to the state as an 'arena' for power competition, rather than as a granitic totalitarian block. Second, that its use of myths ('survivals' of earlier social formations) are central forms of ideology, in Alfred Sohn-Rethel's sense of 'real abstractions' operative in social practice. Third, that desire is important, including in relation to the use of concepts and language. The book's penultimate chapter, which deals tantalisingly if really too briefly with Furio Jesi's oblique claims about fascist language and myth, directly precedes the concluding chapter on fascist desire, gender normativity and sex politics. The adjacency is not incidental.

Toscano says in his Preface that 'This book is a record of my own path through materials from bygone conjunctures and disparate places, to salvage the components of a compass with which to orient myself'. The spatial-topographical metaphor recalls the 'mirror-world' invoked by Klein, and perhaps tacitly endorses her Carollian map of the territory. At the same time, the trope of the disturbing double that appears in Klein's book (hypocrite reader!) is here transposed into the image of a communist 'salvaging', as parts of a theoretical 'compass', components for which fascists are also constantly 'scavenging' for their own metapolitical purposes. Conceptual disorientation (massive topographical space) bleeds into loss of political identity (extreme proximity). In working through this dissonance, Toscano goes a step further than Klein, by implicitly arguing that this combined experience of spatial disorientation and discomfiting loss of identity through proximity *has to be endured*, and that doing so might itself be part of the project of developing an anti-fascist theoretical and political approach.

Much writing about fascism and liberalism speaks about confusionism using topographical-geographical metaphors, and yet is fanatically concentrated on the idea of proximity. Hatred of proximity is the motivating occasion for Klein's book and the organising principle of most liberal theories of fascist 'totalitarianism', in which bourgeois freedom is the 'opposite' of fascist authoritarianism, and maintenance of this social distancing is what politics essentially is. In a review of Toscano's book in the *Marxism and Philosophy Review of Books*, Conrad Hamilton has criticised the work for the contrary form of excessive proximity, this time to liberal identity politics: 'the false hope of a liberal buy-in'.

Fear of resemblance is the phobic root of political thinking that seeks to establish its identity through endless acts of conceptual disavowal: I am not like that, we are not like that, that is different to us. This is theoretical language as a game of looking in the mirror: the endless attempt to establish one's own political and social personhood through the act of staring at oneself in the reflective surface of some undecideable concepts. Toscano's attempt to define 'lateness' as the historical-political point at which 'conceptual definition' becomes a kind of shell-game *opens up as materials for an alternative self-definition* the full gamut of relationships *to* concepts that cannot *not be* contested and self-contradictory: degradation, exaggeration, stereotypy, eclecticism, overstatement, the situated and deuniversalised language that is most often made over to literature, or, worse, poetry, misprision, false particularisation, resemblance, appearance, mimicry. These and other associated terms are all means through which fascism relates to (rather than obliterating) the traditions of bourgeois liberalism, most obviously through its exploitation of a freedom that is both historically produced – a 'function', if we like, of the forces of production – and (to use Toscano's own adjective) highly 'differentially' owned: a freedom that is always and by definition a freedom for some people to inflict harm, inaugurate violent spectacle and fuck up the potential of others. The scarred or scavenged tool of 'anti-fascism' is itself degraded, situated, self-contradictory, eclectic and prone to overstatement, but it is also a means to convert the ineluctable shell-game within a system of overlapping and contested concepts back into a means of self-identification through the medium of relation itself, including to inevitable conceptual proximity. Toscano declines the task of reflecting on 'late' (that is, contemporary) fascism through the degraded materials of personal biography, but there are very few of us who in the recent period of mimetic shock will have been spared the painful spectacle of watching our 'own' contemporaries and ideas becoming warped into what we imagined to be our opposite. In that sense, we are all Naomi Klein (and Naomi Wolf).

This perhaps brings us back to *Alice Through the Looking Glass* and rabbit holes. In fascist thinking, deliberate absurdism has to do with the supererogatory: it is the 'thinking' of people whose practical commitment is to the intensification of whatever is happening anyway. When at the Berlin Biennale in 2016, a poster put up by the fascism-curious curatorial collective DIS asked 'why do fascists have all the fun?', the idea seemed to be about exactly this utopian aspect of ('childlike') irresponsibility: the freedom of thought from the burden of having to make sense, which perhaps is just an extension of the negative idea of freedom ('freedom from') that has always been most appealing to those already in possession of power, wealth and privilege. But if we take seriously that Mussolini's 'super-relativism' means that there are no fascist concepts per se, but only fascist modes of thought, 'stages' or 'stases' that are always passing over into *meta*-stases, what could be the Marxist 'cell form' of these metastases, of the changing sequences of the disorder or malaise?

Late fascism as a mimetic or 'scavanger' tradition can be like anything else; it can be like liberalism or communism or an art biennial in a major European metropolis, and it can also be like money or a career move or a fantastic world involving a mirror. This adaptive character creates a problem that *Late Fascism* approaches using language that will strike some as almost alarmingly existentialist. Toscano talks throughout his work of voids: of the 'tactics of the void', or of a 'pulsating void' at the heart of fascism. This is his main, implied answer to what we might call the Ship of Theseus problem – the accusation that if fascism has no definition and is permanently scavenging new materials, then it is not the same as itself and lacks any meaningful identity. 'Serious scholars' of the phenomenon are unlikely to accept this playfully provocative insinuation. Fascism is, as 'one of the old guard' informed George Jackson, 'an economic geo-political affair where only one party is allowed to exist aboveground and no opposition political activity is allowed', mutatis mutandis and allowing for some fashionable variation in the descriptive vocabulary. The idea that it is a constitutive *absence*, one that defines a relationship to the ideas that it uses, *and that there are no ideas of which it cannot make use*, seems deeply and therefore also suspiciously metaphysical. Fascism has to be something more than a kind of emptiness that makes its way inside the languages – all of them, without respect to political tradition – that have emerged to describe human life in its mediations by capital, technology and the state. Doesn't it?

The question hangs in the air. What becomes of political theory when it cannot free itself from an impossible riddle? To borrow some lines from Karen Dalton's version of 'Katie Cruel':

> If I was where I would be,
> Then I'd be where I am not
> Here I am where I must be
> Where I would be I cannot

This idea comes back in one last metaphor that appears in *Late Fascism* on more than one occasion. In his chapter on fascist freedom, Toscano discusses the fascist 'non-state' (another concept defined by a negation) as 'the *volatile arena* for political and economic power-competitions, driven and legitimated by racial imperialism'. Later, in his chapter on fascist desire, he quotes a long passage from an article by Robin Marasco, in which Marasco argues that fascism 'offers white women an account of their unhappiness and *an affective arena* to express their rage'.

It seems that political concepts too can become 'volatile' arenas, stadia for the 'venting of rage'. But they do this only *after* they have been hollowed out, intussuscepted with a void or absence that itself responds to our own feeling of anger that their original meanings have failed to do what they promised to do, which in the case of political concepts is usually to change our life. The scavenged and degraded fascist concept becomes a hollow arena for the 'venting of rage' only once it has failed to accomplish the transformative or descriptive task for which it was originally designed. This is one reason why fascism itself is always 'late' and why (although it is by no means simply a 'mirror' of liberalism or communism) it has no distinctive philosophy of its own. It is a kind of hole, driven into political ideas that we believe have betrayed us. Its concepts, like its states, are '*non*-concepts', the tools and scars of interpreting and changing the world transformed into empty arenas for the venting of belligerent wounded animosity.

Meaning, apostrophises Naomi Klein somewhere in the middle of her unexpected 'trip into the mirror world', is today undergoing a process of 'radical currency devaluation'. Her book here produces quite unexpectedly a topos basic to intellectual elitism ever since at least the seventeenth century, articulated by figures such as Alexander Pope and Jonathan Swift: we are living through a crisis in values, brought on by the linguistic uses and misuses of uneducated masses of people. The 'fun' associated with fascist mimicry of concepts is just this general tendency towards devaluation intensified into a nihilist comedy of hyperinflation.

Klein is interested in the way that political language comes to seem like mere noise, a background hum that continues reassuringly 'in the media' as the powerless and the weak are tortured and put to death in boats or the concentration camps of 'third country' clients. She is also interested in the way the agents of social murder can speak as if they were their opponents, and she is interested in this 'as if' as a feeling of meaninglessness, as loss of meaning, as directionlessness, as depression.

Toscano's 'lateness' may seem to invoke some of the same tendencies. But the lateness of his degraded antifascism is not about value but about *survival*, and the fact that this distinction is itself hard to hold on to is a testament to the absolute hegemony of ideas of value and respectability in governing the way in which we think about concepts and political identity. The figure in his book of George Jackson as someone *for whom the dominant and 'correct' theory of fascism was always a kind of nonsense literature*, always a rabbit hole leading to an upside down world fantastically purified of tiny electronic listening devices, barely functional plastic tape recorders and especially of steel bars, is its fundamental lesson. The degraded object of an in a sense obviously false Third Position Stalinism became for Jackson a means with which to explain. He did not fear he would be 'like' a Third Positionist Stalinist. Nor did he suffer from the experience of mimetic shock, which in this sense is revealed as a disease of affluence, a discovery that allows the theme of 'class' in *Late Fascism* to come back in, now as the old anxiety about being seen in the wrong company.

Ultimately the value of the thing that helps us to survive is irrelevant. If political speech is experienced now as something which has been drained or evacuated of significance, such that the solecisms of a 'sympathetic

… elderly man with a poor memory' (as one journalist said of Biden) seem to speak an essential truth about the whole thing, then this is perhaps a reflection not of the loss of value of political language but of the irrelevance of all existing systems of value to our own intellectual and political endurance. Toscano's book's open approach to degradation implies this. We may not have our own conceptual space, free from mirrors and rabbit holes and irresponsible desires, but we relate to dead and degraded materials including ourselves with the aim of helping each other to live. Degraded as it is, the anti-fascist Ship of Theseus offers to you, without conditions, as Frank O'Hara once wrote: 'my hull and the tattered cordage of my will'.

Danny Hayward

Farce squared

Naomi Klein, *Doppelganger: A Trip into the Mirror World* (London: Penguin, 2023). 416pp., £10.99 pb., 978 1 80206 195 6

In my initial read of Klein's spiral through a web of mirrors, doubles and doppelgangers, Zionism seemed to be just one instance among many of a right-wing ideology corrupting the language of liberation. But the more I sat with Klein's book, the clearer it seemed that Klein's analysis of Zionism contained the key to all of the other issues of interest. In one way, it is unsurprising that I couldn't get away from Zionism: this piece was written in April and May of 2024, when students and faculty at campuses across the United States, including my own, initiated an impressive protest wave against the continued investment of our educational institutions in profiting from the atrocities unfolding in Palestine. It has been nigh impossible these last seven months to focus on anything else, to write on anything else, to think about anything else. The brutal repression of Palestine has become a filter through which we must see everything else.

At the end of *Doppelganger*, Klein focuses on the rise of Zionism as a perverted double of Western imperialism, 'a doppelganger of the colonial project, specifically settler colonialism'. While it may seem to some that the Israeli state's current atrocities in Gaza, the West Bank and Lebanon are exceptional, Klein sees them as the replication of the repressed atrocities that made the modern world: European colonialism, in all its forms, which used genocide, land theft, racial hierarchy, religious zealotry and capitalist domination to remake nearly every corner of the globe. The truth about Zionism, from Klein's perspective, is that it reflects the normative rule of global power, rather than representing a novel regime of brutality. Tracing a long history of doubles from the extermination of Indigenous peoples in the Western hemisphere to the Nazi death machine to the West's attempted *mea culpa* for antisemitism, Klein reveals the present settler colonial regime in Palestine to be a return of the repressed of Christian, Occidental, liberal societies. Klein could not have anticipated how timely this analysis, which neither exculpates nor exoticises Jewish Israeli domination, would prove to be, as the events of October 7 set in motion a new level of extreme violence on Gaza.

One of the most famous accounts of historical doubling comes from Marx, who wrote in *The Eighteenth Brumaire of Louis Napoleon* that 'Hegel remarks somewhere that all great world-historic facts and personages appear, so to speak, twice. He forgot to add: the first time as tragedy, the second time as farce.' The farcical is a theme that recurs throughout Klein's readings of many unsettling twin stories over the course of the book, and the case of Zionism is particularly acute. At the crest of decolonial movements for independence after World War II, the Western community coalesced around the demand for Jewish people to be granted a national state, and for that national state to be placed in Palestine. While contemporary right-wing commentators try to debate the accuracy of calling Israel a colonial state, Zionists from the 1880s through the 1950s were quite clear that they were colonising Palestine, and despite the growing global resistance to colonisation, many Zionist institutions directly described themselves as a colonial force:

> The tacit argument many Zionists were making at the time was the Jews had earned the right to an exception

from the decolonial consensus – an exception born of their very real extermination. The Zionist version of justice said to Western powers: if you could establish your empires and your settler nations through ethnic cleansing, massacres, and land theft, then it is discrimination to say that we cannot. It was as if the quest for equality were being reframed not as the right to be free from discrimination, but *as the right to discriminate*. Colonialism framed as reparations for genocide.

This twisted strategy emerges as a paragon example of a tendency Klein sees rising to prominence in the contemporary age: a distorted mirroring that the right wing uses to appropriate and reconfigure ideas and strategies traditionally associated with the left. And what better metaphor than an eerie double that is familiar, and yet also somehow *wrong*, than the doppelganger?

Doppelganger arrives at the analysis of Zionism through meditations on a wide range of doubles: pop culture, social media, the alt-right, 'far out' new age spiritualists, trucker convoys and more all emerge as manifestations of a troubling tendency toward distorted doubling. But perhaps the most narratively compelling case is the one that anchors the narrative of the book: Klein's attempt to understand and respond to her own case of mistaken identity. For over a decade, Klein has been repeatedly mistaken for 'the Other Naomi' – Naomi Wolf. Wolf, the once-vaunted feminist author of *The Beauty Myth* and now right-wing media darling, emerges not only as Klein's double, but also as exemplar of the entire 'Mirror World' of far right politics, conspiracy theories and science denialism that has become a centrifugal force in contemporary politics, not only in the United States, but around the world. In tracing Wolf's political backsliding, Klein touches on an all-too-familiar experience that many of us experienced forcefully through the pandemic: family and community members being swept up in conspiracies about vaccines, child trafficking rings, and 5G seemingly overnight. Wolf, once the face of (a certain kind of) feminism, now serving as a talking head on Bannon's *War Room* provides a compelling case study in a broader transformation of social relations.

But Klein has a more personal investment in Wolf because, even after the latter's rightward run, the two Naomis are repeatedly confused for each other. In a stark episode recounted in the book, Klein recalls how, at one point, the two authors were mistaken for each other so frequently that Twitter's auto-complete function routinely *prompted* users to make the mistake. In an attempt to understand her own doppelganger experience, Klein turns to many of the great thinkers of the double: Sigmund Freud, Charlie Chaplin, Carmen Maria Machado, Robert Louis Stevensen and others. The book's narrative meditates on how it feels to literally 'have a double walking around', one possible translation of the German word *doppelganger* (more traditionally, 'double-going'). The reader feels with Klein the anger, frustration, helplessness, humiliation and exasperation of being mistaken for someone else and hence of being, in public, misrecognised and misunderstood.

Circulating through the text is a self-reflective anxiety about uncovering the cause of this conflation: *why* did Klein and Wolf keep getting mistaken for one another, despite agreeing on almost nothing? Klein's gracious explanation – that they are both middle-aged women writers with books on big ideas – feels as unsatisfying to her as to her readers. Klein's mother offers another explanation: antisemitism, pure and simple. It's not that the world can't distinguish two people with the same name or two women writers, it's that in the popular culture both women stand in for another type of doppelganger altogether: the racial or ethnic doubling of the stereotype. Klein's mother's suggestion that no matter how much assimilation Jewish people subject ourselves to, we will always be seen through the projection of an antisemitic double is, of course, the same conviction that underpins Zionism.

In one sense, Jewish people seem to be as assimilated as any minority group could be. At the same time, I lived through frequent bomb scares at my Jewish elementary school as well as a traumatic white supremacist shooting at the Jewish Community Center summer camp at which I was a junior counsellor and where my sibling and cousins were campers. As the far right concretes visibility and power, openly antisemitic chants ('Jews will not replace us!'), hate crimes (the Tree of Life Synagogue Massacre) and conspiracy theories (Elders of Zion, Great Replacement, Soros, etc.) have become more normalised. The gamble made by many in my parents' and grandparents' generation – that assimilation would deflate the haunting double of the Eternal Jew – seems to have failed.

What accounts for this failure? Klein argues that the Western societies we live in are fundamentally unable to confront the violent and traumatic conditions that structure collective life, and that inability creates the condition for the emergence of doppelgangers. Ultimately Klein's diagnosis is analytic (in both senses): a society that needs doubles is a society that cannot bear to look itself in the mirror. Doubling cleaves off uncomfortable truths about ourselves and projects them onto others, turning our own anxieties into monstrous others. In order to deflate the power of the 'Mirror World', Klein suggests, we have to create a world where we can confront all of the insufficiencies and dark tendencies that structure of American and Canadian society – settler colonialism, capitalism, oppression and ecological devastation.

The fact that real antisemitism is on the rise (and that it might in fact play a role in Klein's own doppelganger experience) thus is not due to an eternal, ontological antisemitism, but is a political effect of Western society's inability to confront the oppressions at the heart of its own history. And this is what Zionism fundamentally misunderstands and misrepresents about the character of ethnic doubling in general and the case of antisemitism in particular: what Jewish people, like all people, need to be truly liberated would be a real reckoning with the violences of Western colonialism, capitalism and heteropatriarchy, not the creation of a violent, Western society 'of our own'. Liberation is not joint partnership in domination.

Of all of the doppelganger tales explored in Klein's book, Philip Roth's *Operation Shylock* proves the most insightful (despite Klein's lifelong loathing for the author's incapacity to write multi-dimensional women characters). *Operation Shylock* tells the story of an author (called, in the story, Philip Roth) and an imposter who, using the name Philip Roth, critiques the Zionist project as a world historical mistake, and founds a movement called 'diasporism', urging Israelis to return to the European countries that had attempted to exterminate them less than a century ago. Far from a principled anti-Zionist text, however, Fake Roth more closely resembles a farcical caricature of actual diasporist and anti-Zionist Jewish politics, taking them to 'fanatical and cartoonish extremes'. The author Roth (who Klein calls 'Real Roth') travels to Jerusalem to confront anti-Zionist Roth ('Fake Roth'); hijinks ensue. In order to introduce some distance between himself and his doppelganger, Real Roth 'refus[es] to call him [Fake Roth] by their shared name and instead renam[es] him Moishe Pipik – *pipik* being the catch-all diminutive given to naughty kids and schlemiel-like characters in his childhood home; the name literally means 'Moses Bellybutton' (fitting for all the navel-gazing)'. Real Roth describes the pipikism of his double: 'the anti-tragic force that inconsequentializes everything – farcializes everything, trivializes everything, superficializes everything.'

If Marx in the nineteenth century could already identify history's doppelganger story – first as tragedy, then as farce – what comes after the farce? Klein's suggestion is that we might be living through a kind doubling of the farcical, a kind of farce squared, in which the outlandish and outrageous and brazenly trivial become so meaningless that the very concept of meaning is thrown into doubt. For Klein, the primary upshot of pipikism is its dangerous evacuation of seriousness and meaning. But for Klein, pipikism does more than simply appropriate the terms of the left for deployment on the right; pipikism appropriates in order to toxify. It degrades the ideas and analyses so far that they become unrecognisable and unusable: 'it doesn't just farcicalize what they say; it farcicalizes what many of us are willing and able to say afterward.'

Here is where the idea of pipikism significantly diverges from some of the other theories circling around this problem. While many decry the 'appropriation' of left ideas by the right or the 'incorporation' or 'domestication' of these ideas by powerful institutions, all of these concepts emphasise the *usefulness* of what is stolen. In each of these other ways of thinking about the problem, we could imagine a terrain on which we argue about whose use of these ideas or concepts is right; at the very least we can still use what they take from us. Pipikism is a different concept altogether; it is a use that destroys – for all parties involved. Klein gives a helpful example:

> For instance, when Bannon states that his armed and authoritarian posse is being 'othered' by leftists and liberals, he is appropriating an important term that analysts of authoritarianism have used to describe how fascists cast their targets as less than human, making them easier to discard and even exterminate, But he is doing more than that, too. He is also making a mockery of the whole concept of othering, which in turn, makes it harder to use the term to name what Bannon does as a matter of course – to migrants, to Black voters, to trans and nonbinary youth.

One of the more impactful scenes of online pipikism emerged out of the antivax movement. Vaccine skeptics appropriated language from the feminist movement: 'my body, my choice' – even as some of the same people were vehemently pushing for the rollback of reproductive rights. They also started to wear yellow six-pointed stars, the infamous mark the Nazis forced on to Jews in the Ghettos as a precursor to the 'final solution' of total extermination.

As a disabled Jewish person, witnessing this strategy was (and still is) truly enraging. When the pandemic hit, I was already immunocompromised, and I spent many, many months inside a one-bedroom apartment with only my partner. In the first year of the pandemic, I almost never saw friends – most people who had previously been close to me did not want to take the precautions necessary to be part of a pod with us – and all of those rare social events were outside, masked, at 6-10 feet of physical distance. It was a dark and lonely time in which my predominant feeling was a deep and overriding disappointment: disappointment in the people and institutions in my personal life who couldn't seem to make small changes to protect my life, and disappointment in the larger structures of collective life that failed us all so greatly, so many times. And here was a group of people trying to use this symbol of violence against my people in order to make me less safe.

I can't help but think that the pipikism of real antisemitic violence in this moment of rising antisemitism is laden with more specific import than Klein attributes. For her, the yellow star wearing is yet another instantiation of a general trend of pipikism; it is true that, for example, COVID-denialists, including Klein's doppelganger herself, have also appropriated the language of the Black liberation struggle, likening vaccine passports and mask mandates to Jim Crow laws.

But there is something about the specific conjunction of the pipikism of 'fascism' combined with the creepy philosemitic appropriation of Jewish pain that returns me specifically to the question of Zionism. Over the past few years, there have been increasing attempts to legislate the equation of anti-Zionism with antisemitism. Several US states and European countries have formally adopted the International Holocaust Remembrance Association (IHRA) definition of antisemitism, which explicitly defines almost any criticism of Israeli policy as an act of hate. Recently, the US House of Representatives voted to pass the Antisemitism Awareness Act (AAA) which repeats this same fallacy. A bill is being debated that would strip non-profit status from any organisation that critiques Israel, and students, faculty and staff across campuses are facing brutal repression for their bravery in denouncing acts that, if committed by any other world power, would be roundly condemned by all. In the context of rising *real* antisemitism of the far right, the craven pipiking of the antisemitism poses a unique danger – a danger that has been, for a long time, unleashed on Palestinians, and is now being hurled at activists, students and academics, including Jewish ones.

In January, I had the opportunity to assemble with other activist leaders in Jewish Voice for Peace. Around a campfire, Klein herself led a discussion about how her analysis might be useful in the current moment of uprising against the ongoing genocide in Gaza. Donned with masks and shirts with revolutionary slogans, the conversation, though rife with loving disagreement, focused on the practical ways to try to manoeuvre around the right-wing deployment of pipikism in the form of Zionism. As Jews demanding an end to the onslaught in Gaza as well as the longer-term apartheid in occupied Palestine, we were daily confronting a deranged deployment of the slogan 'Never Again', in which our community's commitment to stop genocide anywhere was being used to justify an ongoing genocide. From legislative houses to corporate policies to universities, we were (and still are) trying to fight the degradation of the term 'antisemitism' beyond recognition to mean *any* critique of the Israeli state – and we were constantly being attacked with vile terms like 'antisemite', 'self-hating Jew', 'kapo' and 'Judenrat' for holding fast to Jewish values like social justice (*tikkun olam*), the sanctity of life (*pikuach nefesh*) and solidarity with others (the most frequently commanded law in all of the Torah – an auspicious 36 times!). In the midst of an uprising, a cross-class, intergenerational group of activists saw in Klein's book a more helpful diagnosis than mere appropriation. The Jewish community was being pipiked by Zionism as we spoke.

Critiquing the appropriation of leftist ideas by institutions is not new; activists have warned for decades about the dangers of pursuing social justice in collaboration with state governments, corporations, large non-profits, and universities, even when they seem to generate real successes. For example, the establishment of new programs of learning, in Women's Studies, Black Studies, Critical Ethnic Studies, Queer Theory, and others, constituted a real achievement for identity-based social movements, to say nothing of the ways that queer, feminist, anti-racist and decolonial topics and methods became available for study inside some of the more traditional disciplines. In conjunction with other strategies of power-building outside of the academy, the institutionalisation of new departments and areas of study massively transformed public discourse. Klein discusses how new proximities to institutionalised power, alongside new social media technologies, gave grassroots organisers larger audiences than ever before, leading to 'huge victories in transforming the way we talk about all kind of issues – billionaires and oligarchic rule, climate breakdown, white supremacy, prison abolition, gender identity, Palestinian rights, sexual violence – and I have to believe that those changes represent real victories, that they matter'. These changes have been so widespread that nearly every institution of collective life – universities, governments, boardrooms – have adapted themselves to the new lingua franca, hiring a new coterie of consultants and vice-chairs to integrate this language into their operations. The wide uptake of some left ideas is not nothing. It is a win of a certain kind. But, as Klein remarks, these wins have been coupled by a real rollback in the material rights and entitlements that, for lack of a better term, make words *matter*. We seem to have won the discourse war, Klein laments, 'at the precise moment when words and ideas underwent a radical currency devaluation ... [in] a torrent that assiduously amplifies the more operatic forms of virtue performance and the most cynical forms of pipiking'. To borrow a distinction from Gramsci, we are winning the war of position, but losing the war of manoeuvre. And as Gramsci knew well, successful revolutions need to win on both fronts at once.

As much as Klein's analysis of pipikism and the 'Miror World' clarify the current political conjuncture, she often places the boundary between 'our world' and the Mirror World in a surprising place, folding liberal politicians and institutions into 'our side' of the divide. But I think many on the radical left see more continuity between Biden and Bannon than Klein's analysis allows. Certainly, we live in a time of political polarisation, but on many of the key questions of our time – capitalism, environmental protection, abolition, Zionism, decolonisation, etc. – there aren't many real *material* differences in policy or analysis, but rather what Freud called 'the narcissism of small differences' over relatively minor tweaks to what French philosopher Jacques Rancière once diagnosed as a fatal 'consensus' of governing parties. It was, of course, Biden and Trudeau governments who presided over the mangled 're-opening' procedures that caused so much confusion and left frontline workers exposed to death, often without even meagre labour protections. Some of the most consistently violent police forces run basically unchecked through democratically-controlled cities like LA, Chicago and New York. And it has been Biden and Trudeau who have continued to send money and weapons to the Israeli military actively perpetuating a genocide in Gaza. I do not disagree with Klein that 'our side' is fighting against another side that views the world in completely distorted terms, but I am not sure we agree on who constitutes 'our side'. I am mindful (and agree) with Klein's wise caution against the left tendency toward fracture into ever-smaller political echo-chambers of agreement. Movements must hold spaces for substantive disagreement, and litmus-tests of ideological purity limit the power and appeal of movements that need broad participation to be successful. In their best moments, I have witnessed the transformation of people's politics that comes from simply working in proximity and trust with a heterogeneous cross-cutting coalition of groups and interests, working toward a common goal. But I fear there is more pipikism on the so-called 'left' than Klein seems to admit. As the strategy has been taken up across the radical right, it has also become mainstreamed, with politicians, pundits and party strategists on both sides leaning in to pipikism. This is nowhere more evident than in relationship to Zionism and antisemitism, in which the pipikism I have outlined here is being touted as justice by a bipartisan consensus.

For Klein, the ultimate political devastation this form of pipikism unleashes on the world is its evacuation of meaning, or, in her terms, 'the all-out war on meaning that this new stage of progressive-cloaked capitalism represented.' This is the heart of the problem for Klein: 'If nothing means anything and nothing follows from anything else, then, as Hannah Arendt warned, everything is possible. Reality is putty to be shaped and molded at will.' While I am sympathetic to Klein's frustration over the death of meaning in some ways, I'm not convinced that this is the real problem. Nearly every generation has dealt with its own version of the crisis of meaning. Perhaps the most famous retorts to the death of meaning came nearly a century ago with the rise of existentialism. In the face of the wanton violence of the World Wars, the obvious failures of capitalism in global crashes and rising agitation against the coercive institutions of state and church that had previously provided stable meaning, philosophers like Sartre, Fanon and de Beauvoir responded to the death of meaning with a defiantly glib, 'so what?' If meaning is up for grabs, if it is no longer moored to unwieldy institutions of power, might that not, in the end, work in our favour?

If, as Klein says, 'everything is possible', isn't that ultimately the single, most necessary development for revolutionary thinking? In an age conditioned by post-Soviet, neoliberal malaise in which, as Frederic Jameson famously wrote, 'it is easier to imagine the end of the world than the end of capitalism', the idea that anything is possible might be the most precious idea imaginable. Marxist analysis reopens the question of just such a possibility. The upshot of Marx's analysis is that capitalism as a social system and the domination it entails is fundamentally a social system, not a natural one, one that human beings made and continue to reproduce. The conviction that, because we are the ultimate authors of our circumstances, 'anything is possible' means that we have the power (or at least the potential) to make a world beyond domination, beyond oppression, beyond fate.

For Klein, all doppelganger stories can figure as a kind of portent, a sort of future anxiety. She writes, 'For centuries, doubles have been understood as warnings or harbingers'. The warning of Zionism might be that the Era of the Mirror World is quickly coming to a close. There may no longer be a clear or easy separation between those of us living in reality and those who see the world through the distorted lens of denial, repression and pipikism. In this sense, the formation of Zionism as a pipikism that cuts across both sides of the mirror world may contain the seed of a future made all the more dangerous.

But a warning is also a possibility. We do not have to imagine that we greet the harbinger as Cassandra, doomed to see the future but powerless to change it. The political organising around Palestine these last months provides a different orientation. If the world we live in is built on settler colonialism, capitalism, racism and antisemitism, then we must join together to interrupt these processes. In doing so, we can try to build a different world and in that process, address and repair the repressed past that violently haunts the present. If we can see and name clearly the path we are on, that is always the first step in being able to shift course. Klein's theory of pipikism provides an important tool – it sounds the alarm of the world we are living in. It will be up to us to decide how to respond.

Ashley Bohrer

Beyond bread and butter

Richard Seymour, *Disaster Nationalism: The Downfall of Liberal Civilization,* (London: Verso, 2024). 288pp., £20.00 hb., 978 1 80429 425 3

Why does the right appear to have been the main beneficiary of recent crises, and why do all tributaries seem to flow into the reservoir of nativist reaction? The more uninspiring impulse in left analyses is to see some sort of neat relationship between the dispossession of the working classes and the appeal of nationalist revanchism. The solution then is a focus on 'bread and butter issues'. Richard Seymour's *Disaster Nationalism* shows just how unsatisfactory such a response is.

> It *isn't* the economy, stupid. It isn't even physical survival. In India, the Philippines, Brazil and the United States, pogroms, death-squad populism, far-right militias and police and paramilitary violence are the driving force of nationalist success. They offer not growth, but the chance to destroy a neighbour. Isn't this what happens as civilization falls away?

Seymour takes the seductions of disaster nationalism seriously, mapping their libidinal force and their vectors of contagion.

Disaster nationalism is not quite fascism. Or, more to the point, disaster nationalism, is *not yet* fascism. As Seymour explains in the introduction, 'I think disaster nationalist leaders are pathfinders for a new type of fascism, because in a manner of speaking we are always *pre-fascist* as long as the conditions for fascism have not been abolished. But whatever emerges will not be cosplay of the 1920s and 1930s.' Disaster nationalism makes no claims to revolutionary anti-capitalism – as interwar fascism did before taking power – but instead pursues a kind of muscular capitalism unshackled from the constraints of liberal international agreements and human rights law. The strongmen at the centre of Seymour's analysis – Modi, Trump, Duterte and Bolsonaro – were voted in by electoral means, not military coups. And with the exception of Modi, these leaders have no strong civil base; their social and institutional roots are weak.

In any case, Seymour's comparisons with 1920s and 1930s fascism remain only a sidenote on the way to a highly original reckoning with the contemporary. (Alberto Toscano's *Late Fascism* [reviewed elsewhere in this issue] provides a deeper dive into fascist historiography.) Seymour has been circling around the question of fascism in his Patreon blog posts over recent years – many of which find their way, reworked, into the text of this book – describing our moment in terms of inchoate fascism, incipient fascism and not yet fascism. In whichever formulation, the idea that the forces of disaster nationalism are pathfinders to a new kind of fascism is as compelling as it is troubling.

The conditions for the rise of disaster nationalism have been largely negative, based on 'the stalemate of parliamentary institutions, the declining authority of the old establishment and the breakdown of social life'. It is the latter point which most exercises Seymour: social decay and the attendant psychoanalytic questions that are raised by the collapse of public sentiment and democratic possibility. *Disaster Nationalism* is concerned with micro-fascisms, which means attending not only to far-right political movements but also to seemingly spontaneous acts of individual and communal violence: the lone wolf and the pogrom are central themes in the book. His argument is that Trump, Duterte, Modi and Bolsonaro are symptoms of a wider malaise, one which runs deeper and which requires a theory of the passions. Bread and butter start to look quite plain when you think seriously about what people are willing to kill and to die for, which has always been *the* question for scholars of nationalism.

Seymour's attention to psychology and his reading of psychoanalysis proves especially generative. He echoes Naomi Klein, in her 2023 book *Doppelganger* ([also reviewed elsewhere in this issue]), when arguing that calling people stupid or disproving right-wing misinformation misses the psychological power and cataclysmic appeal of conspiracy, vigilantism and mob violence. The book is concerned with and by the 'wild and whirling winds of neighbourly hate' that mobilise the passions of millions of people. Building on his 2019 book *Twittering Machine*, Seymour demonstrates that our digitally mediated world cannot be analysed or even named without a series of terms that command psychoanalytic inflection: conspiracy, attention, desire, nostalgia, addiction, apocalypse, sex, death, anxiety. The question for Seymour is, 'how do such emotions become politicised by salvific nationalism?', where pervasive anxiety and depression are fixed to 'a series of phobic objects (Muslims, communists, globalists, Jews and so on).' The challenge is to theorise how the cruelties and subversive pleasures inherent to late capitalism feed disaster nationalism. Founding political appeals in people's material interests represents a form of wishful thinking; the perverse desires for repression (of oneself and Others), purificatory violence and for the end of the world do not answer to such instrumentalist strategies.

Put simply, people rarely vote with their interests (indeed, Seymour nicely traces how the notion of self-interest was advanced by liberal philosophers as a means of advocating the value of greed and avarice against the passions of lust and ambition). In fact, people are animated by the things that they love and they love the things they have to make sacrifices for. It is therefore apposite that the first substantive chapter, 'Class: Not the Economy, Stupid', establishes a more sophisticated analysis of how disaster nationalism thrives on class violence and *ressentiment*. While resentment itself can be a good thing when mobilised toward the struggle against injustice, that healthy consolidation of class hatred we might call consciousness, *ressentiment* is that kind of resentment which remains enthralled with a sense of its own powerlessness and victimhood. These feelings have proliferated with the decimation of the left – falling trade union membership, widening inequality, increased uncertainty and precarity, social atomisation – so that the injuries of class are made invisible and apolitical. Interestingly, the evidence suggests it is not the most deprived workers who are most vulnerable to the nationalist contagion but those higher up the class hierarchy – those who have something to lose, the downwardly mobile middle, business and professional classes. It is not deprivation, then, but a trajectory of decline that most predisposes people to disaster nationalism. We are not talking here about 'a class, properly speaking, but a passively resentful conglomeration of individuals who believe they obey the law, respect authority and resent queue-jumpers and outsiders'. Seymour then shows how this twenty-first-century brand of authoritarian populism is put in service by political leaders and parties who on the whole seek to instigate capital accumulation without the guardrails – from India to Brazil, the Philippines to Argentina.

Seymour's psychoanalytic flair is most fully realised in the chapter on sex, where he asks what kind of arousal the erotic catastrophe of disaster nationalism produces in its adherents. He writes, 'pornonationalism promises to eroticise social life, not only by reviving repression but also by liberating sexual violence. It brings disaster and death into the mix. And it promises the impossible: by killing the sexually nefarious and terrorising women and LGBT people into retreat, it claims to be able to restore an era of glamorous male sexual power'. He sketches lines of connection between disaster nationalism and misogyny, but not in a schematic way; this is not about intersections or analogies but ressentiments that are formed out of the same anomic sludge. The desire for order, hierarchy and repression relates as much to gender and sexuality as race and nation. But amidst the incel's complaint about their unfuckability, Seymour remarks that it is not sexual gratification that is collapsing but desire: 'Something about late capitalist civilization and its diminished sociality is just not very sexy'.

This analysis of incels and the manosphere is one more example of Seymour's insights into the online spaces where reaction is nurtured. *Disaster nationalism*, then, is fundamentally a story about digitally mediated nationalism, where cyberwar offers the most concrete case study. While Trump is a kind of one-man troll farm, and Modi 'reward follows' his most virulent citizen-trolls, Duterte spent hundreds of thousands of dollars on a particularly advanced 'disinformation architecture'. This architecture was absolutely central to his ascendance, which relied on hundreds of workers disseminating his key messages via troll accounts and fake online profiles:

> The trolls did not simply start blasting propaganda. Rather, they worked to establish a rhythm. Those who seeded Facebook groups based in local communities, for example, would start by posting regular material in the local dialect without an obvious political slant. They built up memberships approaching 100,000 each. As the election neared, because Duterte's issue was crime, they began posting one news story about violent crime per day. And because Duterte's specific appeal was the drugs war, they would usually leave a comment blaming drug dealers. Then, as the election drew closer, the rate of

posting would increase to two news stories per day. Then three. Then more. They generated a rhythm of seemingly spontaneous, locally rooted, apolitical 'concern'. A few thousand well-orchestrated accounts with professionally built audiences was sufficient to game the algorithms by forcing hashtags and 'trending topics' up the agenda, changing what the social industry platforms showed to users and forcing media coverage.

Of course, digitally mediated cultures of ultra-nationalism do not stay online (if only). The online shit-storm gets armed and takes to the streets; the social media mob materialises in 'meatspace'; the keyboard warrior becomes the lone wolf. Previous tensions between electoralism and collective violence no longer appear to hold; mob violence is not damaging to political leaders, but rather becomes their chief selling point. In the words of Duterte: '*Hitler massacred three million Jews ... there's three million drug addicts ... I'd be happy to slaughter them*'. Duterte's deathsquad populism has been extremely popular, with 84% supporting his campaign against drugs in 2020, 'despite the fact that a similar majority (78 per cent) were either "somewhat worried" (33 per cent), or "very worried" (45 per cent) that they or someone they know could be a victim of an extrajudicial killing'. Duterte publicly boasted about killing drug users himself, and incited members of the public to take revenge: 'If you lose your job, I'll give you one. Kill all the drug addicts'. It is this brazen call to vigilantism and summary killings that seems to characterise disaster nationalism, wherein the only response to social breakdown, in this case manifest in drug addiction and petty crime, is via recourse to extreme and unaccountable violence.

Seymour argues that the canary in the coalmine, as far as this trend in recent history goes, is the 'Gujarat model'. In 2002, the carnival of violence against Muslims, in which thousands were killed, raped, tortured and burned alive in an orgiastic pogrom, catapulted Narendra Modi, Chief Minister of the state of Gujarat, to his now well-established status as father of the (Hindu) nation. 'It is in this calculated use of mobs, vigilantes and lynchings, from Delhi to the West Bank, that disaster nationalism accumulates much of its strategic force, as well as its "anti-systemic" credentials ... the trend is towards a fusion between legal violence and far-right extra-legal violence'. In India, majoritarian mob violence would go on to find legislative voice in India's Citizenship Amendment Act, which critics worry has made possible the mass disenfranchisement of a significant number of India's over 200 million Muslims. The chapter on 'the armed shitstorm', framed by the 'Gujarat model', then opens out onto an account of disaster nationalism in Israel and the unspeakable horrors of the last twelve months. The argument here is that, ultimately, disaster nationalism spells genocide, because it offers a 'vision so unrealisably remote that the desire it expresses can never be satiated and can never stop short of disaster'.

To conclude, Seymour asks how climate collapse – 'a force multiplier testing the very energetic foundations of contemporary civilization' – intervenes in this dismal story. If disaster nationalism erodes democracy through its hateful longing for ethnic struggle as a means of restoring order, then climate change everywhere places enormous stress on its material foundations. And yet this final chapter is not all doom; it is also where Seymour reminds us that the left has its own passions, however embattled: 'if workers are drawn into struggle by a combination of need and hope, pulled into the rhythms and contradictions of the historical process with its volatile upturns and downturns, conceive of themselves as part of that history and form the radical need for community and universality, then they are to that extent inoculated against the paranoid, anti-social and vengeful passions of disaster nationalism'. And it is not only organised workers but also activists in social movements who know that sacrifice. Communal fellow feeling, love and rage make it possible for us to do things with and for one another. 'Disaster nationalists need not be the only ones to benefit from the crisis of liberalism'.

Seymour describes our current cycle – defined as 'a period of some decades in which a set of social changes or conflicts germinates, develops and matures' – as one of 'nationalist revanchism'. Nationalism is therefore *the* question for our times, connecting the book to a larger archive of critical work on nationalism. For example, sociologist Sivamohan Valluvan reminds us that nationalism always involves self-definition through the exclusion of ethnoracial outsiders and minorities; the buzzword most invoked to name our present cycle, populism, therein becomes a stunted misnomer, distracting from the larger and more enduring problem of nationalism, which is inherently majoritarian and exclusionary. In the words of Arjun Appadurai: 'the road from national genius to a totalized cosmology of the sacred nation, and further to ethnic purity and cleansing, is relatively direct'. With this wider tendency in mind, we might ask some clarificatory questions. Most crudely, when does nationalism become disaster nationalism?

This relates to Seymour's selection of cases, which is not supposed to be exhaustive but invites the question as to why some states are included and not others. Russia's omission seems worthy of comment, as does Turkey's. Not unrelatedly, I felt the chapter on Israel-Palestine fit somewhat awkwardly, with long sections on the *sui generis* history of Israeli state formation and settler colonial violence that seemed detached from the flow of the argument, even if Seymour's desire to situate the genocidal war in Gaza within the frame of his argument is understandable. The point that disaster nationalism ultimately leads to genocide is well made, but urgent and dire circumstances may have rushed the analysis.

In a very different vein, how do we square nationalist revanchism with other characteristic features of our time – digitally mediated nihilism, post and anti-politics, and social dissolution – especially those that don't feed nationalist feeling but result in desultory apathy? After all, most people are unlikely to partake in an armed shitstorm, more likely to collapse into a screened fugue, only passively dreaming about the nation's restoration and its promise of order. The point is that Seymour's impressionistic style can necessarily be critiqued for a lack of definitional, typological work. Such a critique can be stale – bemoaning what authors don't include is much less interesting than working with what they do – but here it might raise useful questions about the global conjuncture.

In any case, Seymour is highly original in his attention to new geographies of the radical right, which is both a testament to his mode of restless critique and an indictment of much popular critical thought. Identifying synergies between India, the Philippines, the US and Europe is suggestive, although we need more work on how these proto-fascist formations materially relate to one another and how they travel. Still, there is a lot of emphasis on the US context in *Disaster Nationalism*, especially regarding the disturbing particularities of North American conspiracism (e.g. QAnon), which feels idiosyncratic, even if of undeniable global relevance (especially in light of Trump's re-election). Understandably, this emphasis in the book likely reflects the relative ease with which Seymour can access a larger and richer archive on US politics – assuming he is reading mostly in English – but it is a reminder of the immense challenges of theorising from the South and East (the examples I have cited here gently counter that preponderance of US examples, if for no other reason than because I am less interested in that particular horror show). With that in mind, we might turn to theorists writing from the African continent who have provided us with a useful set of provocations. The Comaroffs have made a compelling case that the twenty first century requires 'theory from the South':

> contemporary world historical processes are visibly altering received geographies of core-and-periphery, relocating southward not only some of the most innovative and energetic modes of producing value, but the driving impulse of contemporary capitalism as both a material and cultural formation.

Or note here how closely Achille Mbembe, writing in 2016, resembles Seymour:

> Almost everywhere the law of blood, the law of the talion, and the duty to one's race – the two supplements of atavistic nationalism – are resurfacing. The hitherto more or

less hidden violence of democracies is rising to the surface, producing a lethal circle that grips the imagination and is increasingly difficult to escape. Nearly everywhere the political order is reconstituting itself as a form of organization for death.

Such resemblances suggest that a fitting supplement to the terrain already sketched by Seymour is to fold into the analytic remit, with even more emphatic resolve, the events, circumstances and attendant theorisations unfolding in Asia, certainly, but also Africa.

Seymour remains extremely convincing on his main point: that we need to think about the reactionary passions and desires being animated by our current order. That said, I wonder about the link between psychology and culture. After all, it is through cultural analysis that the left has built a tradition of critiquing crude materialism while attending to the symbolic and to processes of subjectification. Perhaps Seymour thinks cultural studies approaches are less suited to a digitally mediated world, but it cannot be that he hasn't thought about it, and it would be interesting to hear him reflect on the study of culture today.

We might also consider the less spectacular ways in which popular culture mobilises various forms of microfascism. Anna Kornbluh's recent book, *Immediacy, or The Style of Too Late Capitalism* offers some ways in here, in its attempt to read our contemporary malaise through culture: fitness and wellness culture; the aesthetics of Netflix; the gamified paralysis of dating apps; the way music is produced for atomised listeners and watchers on Spotify and YouTube; and the viscerally affecting but always solipsist first-person realism popular in today's literature. But we also need to track the rhythms of and in people's lives; the everyday which is not amenable to the analysis of online content and large-scale surveys. What we discover from such an ethnographic sensibility will likely be both better and worse. Better because most people do not join the mob; worse because the nation still retains a hold over their political and cultural imaginations. What is it about the broader terrain which channels so many unfulfilled desires into nationalist longings for order, and makes hopes for substantive democracy increasingly beleaguered, even if this nationalism falls short of civilisational downfall and apocalyptic longing?

Perhaps this is merely another way of staging my earlier query: what is the relation between nationalism in general and disaster nationalism? Seymour might reply that disaster nationalism is not a type that he wants to distinguish from non-disaster nationalism, but rather a tendency, one defined by a particularly unstable and intense set of myths, passions, violent longings and practices. This is the best way to read the book, as a theoretically searching text, an attempt to capture something emergent, the character and texture of incipient fascism rather than a new theory of nationalism. All that being said, I retain some reservations about the method which views lone wolves and the armed shitstorm as portents of what is to come – or maybe I'm just in denial. Either way, this approach can be complemented by attention to the ordinary and the mundane – both to observe how microfascisms permeate the everyday, and where they don't.

This means journeying to the ordinary places where the rhythms of living with one another mitigate isolation and anomie, places where the false allure of race and nation lose their hold. There is certainly a point to be made about building institutional power – party, union, state – which can be phrased in familiar oppositional language, but Seymour's attention to desire, passion and subjectification also suggests the cultural as a terrain of struggle. Politically, the fight is always to convince people that nationalism is not in their interests, even when they are being included. But to combat 'wild and whirling winds of neighbourly hate' we also need *cultural* resources of hope, and it might be through attention to lived, popular and alternative culture that we can best identify counter currents, polyrhythms and sites of sociality and humaneness in the everyday.

Luke De Noronha

Technologies of impotence

Elsa Dorlin, *Self-Defense: A Philosophy of Violence*, trans. Kieran Aarons (London: Verso, 2022). 250pp., £17.99 pb., 978 1 83976 105 8

'To begin from muscle rather than from law', proclaims French philosopher Elsa Dorlin in *Self-Defense*, her first monograph to be translated into English. (An extract was originally translated in *RP* 2.05 (Autumn 2019).) Variously describing her own intellectual project as a phenomenology of violence, a genealogy of violence and a constellational history of self-defence, Dorlin adopts a distinctive Foucauldian perspective on the co-constitutive relation between corporeal self-defence and political empowerment, whilst interrogating the carceral origins of the juridical distinction between legitimate and illegitimate violence. Dorlin's intersectional lens successfully challenges the liberal fantasy of a moral economy that perpetuates an *a priori* distinction between the shielded and the armed. Less directly though no less categorically, *Self-Defense* also takes issue with femocratic forms of empowerment, rightly condemning the humanitarian conflation between material need and the need of protection, especially as the latter pertains to the treatment of racialised women in a colonial context. Undoing the oppressor/oppressed binary while foregrounding the difference between those subjects whose right to use physical and armed force is defensible, and those whose access to arms is pre-juridically criminalised, Dorlin reimagines biopower through a prosthetic imaginary where racialised gendered subjectivation occurs via a dialectical movement between weaponisation and disarmament.

Unlike Foucault's docile bodies, Dorlin's weaponised (dis)armed bodies are activated, stimulated and roused: 'It is a matter of *conducting certain subjects to annihilate themselves as subjects*, arousing their power of action to better guide them towards their own ruin. It is a matter of producing beings who in defending themselves destroy themselves' (original emphasis). In this particular form of subjectivation posited by Dorlin, technologies of power produce impotence, corporeally and politically, as the subject of self-defense is always already criminalised. Otherwise put, this process of subject formation is a process of becoming-defenceless through self-defence. When working to undo the binary logic of victim/aggressor and prey/predator, Dorlin's analysis is indebted to Gayatri Chakravotri Spivak's foundational observations on the imperialist philanthropy of 'white men [...] saving brown women from brown men'. In this respect, it could be argued that Dorlin's proposition of (dis)empowerment as a technique of the self sits in marked contrast with recent feminist discourses on the agentic potential of vulnerability (see for instance, Leticia Sabsay, Victoria Browne, Ewa Ziarek and indeed Butler). The message that women of colour need no white male saviours is pronounced loud and clear and, despite her detached authorial voice, and at times historicist facticity that appears over-reliant on secondary sources, Dorlin punches back against the current swelling tide of liberal, reactionary and fascist white feminisms.

Originally published in French in 2017, *Self-Defense* predates Judith Butler's *The Force of Non-Violence* (2020). This bibliographical reference is significant because Dorlin's engagement with biopolitics closely follows Butler's humanist ethics of preservation of life as articulated in *Frames of War: When is Life Grievable?* (2009), and I would suggest that it is with reference to, and as an extension of, the Butlerian 'grievable' that one ought to read Dorlin's proposed category of the 'defensible'. Such an extension enables Dorlin to convincingly put forward a novel conception of the constitutive relationship between disempowerment and powerlessness, with the emphasis now placed on the self-reflexive character of what might be understood as 'passive agency'. Exemplary illustrations are offered through the techniques of torture endured by the bodies of Millet de la Girardière and Rodney King, accompanied by other instances of individual resistance, such as the fictional heroine of Helen Zahavi's 1991 novel *Dirty Weekend*. When Dorlin's prose strikes successfully, the Francophone reader encountering the text in English can imagine the analytical role that Dorlin's alliterative associations play in the construction of her argument, as is the case through the aural proximity of the words *coupable* (i.e., guilty, culpable) and *capable* (i.e., able, capable). More pressingly perhaps,

because there are no translator's notes in the English edition, and because Dorlin does not explicitly distinguish between *puissance* and *pouvoir*, one is left uncertain as to whether the conceptual difference between 'power-over' and 'power-to' would have been linguistically and conceptually discernible in the French original. Dorlin is curiously silent on the formative function of epistemic violence in sustaining colonial and state oppression, and the opportunity to mobilise Fanonian radical psychiatry for a psychosomatic reading of defencelessness is regrettably missed. Moreover, despite the book's emphasis on corporeal power and counterpower, Dorlin's racialised gendered bodies are always already able – and able to take up arms, if given the correct training. This able-bodied premise notwithstanding, scholars working within critical disability studies who may not be in dialogue with Black feminist scholarship can find in *Self-Defense* a useful starting point for analysing crip subjectivation, especially with respect to the corporeal double-bind experienced by a person interpellated as defenceless and dehumanised.

It is worth noting that Dorlin's genealogy does not suggest a categorial distinction between modes of subjectivation produced in quotidian instances of self-defense undertaken by sole individuals, and modes of subjectivation produced in historical moments of collective uprising. Although the book's ideological preoccupation appears to rest on the latter mode – a key chapter is dedicated to the rhetorical and tactical function of armed self-defense in the Black Panther Party – the manner in which Dorlin transhistorically poses the political subject with respect to citizenship and citizens' rights, and the constitutional right to bear arms and to train to bear arms especially, betrays an unexpected un-Foucauldian allegiance to the philosophical primacy of the state. Dorlin argues for a conception of US vigilantism that would historically situate it 'as part of a process of rationalizing governmentality' and follows the same line of argument when discussing militarised self-defense in the nation-state formation of Israel. Dorlin's metonymic move from individual-self to collective-self is narrativised compellingly across several chapters that revisit the familiar imaginary of the American national subject as constituted by the right to armed self-defense. Whilst doing so, however, Dorlin inadvertently overemphasises a genealogical continuity between the subjecthood of the slave and the subjecthood of the freed Black person in the antebellum period. This continuity is further extended into the present moment through mobilising a political conception of Blackness which, although serving to analyse instances of neoliberal carceralism by revealing the vigilantist origin of Neighbour Watch voluntarism for instance, presupposes the racialised subject as the racialised citizen, with the voices and bodies of the racialised stateless, as a consequence, excluded.

Dorlin's engagement with the role of the military and militarised subjectivation raises further unresolved questions about modes of coercive and coerced citizenship. Drawing on the Abu Ghraib documents examined by artist Coco Fusco in *A Field Guide for Female Interrog-*

ators (2008), Dorlin proposes that we consider such acts of imperialist sexual violence in the same genealogical lineage, or what Dorlin calls a 'citational relationship', as the white supremacist violence undertaken by vigilante groups in the late eighteenth century. Dorlin's argument is that self-defense here stands for collective self-defense in the name of the American nation, where feminised, sexually aggressive white bodies ('blonde' female soldiers) rape male racialised prisoners of war. Dorlin traces the changed biopolitical role of the 'white woman' in such race relations, from the position of a white female body assumed fragile and in need of protection, to the position of a white female body assumed assertive and carefully deployed as an instrument of torture. As indisputable as such a genealogical narrative might be, it nonetheless remains unclear – especially given the political import of her publication – why Dorlin does not differentiate between modes of subjectivation that emerge in the organisational context of small-scale clandestine armed struggle and those that emerge in the expansionist context of global military operations.

This reservation brings me to my final point, which concerns Dorlin's genealogical method. *Self-Defense* is organised in a manner that appears to fluctuate between snapshot episodicity and linear historicism. It is unfortunate that the selected corpus of material is at once too geographically limited and too eclectic for the overarching discussion to not feel inexhaustive. The majority of examples are derived from experiences of racialisation and subjectivation through criminality in a US historical context (key exceptions being her narratives on the *krav maga* in the Warsaw Ghetto Uprising and jiu-jitsu in the Suffragettes). Although perhaps the book's original intent was to bring 'American' Black studies to France, for Anglophone readers at least, it is a lost opportunity that the investigation restricts its genealogy of French colonial violence to introductory comments on the *Code Noir* and does not incorporate analyses of contemporary Afro-French and Arab-Muslim subjectivation. Dorlin's citational approach does not call for the deployment of case studies or representative samples in a quantitative social-science sense, of course, yet a theoretical justification over the suitability of the chosen material would have enhanced the book's overall readability and intellectual cohesion. Lastly, the absence of a crisp narrative that foregrounds the historical relationship between those selections – whether such a historical relationship is to be understood causally or otherwise – means that Dorlin's non-linear rendering often collapses into a timeless contemporaneity.

As a genealogy of disempowerment and counterpower, rather than as a philosophy of violence (in a Fanonian, Sorelian or Benjaminian vein), *Self-Defense* attempts to develop new feminist conceptual tools such as 'dirty care', 'phenomenology of prey' and 'thanatoethics' but, disappointingly for a reader who expects a philosophical proposal, it does not put those conceptual tools to use. Dorlin's intellectual project is also arguably best understood as indexically Barthesian, rather than phenomenologically Fanonian. Dorlin may not begin 'from law' (although in the case of *Code Noir* she does) but neither does she begin 'from muscle'. It would be more accurate to say that Dorlin begins from her gut – from her own anger, which then informs her discursive analysis of mediatised episodes of police violence; contemporary popular visual and literary culture; and, for the majority of the publication, archival material of clandestine organising (primarily accessed through previously published accounts). Despite its philosophical shortcomings, *Self-Defense* does cover significant ethical terrain, especially when it exposes political contradictions such as the development of neoliberal homonormativity's relationship to whiteness (see her discussion of the Gay Liberation Front in early '70s San Francisco and The Lavender Panthers in the penultimate chapter). Once again, perhaps Dorlin's intent had been to sketch a historical and political continuity between neoliberal racist homonormativity and fascist homonationalism, but much is obfuscated in her account and such a crucial point of argumentation is never made explicit. At a historical conjuncture when extra-parliamentary far right formations, actively supported by nationalist governments and states, have a discursive and financial monopoly on legitimising and enacting racialised and ethnonationalist violence, Elsa Dorlin's *Self-Defense* may not be essential reading as such, but it nevertheless rightly insists on calling for an end to such abuses and dehumanising technologies of power.

Chrys Papaioannou

The necessity of strategy

Vincent Bevins, *If We Burn: The Mass Protest Decade and the Missing Revolution* (London: Wildfire, 2023). 352pp., £25.00 hb, 978 1 03541 227 3

Vincent Bevins is quick to point out that he's neither a philosopher, nor a historian, nor a revolutionary. Instead, as he repeatedly reminds us, with more than a whiff of Socratic ignorance, he's 'just a journalist'. It is true that a real strength of this book comes from its journalistic inflection. *If We Burn* is rich with sympathetic and exhilarating vignettes of the experiences of the activists who took part in the 'mass protest explosions' of the second decade of the twenty-first century: in Tunisia, Egypt, Bahrain, Yemen, Turkey, Ukraine, Hong Kong, South Korea, Chile, and especially Brazil. Yet, this is not solely a work of journalism. In *If We Burn* Bevins makes a clear and provocative *argument* that is highly pertinent for contemporary social and political theorists and for political philosophers. The argument is both implicit in his rich narrative presentation of the uprisings and then explicit in the final two, more theoretical, chapters. He convincingly submits that the dominant strategy adopted by the large protest movements in the period 2010-2019 was ill-conceived and self-limiting. He rejects their ideological commitment to horizontalism, consensus decision-making, and the strategy of spontaneous mass demonstrations and occupations. Instead, Bevins argues that left-activists engaged in future protests should return to appointing democratic representatives and should adopt a clear organisational structure. Perhaps most significantly, he calls for a recalibration of priorities: more energy and time should allocated to strategising how to achieve desired 'ends', rather than obsessing over 'means'. There is a warning writ large throughout the book too: that the past lack of a long-term strategy and the weaknesses of the tactics deployed by these movements led not merely to their failure to achieve their objectives, but worse, it led to a world being fashioned which was diametrically opposed to the values of the left-leaning protestors. Millions of activists getting 'fucked up on revolutionary *élan*' failed to enable progressive social transformation. As Bevins argues, many of 'these countries experienced something worse than failure. Things went backward'. Crucially, the mass protests movements discussed are understood as part of a story which ends in more repression, more neoliberalism, more inequality.

The title, *If We Burn*, is a nod to Finn Lau, a democracy campaigner in Hong Kong, and a user of the LIHKG forum, who advocated 'Lam Chau', which translates literally as 'embrace fry', or mutually assured destruction. This was rapidly converted to a more popular Western rendering, linked to a line from *The Hunger Games*: 'If we burn, you burn with us'. Bevins commences his analysis with a tragic fire, the self-immolation of Mohamed Bouazizi, a market trader in Tunisia, in December 2010. This marked the start of the 'Arab Spring' and the pattern of mass protest movements that swept the world throughout the decade. In 2010, Tunisia, Egypt, Bahrain, Syria and Yemen could all be categorised as 'authoritarian-neoliberal' states (this is equally the case in 2024). Following brutal 'structural adjustment' programmes their populations struggled with stripped-back public services, political repression, poor employment prospects, corrupt officials and spectacular wealth inequalities. It is thereby highly symbolic that Bouazizi was driven to his desperate act by a illegitimate seizure of his goods by a police officer as he struggled to make a living.

While Bevins should be commended for his attention to detail across his portrayal of the various uprisings of the decade, the argumentative power of the book comes from Bevins implicitly showing what unites all of these revolutionary movements, rather than by his impressive knowledge of their particularities. His method is essentially to show, with delicacy and sensitivity to specifics, a common dynamic. His argument is presented at first through a delicate form of disclosing analysis, showing rather than telling. To this end, I want to draw a crude ideal-type of a movement in this period, abstracting the commonalities that Bevins discloses.

Across the ten mass protest movements Bevins details, one can see the following pattern recurring:

1. A heterogeneous mass of people who are dissatisfied with the status quo converge in public, in a leaderless,

horizontal movement.
2. At first this group constitutes a significant proportion of secular progressives, opposed to authoritarian-neoliberalism.
3. Well publicised instances of state-repression drive further people on to the streets to swell their numbers.
4. These protests are characterised by a commitment to 'no stage', to having no leaders, and they have no clearly articulated set of demands.
5. As they gain critical momentum, the protestors become more heterogeneous, their ranks swelled by organisations with more conservative, nationalist, religious and neoliberal orientations.
6. The protestors ultimately unite, or are read as uniting, behind a call to topple a 'corrupt' and authoritarian leader.
7. The leader is ultimately toppled, with the mass of people initially celebrating, expecting this to lead to improved conditions.
8. In the aftermath of the regime falling a coalition of organised reactionary elements cohere to reinforce neoliberalism and authoritarianism, out-manoeuvring horizontally organised left-wing activists.
9. These left-wing activist suffer burn-out and depression, or are arrested.
10. Interviewed with the benefit of hindsight, the left-leaning activists state they wished they had had a clearer long-term strategy and had been less obsessed with horizontalism.

I stress again, that this is obviously an ideal-type abstraction, not one presented by Bevins himself. However, the above abstraction is the story which is told, at its core, over and over in *If We Burn*: in Tunisia, Egypt, Bahrain, Yemen, Turkey, Ukraine, South Korea. The implicit argument is simple: look at what happens when you try a leaderless approach devoid of long-term strategic thinking. Look at what happens over and over and over again. Failure, burn out, entrenched authoritarianism and neoliberalism.

I am not an international relations or a political science scholar, so I shall leave it to those more qualified than me to comment on whether Bevins' portrayal of each uprising is accurate, or whether any of the states discussed are actually closer to meaningful democracy than they were before 2010. With those caveats aside, I found Bevins' narrative convincing and I thus turn to the final, more theoretical chapters ('Reconstructing the Past' and 'Building the Future'), where he presents an explicit argument on strategy, impressed and receptive. In these final two chapters, I read Bevins as making three convincing arguments: a) a rejection of both horizontalism and of b) amorphous spontaneous protest, and instead, drawing out of this, c) an appeal for democratic, structured left-organising, with clear representatives, engaging in pre-meditated, long-term strategic thinking.

Bevins' rejection of horizontalism is not to be misinterpreted as a call for some Leninist vanguard. Instead, he urges left-activists to have clear structures of democratic representation so they are capable of articulating their demands and can fight back against co-optation. Bevins advances this argument delicately throughout the whole book, but it comes most clearly through the voice of the Egyptian human rights activist and investigative journalist Hossam Bahgat, who, in hindsight, laments: 'we thought representation was elitism, but actually it is the essence of democracy'. Through Bahgat, Bevins is pointing to a rejection of an ideological commitment shared by the protest movements of this period: to having no fixed representatives, to a rejection of hierarchy, to an ideological horizontalism. This was typified by the slogan 'no stage', which captured the sentiment that nobody should be in control of the movement, neither speaking on its behalf, nor controlling who has the capacity to speak for it. Across his analysis of the various movements, Bevins demonstrated how an aspiration for true horizontality left the uprisings without a coherent voice. This did not mean that plurality and ambiguity was communicated to the world and to those in power. Rather, both international journalists and those with institutional traction on the ground, served to create and shape a narrative, displacing the concerns of the initial left-leaning activists. International journalists framed the uprisings as part of a broader liberal teleology, 'toppling a brutal autocratic leader', and as part of the ushering in of liberal modernity in the form of human rights and a free market order. They were provided ample assistance in doing so by the various NGOs on the ground, who were funded to operate within a similar liberal-capitalist horizon. (As Bevins comments, the Eurocentricism of the media coverage is reflected in the name 'Arab Spring' itself: 'spring' is not a cause for celebration in the Arab World, it means temperatures are about to soar). More problematically still, organised right-wing factions on the ground were able to articulate and communicate demands proficiently to local media outlets and to the executive, co-opting the movements' energy and displacing calls for economic justice.

It is not merely the case that these uprisings rejected having nominated representatives to articulate the peoples' demands; rather, on principle, many had no organisational structure whatsoever. Indeed, their amorphous fluidity was held as a virtue. Tahrir Square was famously presented as a carnivalesque of prefiguration, where a new world was swimming into view. To enforce structure would be sacrilege, reactionary, authoritarian. The problem is that across all the uprisings Bevins discusses, while left-activists refused on principal to organise and hierarchise, established right-leaning forces did so to great effect. In nearly every case, organisations with a clear hierarchical structure, whose existence predated the movement itself, were able to shape the protest and steer the uprising into a direction that suited their interests. Hossam Bhagat is again turned to here, for words of sage reflection. What should activists do today? 'Organise. Create an organised movement'. Bevins is also clear on the importance of premeditation here. Activists should not wait for a spark to organise. This is where he is perhaps most didactic and explicit, offering a clear injunction: do not wait for a mass uprising to form an organisation. Rather, 'it was the groups that were already there, prepared, that did the best when the explosion came – whether they were Hoxhaist Communists in Tunisia or the nationalist extremists in Ukraine, these groups punched above their weight'.

For Bevins, 'organizations are effective and representation is important'. Activists should acknowledge that leaders and 'vertical structures, and hierarchies tend to emerge in large groups of people', the solution is not to prevent this, but to 'construct a self-consciously democratic organisation that ensures this happens in the most

legitimate and transparent ways possible'. His rejection of horizontalism is therefore largely based on historical precedent (look: it fails) and efficacy (it fails because it is not as effective). But there is also an interesting further argument against horizontalism, which emerges briefly and that deserved further space in the book. Horizontalism is also poor because it is *too individualistic*, and in this it reflects a pathological neoliberal subjectivity. Everybody wants to be the leader, everyone wants to have their own understanding of why they are protesting, nobody will sacrifice a portion of their autonomy to be part of a broader, organised movement. It becomes an impotent cult of collective individuality. I would have been interested to have seen this argument fleshed out further.

Personally, I am convinced by Bevins that what is required, learning from the 2010s, is democratically structured organisations, with clear representatives, who are committed to strategic thinking. Thinking about what happens the day after the regime falls matters. When the power vacuum emerges: how are progressive groups going to ensure their values and policy aspirations win the day? For too many groups there was a naïve belief in the glorious victory following the fall of the dictator. As Egyptian activist Mahmoud Salem described it, there was a sense that everything would melt away when Mubarak had gone. Salem compared his innocent belief to a view that all evil would instantly be purged from the kingdom, akin to the destructions of the forces of Sauron when the ring is thrown into Mount Doom in *Lord of the Rings: The Return of the King*. Bevins is obviously correct: history shows that is not what happens. Left-activists must strategise how to take control of the political vacuum, merely creating one does not guarantee a progressive future. As Bevins argues, you cannot just burn your car and just hope a better one will come along and replace it. Detailed, situation-specific, dynamic and adaptive strategising is required. In light of insurgent neo-fascisms and the impending existential threat of climate change, and the total failure of neoliberal parties to engage with either meaningfully, the questions Bevins poses are only going to become more relevant for left activism in the years ahead.

Neal Harris

Streaming hammers

Paul Rekret, *Take This Hammer: Work, Song, Crisis* (London: Goldsmiths Press, 2024). 200pp., £36.00 hb., 978 1 91338 016 8

The headphones come off. Sore ears. The promise of lively distraction wears thin, and playlists lose their already limited lustre. The troubled relation between labour and leisure spirals, unresolved, forever onward. In *Take This Hammer: Work, Song, Crisis* Paul Rekret mines this familiar tension, tracing the unease with which we encounter music both as circulating commodity and as aesthetic experience which *might* move us against the near-universal drudgery of waged and unwaged labour.

Take This Hammer draws its title from the 'hammer songs' of primarily Black, predominantly forced, labourers across the nineteenth and twentieth centuries, each sung to 'animate and pace a hammer striking steel, an axe splitting wood, a hoe shaping soil'. In the titular variation a worker exclaims in rejection: 'This old hammer killed John Henry / But it won't kill me, Oh boys, won't kill me.' Rekret posits that in this chronicle of social life in flight from the brutality of segregation, there is no attempt at reconciliation with work, but instead only an insistence on escaping from labour altogether. In varied meditations on 'the song', moving from synthetic New Age experimentation to the equivocations of Vaporwave, Rekret sketches how any such oppositional culture may still be heard in the disorienting space-time of our post-financial crisis economy. As an 'unstable vessel', which bears that which is 'unallowed, insurgent and perverse', he attempts to make sense of how 'the song' may yet still continue to function as a site of struggle. With a commentary on the fragmentary paths of modernism as a background, this is above all suggested by Rekret, albeit at points elliptically, in how music may initiate a 'different experience of time' that in myriad ways opposes the 'capitalist-time discipline' which formats the uneven flows of daily life.

Concerned less with any untempered philosophical speculation on 'pure sonority' and sound, it is the violence and antagonism which conditions music, and casts its horizons, that comes to the fore. If Theodor Adorno famously fretted over our capacity for a poetic celebration of the 'actuality of nature' when the din of jet engines clouded all but 'the most remote forests', Rekret worries over the truth contents of an aesthetic practice whose object is rapidly collapsing: how are the artistic practices of field recording – attempts to document and represent the sound of the natural world – mutating as its source is facing total ecological devastation through the proliferation of the 'lithium and copper mines, the chipboard assembly plants, [and] e-waste dumps' necessary to sustain its own musical infrastructures? The social violence which underpins our recording and listening practices are interrogated in a related vein: how can we ever imagine them to be free of capitalism's imprint when neo-colonial regimes ensure music technology is primarily 'produced, assembled and disposed of in the global South' and the 'overwhelming majority of the world's intellectual property is held in a small number of overdeveloped states in the global North'? Housing crises, financialised debt and the 'racialised and gendered global division of the pleasures and pains'; all are suggested as inextricable from any assessment of the shapes of contemporary music, and the implications and costs of autonomous expression are to be accounted for.

Rekret's range of interlocutors in the book is certainly wide, and extended engagements with feminist theory and thinkers from the Black Radical Tradition structure Rekret's analysis throughout, as he works to consider how the social reproduction of life under perpetual economic crisis and exclusionary violence is resisted and registered in music's expressive forms. This is most acutely felt in his reading of trap music and its ascent into pop hegemony. Although hip-hop and its many sub-genres all reflect upon capitalist crises in distinct ways, Rekret posits that 'only trap ... explicitly starts from the problem of work' through its producers' multi-valent focus on the compulsive tempo of making and spending money in US cities and suburbs. This specific question of work is also, however, necessarily folded into a wider address of capital's transformation of the US's spatial reality. The name of the genre itself originates from the mass of foreclosed and abandoned houses which have proliferated since the early 2000s, and Rekret situates the genre in relation to a profoundly unequal system of housing almost totally subsumed under racialised and market logics. Trap is, ultimately for Rekret, a genre which 'accumulates a seemingly contradictory load of premises' in that it simultaneously 'gestures at a mode of life within and against capital' through resistance to capital's disciplinary regimes, at the same time as it is abstracted into a musical commodity and channelled toward mass commercial influence.

This complex dynamic of production and commodification is further excavated through Rekret's reading of 'authenticity' and its place within the political economy of 'new world music'. A 'ceaseless pursuit of an Other' currently fuels sections of collector-oriented, tourist-like network of labels and archival projects which circulate recordings from musicians, primarily outside the West, which tend toward compositional and technical experimentation in hybrid forms. Rekret highlights that one primary consequence of this mode of consumption is how it promotes a total evacuation of the political stakes of the music itself, rendering it invisible or just as an additional selling point; the complexity of Francis Bebey's oeuvre, for example, is compressed into a simple 'eccentricity' that can be enjoyed at a distance, where his extensive participation in decolonial cultural politics, musical as well as novelistic and pedagogical, is continually disappeared.

While sites like clubs are a prominent setting for Rekret's study, the collective dimensions of music today are unfortunately addressed in less detail. We might want to consider, for example, the dynamics of an ever-growing but always fraught live music sector in the UK, and its social function as a site of both pleasure and obstinate toil. Given 'refusal' is articulated through both individual and shared practices, and often in a messy blend of the two, the place of music within our vanishing shared lives is left somewhat unclear; our enjoyment of music both emboldens modes of communality which work against the seriality insisted upon by capitalism's divisions of labour, while also threatening to reinforce the intrusion of isolation into all spheres of life. I'm reminded of a development which Laleh Khalili records in her intimate account of life on tankers and ships, *The*

Corporeal Life of Seafaring, where she notes how ships' crews increasingly disappear into the solitude of their cabins for online streaming, when they might have once endured stormy seas through late-night sing-alongs. Access to a karaoke machine was previously demanded by workers as a condition for their work, but now mutual revelry in song and performance increasingly dissipates through ubiquitous satellite internet connection.

On this, Rekret's engagement with streaming culture is perhaps more clarifying, as he documents the perpetual encroachment of streamed music as a functional salve to the hardship of precarious jobs and socio-economic instability. With the rise of the curated playlist as a background presence for life's every moment, Rekret sees the ambient-ification of our experience of music at large: shorter songs, less key changes and front-loading of hooks to ensure listening beyond the 30-second mark which triggers payment to an artist. A predictability in sound and style seems to be a compelled telos of our current musical epoch. While the logic of experimentalism which guides ambient music itself has always been up for debate, with the expansion of 'chill' into every terrain, Rekret sees primarily an extension of digital capitalism's mechanisms of capture. Computational algorithms collate songs through quantitative meta-data, all transmitted through 'ambient computing' systems that can ensure constant access, with an appropriate playlist always at hand and ready for consumption. It is through these hostile conditions that the radical, propulsive force of any music, popular or otherwise, will have to sound out. What to think, then, as I sit on my daily commute, gladly accompanied by the gentle intensity of ambient recording works like KMRU's *Peel* or *Dissolution Grip*, with the sampled city noise of Nairobi and Berlin blurring with the drone of London? Engaged, momentarily, in escaping the clatter of one metropolis for another and, hopefully, able to reckon with the clear insight of the projects themselves, even if a practice of refusal feels highly uncertain.

Rekret himself does not rally toward any specific aesthetic programme, or pose any politically-inflected imperatives. The grandeur of political or musical strategy or polemic would likely stick out awkwardly within the book's critical gaze. Given his recurrent stress on the universalising, but differentiated, effects of capital's subsumptive processes, a wider global, comparative frame of contemporary listening practices and musical cultures may be a further track to follow, particularly in relation to current movements of struggle and revolt (as a way of making sense of the important place of song and sound in on-going solidarity movements against the genocide in Palestine, for example). Left without a definitive balance-sheet of our musical moment, the lack of a concluding chapter perhaps instead extends the open form of the song, which he suggests may still yet harbour a negativity capable of affirming life beyond capital's rhythms, but which cannot be foreclosed, or easily systematised. No easy answers, of course. Yet, as the crises Rekret foregrounds continue unabated, we will need fresh tools and texts to make sense of future compositions of music and resistance that may come to mediate the dissonance of everyday life - and *Take This Hammer* should be amongst them.

Dante Philp

Against autonomy as Idea

Grant Kester, *The Sovereign Self: Aesthetic Autonomy from the Enlightenment to the Avant-Garde* (Durham, NC: Duke University Press, 2023). 280pp., £21.99 pb., 978 1 47802 042 4

Grant Kester, *Beyond the Sovereign Self: Aesthetic Autonomy from the Avant-Garde to Socially Engaged Art* (Durham, NC: Duke University Press, 2023). 296pp., £23.99 pb., 978 1 47802 042 4

Much like Western civilisation in general, aesthetic autonomy would be a good idea. Or would it? The first volume in Grant H. Kester's diptych on the interrelations between art, autonomy and political action, *The Sovereign Self: Aesthetic Autonomy from the Enlightenment to the Avant-Garde*, presents an ambitious critical genealogy of the notion of aesthetic autonomy from the eighteenth century through to the present. In it, Kester is concerned with demonstrating the continuity of what he argues to be the discursive structure of aesthetic autonomy in thought on the relationship between art and political emancipation over some two centuries. As the title suggests, this also involves an interrogation of the dominant form of subjectivity attendant to this discursive structure.

Aesthetic experience and thought, Kester demonstrates, emerged for thinkers like Schiller and Kant as a privileged site for theorising the mediation and conciliation between a burgeoning bourgeois insistence on personal liberty, on the one hand, and the simultaneous emergence of larger social wholes (institutions, states) to which the individual must wilfully subject themselves, on the other. The aesthetic, it is shown, assuages this contradiction in that it becomes the domain in which something approximating political freedom may be temporarily sampled or prefigured, absent the historical conditions of actual emancipation. As such, it may at best inspire or incite political agency, and at worst perpetually defer it by functioning as its surrogate or as a distraction.

Equally, the aesthetic's reconciliatory capacities in fact rely on a profound philosophical devaluation of sensory and physical experience, which must always remain subordinate to the regulative force of the subject's cognitive capacities. Kester shows that this hierarchy – in which it is not hard to recognise the opposition of materialism and idealism – is also instrumentalised in Enlightenment discourse to justify the oppression of entire groups of people: it is because the working class, women, and colonised peoples are presented as all body and no spirit, mired entirely in the immediacy of sensation and incapable of reflexive self-regulation and governance, so necessary for political autonomy, that they may legitimately be dominated.

The figure of the artist, by stark contrast, comes to function according to Kester as the paradigmatic example of the sovereign self, capable of grasping and giving form to the tensions of their times, and of transcending them in the process. In order to do this, however, the inner subjectivity of the artist must remain uncompromised by any form of attachment to the outside world. The artist must become a monad, enclosed upon itself and eschewing any form of relationality, including direct political engagement. The successful artist may, and will, influence and steer the consciousnesses of others and as such impact the course of history, but this process is emphatically not to be reciprocal. The celebration of such unrealistically heroic and hubristic forms of artistic subjectivity is especially apparent in the historical avant-garde, where it reaches its high point, Kester argues, but persists among present-day practitioners as well (albeit generally in refracted, less high-fatulin' forms).

If this seems like an incisive yet somewhat one-sided representation of how the aesthetic domain and artistic subjectivity has been dealt with in Western thought, then that's because it is, and Kester is fully aware of this. In some of the more interesting and fruitful moments in the volume, he effectively manages to 'preserve an understanding of the aesthetic as a discourse that is both with and against the Enlightenment', retaining a more dialectical understanding of autonomy itself, as well as a more complex positioning of the aesthetic vis-à-vis dominant modes of thought – as well as real instances of historical domination and violence. Discussions of Herder's Romantic theorisation of the importance, for the artist, of *Einfühlung* (commonly translated as empathy, but really a feeling with and within the other), of Piscator and Brecht adjusting their plays in dialogue with working-class commentators, and of the *Tucumán Arde* exhibition/manifestation, are at once highlights in and important correctives to Kester's exposition.

But such moments are relatively few and far between, and certainly it is fair to say that the core argument in *The Sovereign Self* remains that, *mutatis mutandis*, this model for thinking about the role of the aesthetic and the position of the artist in (non-)relation to political change stays both dominant and essentially consistent to this day. In a chapter on the parallels between the relations between the historical avant-garde and vanguard party politics, Kester compellingly argues Lenin's thought and the aforementioned schema of aesthetic autonomy to coincide near-perfectly. Subsequent chapters attempt to do much the same thing for Adorno and the critics and theorists affiliated with *October* journal, but also show how the discursive structures of aesthetic autonomy and the sovereign self underpin the work of neo-avant-garde collective 'Chto Delat?' or Thomas Hirschhorn's *Gramsci Monument* (2013).

If *The Sovereign Self* is a critique of the discursive structure of aesthetic autonomy, then the second volume, *Beyond the Sovereign Self: Aesthetic Autonomy from the Avant-Garde to Socially Engaged Art*, is a re-affirmation of the politicised and activist artistic and aesthetic practices that have been at the core of Kester's scholarship to date. Picking up where its counterpart left off, this second volume is concerned with showing that such practices have been historically misunderstood and underappreciated, precisely because they challenge deep-rooted assumptions about art's relations to the political domain and the subjectivity of the artist. To this end, the volume opens with an extensive critical engagement with the work of Chantal Mouffe and Jacques Rancière, which feels like an extension of *The Sovereign Self* in that Kester demonstrates how these aforementioned assumptions are operative in their theoretical work – and, equally importantly, in the artworks that they champion.

Kester's counterproposition in *Beyond the Sovereign Self* will be that socially engaged practices of the last thirty years or so productively violate notions of autonomy and sovereign selfhood. This is first, Kester argues, because these practices actively seek to transgress the boundaries (institutional, discursive, symbolic) that demarcate and sequester the artistic field, directly engaging directly in political action. Second, these practices are not authored by artists bent on individualism and isolation, but are initiated and maintained by people and groups in open and dialogic intercourse with one another. Finally, a third theme arises here as well: these are practices that all insist on the necessity of more or less direct forms of political action and position-taking in the present. This, Kester claims, is in contrast to a totalising insistence (in the discourse of aesthetic autonomy) on an all-or-nothing revolutionary form of political change – for which it is perennially too early or too late (or both), and in comparison to which any practical engagement with politics will always appear compromised, futile or doomed to recuperative instrumentalisation.

Such practices, it is argued, issue from and critically elaborate on certain aspects of the turn to dematerialised art 'objects' in the 1960s and 1970s. They may involve attempts to transform individual or collective consciousness, experiments with group formation and collective artistic production, concrete challenges to repressive regimes, counter-institutional organisation, and interventions in policy and decision-making, among other things. While some are recognisably 'artistic' (and have been marked as such), many others are more commonly thought of as popular culture (like Chilean *Arpilleras*) or are intrinsic to the social movements with which they co-emerged (like artistic contributions to Black Lives Matter or initiatives to decolonise public spaces around the world). Certain practices are only ever mentioned in passing, to exemplify Kester's broad understanding of socially engaged artistic practice, but others are engaged with more in-depth, like Saba Zavarei's *Radio Khiaban* (a podcast on the politics of gender and space in Iran), or a fashion parade organised at Makerere University in Kampala, Uganda, to express discontent with Museveni's dictatorship.

Simultaneously, *Beyond the Sovereign Self* also wants to establish an alternative theoretical lineage, and to expose a tradition of thought concerned not so much with autonomy-as-absolute-autarky, but rather with collaborative, processual and action-based ways of negotiating and wresting away greater degrees political freedom under concrete circumstances, both within and beyond the cultural domain. Given the emphasis on relationality, it is not surprising that Glissant emerges as a figurehead; the work of Mikhail Bakhtin and Habermas's theory of communicative action (some aspects of which Kester remains sceptical of) feature very prominently as well. Taken together, the ideas of such authors form a framework that would allow for an adequate evaluation and analysis of the kinds of work that interest the author.

It is important to stress that, like *The Sovereign Self*, *Beyond the Sovereign Self* features moments that usefully complicate or ease the overly binary oppositions that do emerge between artworks and practices that would either reaffirm or contest what Kester argues to be the dominant paradigm of aesthetic autonomy and its accompanying ways of thinking and imagining the societal position of the artist. Towards the end of the first volume, for instance, Kester writes:

> How do we decipher the complex modes of both resistance and ideological manipulation that emerge in contemporary artistic production (socially engaged or otherwise)? I would suggest that it requires a situational analysis of both the immanent forms of power operating at a given site of practice and the artist's strategic, creative, and improvisational response to them.

One would be hard-pressed to find or articulate a more lucid and sensible programme for the critical theorisation and historicisation of artistic work – as well as its political aims, ambitions, and agency – today. However, precisely because of these instances in the texts, it becomes all the more remarkable that Kester's readings and analyses of specific artworks invariably appear rather less fine-grained and nuanced than this programme would necessitate. My contention here is not necessarily that Kester's critique of, say, Hirschhorn's *Gramsci Monument* misses the mark; it's quite clear that someone like Hirschhorn presides over his purportedly relational and radical projects in a manner reminiscent of enlightened despotism, working not so much with but rather *on* the social, treating groups of people (the artist's 'masses') as so much inanimate matter to be sculpted, moulded and (re)composed.

Rather, it is just that one is ultimately left wanting for discussions of works that actually do demonstrate and engage the intricate imbrication of resistance and ideology – of autonomy and heteronomy. Ultimately, all concrete artworks and practices that Kester touches upon seem to fall wholly within either the 'autonomous' or the 'socially engaged' bracket, and to function as more or less equivocal examples of these two opposing paradigms. This becomes especially blatant when Kester specifies that these paradigms, 'the conventional avant-gardist orientation we encounter in Adorno's work and what we might term a "dialogical" aesthetic paradigm evident in James's writing, Proletkult, and elsewhere', can coexist in a single artist's body of work, without ever really showing how the two can – and in fact almost always *do* – come together in specific artworks. Thus, even though the works are from the same year (1968) and both are a clear response to the Onganía dictatorship in Argentina, Graciela Carnevale's *Acción del Encierro* (in which Carnevale locked visitors to her exhibition up in the gallery space, forcing them to finally break themselves free by shattering the building's glass facade) becomes a perfect illustration of the arrogance of the artist who deems herself autonomous, instrumentalising and homogenising the public to get her point across, whereas the aforementioned *Tucumán Arde* manifestation, to which Carnevale contributed, becomes a reference point in the alternative lineage – effectively a counter-canon – of engaged, dialogical practice.

When one considers the many artworks and forms of artistic activism, from vastly differing geographical, historical and cultural contexts, that Kester considers to make up this counter-canon in *Beyond the Sovereign Self*, it becomes evident that the fact of their non-adherence to essentially eighteenth-century European ideas about political autonomy and selfhood may not always be the most interesting or relevant thing that there is to say about them. Inversely, supposedly autonomous and monologically authored practices are inevitably socially and historically situated, as Kester is well aware and recognises at several turns. One way, then, of shattering the illusion of absolute aesthetic autonomy and its concomitant claims is to read artworks (including the most apparently formalist and detached ones) for the political consequences and implications of this situatedness. Seemingly having little patience for such mediations, Kester generally takes the opposite approach of taking claims of autonomy very seriously – one might also say: at face value – and of tracing what he takes to be their performative historical effects. Throughout the two volumes, this results in an insightful, well-documented and often convincing critique of a certain *idea* of aesthetic autonomy; Kester's is a 'strong' theory, the strength of which lies in its reading and re-evaluation of key philosophical and art theoretical texts, more so than in the heuristic purchase it demonstrates on artistic – and political – practice, past or present.

Steyn Bergs

Graffiti horizon

John Lennon, *Conflict Graffiti: From Revolution to Gentrification* (Chicago: The University of Chicago Press, 2021). 296pp., £27.00 pb., 978 0 22681 569 5

We seem to have reached a point in the development of the idea of 'centring the victim' where even a study of graffiti is compelled to declare that it 'centres the walls themselves'. This begs any number of questions about the adequacy of the practice of 'centring' and its extension or application, not least that regarding its capacity to alter the conditions that produced the victims. In this particular case however we are confronted with an awkward spatial metaphor – walls in the centre of what, exactly? – that speaks as much to an apparent tendency toward metaphorisation in writing about graffiti as it does to any wider scholarly convention. Graffiti, that is, appears peculiarly bound to something like Walter Benjamin's notion of baroque allegory, where the word tends toward the image and history fades into the landscape.

In *Conflict Graffiti*, John Lennon asks the related and intriguing question of the evident connection between social crisis, whether ruin or riot, and the practice of aerosol graffiti. Why in the midst of rebellion or catastrophe would someone stop to spray a picture on a wall? Can it even be considered stopping, taking a break from the action rather than a form of participation in it? Lennon's book suggests it is not, that no matter the message, no matter how ambiguous, something is being actively added to a discourse. Taking a note from peace and conflict studies, Lennon approaches graffiti through its discursive and its violent character. The basic argument is, 'In short, graffiti are messy politics.' This mess of conflict can be organised, as Lennon sees it, in 'waves' of graffiti: the first wave is anticipation, the second is eruption, and the third is suppression. Perhaps most importantly: 'they crash down upon a particular area.' Place, geographically delimited location, is for Lennon the foundational consideration. Some tension or contradiction persists between this insistence and the arc of the book, which, as its subtitle *From Revolution to Gentrification* suggests, follows the crash of the waves, yet does so through or across or above the various sites of conflict. The wave metaphor, a handy image drawn perhaps from the chapter on New Orleans in the time of Hurricane Katrina, cannot quite encompass the movement of history. Place is made to compensate such that territorial defence is raised to an honour or ethic, rather than understood as a result of damage done.

An example occurs in the section on artist Tyree Guyton, who turned the overgrown lots and abandoned houses of his Detroit neighbourhood into a kind of installation, painting murals of whimsical dots and Martin

Luther King, transforming waste into sculpture by nailing a wall with thousands of shoes or parking a yard with hundreds of vacuums. Another long-time resident, upset seemingly more at Guyton than at the flood of tourists drawn to the neighbourhood, asks, 'Who gave him permission?' Lennon frames it in a passage of doubt over the artworks' capacity for 'community enrichment'. Rather than drawing out the real social fear lying behind the neighbour's question, it is left to stand in judgment on art's insufficient productivity.

Notwithstanding, such narratives of localised dispute are Lennon's strength. The chapter on Detroit, which is also about Baton Rouge, Miami, Philadelphia and São Paulo, includes a story about a gentrifying mural project that transforms into – decays or advances, take your pick – a 'graffiti war'. In the chapter on the 2011 Egyptian Revolution, which also takes a detour through Beirut, Egyptian artist Ganzeer, now living in Brooklyn, describes following the progress of a protest march in Cairo online as it wound its way toward his friend's apartment where they waited and watched until it came too close to wait any longer, drawing them down to the streets and into the nascent revolt. The chapter on New Orleans visits Skylar Fein, who grew up in the Bronx, joined the Socialist Party at twelve, travelled to the Soviet Union in his twenties, taught nonviolent resistance with the Quakers, moved to New Orleans to attend medical school but dropped out soon after the disaster to dedicate his time to making art, later writing a manifesto in defence of graffiti. For Fein, graffiti exists outside the relations of capitalism. While Lennon seems sympathetic to this position, he does not attempt to theorise how exactly that might be the case.

Lennon's method, rather, while not quite ethnographic, depends on travel and dialogue, on recording the words of participants and witnesses. Lennon travelled to Detroit, New Orleans, Lebanon, Egypt, Israel, Palestine, Germany and Sweden, interviewing dozens of graffiti writers, artists, activists, business and property developers, residents and so forth. Many of his photographs are included, along with those taken by others. Yet conflict is the focus, with graffiti acting as frame or window onto historical antagonisms. Often a picture or image will provide the entry to a place or conflict, but not in any systematic way, nor with much attempt at the kind of exhaustive interpretation that might threaten to lead the study away from politics into aesthetics. A still from the series *Homeland* is read in a manner almost indistinguishable from how a painting by Norman Rockwell is read. By pivoting on the appearance of graffiti in each, the contours of social conflict contained or concealed within can be sketched. Yet this is done primarily in terms of content, eliding the formal and historical difference between images. The interpretive comparison of two coffee table photography books on the aftermath of Katrina, one that spotlights graffiti and one that does not, falls short largely because, possibly due to copyright issues, not a single photograph from either is included in the argument. The opportunity to consider photographs as more than simple documents for the distribution of content or information, in this case graffiti, is largely missed. Again, this reflects the determination to draw clear lines between politics and aesthetics, or to attach a particular understanding to each.

One of the functions of the idea of the 'graffiti wave' is to roughly distinguish between expressions of political desire and exhibitions of 'fetishized aesthetic objects'. The distinction is further developed, and may even originate, in the division between graffiti and street art, a common and almost compulsory confrontation in the study of graffiti. Here Lennon turns decidedly partisan: 'In urban areas, graffiti makes visible the lives of those who have been rendered invisible; street art is used to bolster the value of the properties lining the streets of the city.' Graffiti is an attack on the private property which street art celebrates. The principle might be made diagnostic: if the property value declines, it's graffiti, if the value rises, it's street art. But then the lines get messy, as Lennon's narratives attest, not least because the graffiti writers throwing up 'authentic' or political work are often the same people recruited by developers to make the wall of a warehouse 'beautiful'. 'Beauty' is here a byword that assimilates the category of art and acts as trigger for suspicion of the profit motive. There is little attempt to theorise the history of graffiti's development as a practice, a history that converges with that of the changing category of art in more than just the appearance of the label 'street art'. As the aesthetic theories of Benjamin, to name one example, attest, the 'high culture' to which art belongs and the 'lower culture' of everyday life continue to undergo a profound historical change in the character of their relation, a change that affects the composition of both categories. Neglecting this shifting relation fixes the surface in place, forgetting the movement of history.

The strict division between aesthetics and politics, with favour lent to the latter, also becomes an argument for instrumentalisation. 'Resistance graffiti' is 'a tool for progressive social movements'. What matters is that it functions, that it communicates, that it directly expresses this or that political desire in the public sphere. Yet the appearance of Sad Panda, a seemingly apolitical painted figure found among the more explicit 'revolutionary desires' expressed in the wall writings of Cairo, presents a curious limit or vanishing point for signification. Lennon, for his part, does not try to fix the Panda's meaning, leaving it open but included simply because it appeared on the wall. It's in the public sphere, it must mean something. The concept of the 'public sphere' is considered in the first chapter along with walls and streets – that is, divorced from the consideration of media. Lennon sets the theory of Jürgen Habermas, who understands the public sphere as a space where consensus is built through rational discourse, against that of Chantal Mouffe, who rather sees it as a locale for competing ideologies working toward 'dissensus'. He suggests we understand graffiti as pushed and pulled between, but then immediately identifies graffiti with the antagonisms of the latter, consistent with the anti-authority, anti-state, anti-party politics that is the general tone throughout.

Conflict Graffiti's argument for place-based contextualisation of graffiti's political desires remains at odds with the book's implicit attempt to construct or describe a tentative counter-public grounded in the international practice of graffiti. Or, if not at odds, then the full relation between, say, local production and global distribution has not been developed, suggesting a need to return to public sphere debates about the historical character of political experience. One major blind spot of that approach here is that nearly everyone given page time is a man, reproducing unreflective assumptions about and gendered divisions constitutive of both the practice of graffiti and the notion of public. Lennon is aware of the problem: the chapter on Banksy in Palestine notes the competitive machismo that propels graffiti writers to 'get up' in more and more difficult, inaccessible spots. Still the blind spot persists in the heart of the book's understanding of place. Banksy's 'activist graffiti tourism' is justifiably criticised. Its echoes in the story about the Detroit graffiti war that started because an 'outsider', not a local, painted a mural, are evident. Yet an uneasy gap remains between understanding the walls of a home as a 'commonplace visual security blanket' and a border wall as 'physical and ideological barrier'. Lennon meets a Palestinian refugee whose home is no longer a refuge, whose walls have 'lost their security' and who finds 'his private space melding into one amorphous dangerous public space.' The implication here is an absolute split between public danger and private safety, yet one that cannot be entirely attributed to the condition of war. A conception of the public sphere that neglects the gendered (and racialised) violence which troubles the heart of the concept, as Nancy Fraser, Joan Landes and others have argued, tends to repeat that violence. Here it recurs in the notion of private sphere as sanctuary (and locale of purity), as an enfolding safety suggestive of the domestic realm occupied by wife or mother, both potential victims and ultimate protectors. It contains, in other words, an image of origin. There is no counter image in this book where refuge is the result of escape.

Lennon, a professor of English at the University of South Florida, claimed in his earlier book, *Boxcar Politics: The Hobo in U.S. Culture and Literature, 1869-1956*, that flight, escape, migration, was 'a distinct form of resistive politics.' Such an argument is now absent. In like manner, one of the few places where the 'merging of the political with the aesthetic' appears acceptable to him is when, in the work of Yazan Halwani, the aim of art is 'to unite Beirut'. We might ask: unite against what? The question of graffiti in times of crisis is also the question of culture, which continues to pivot on whether culture means preserving identity or risking its loss, the defence of a familiar position or the dialectical cultivation of the human.

Kyle Proehl

Mannerism's metamorphoses

Sjoerd van Tuinen, *Philosophy of Mannerism: From Aesthetics to Modal Metaphysics* (London and New York: Bloomsbury Publishing, 2022). 240pp., £85.00 hb., 978 1 35032 248 6

Mannerism has often been ignored in the field of art history. It has been seen either as that which does not correspond to classical art, in the sense of a divergence from it, or sometimes has been read in relation to the Baroque. The question that follows, and probably these are questions proper to the field of art history, is whether mannerism is a historical period or a style which can then be read in moments across history. If it is a style then the historical period corresponding to it would indicate an accumulation or circulation of these styles when they become the rules of production of art. This is much clearer with the Renaissance where the perfection of the human body and its relation to nature is represented in a specific form – the use of perspective and Alberti's rules of construction, of not only the pictorial space but also elements that would occupy this space – are specified. However, mannerism appears to be an anomaly in this attempt of art history to provide it with specific rules and hence it also resists historical periodisation. This is because it is the practice that exceeds thought and hence rules are not sufficient to formalise the work.

Sjoerd van Tuinen rightly points out that Vasari's book on the artists is called *Lives* rather than Rules. It is this way of practice of construction that he seems to be interested in because this, I think, also relates to his main attempt in the book – to not provide new ways to understand mannerism but new ways to perceive and live manneristically. Hence, it would be wrong to think of The *Philosophy of Mannerism* as a book of art history, though matters related to art history are sufficiently discussed, but rather it is a book of philosophy – that is, what we understand from Gilles Deleuze as that which concerns itself with the creation of concepts. It is through philosophy that it is possible to think of the singular as opposed to the generalities of art history. It is this thinking of singularity which allows for the discovery of a novelty within the historical moment itself, because singularities, though emerging from history, cannot be reduced to the history itself. So the task is, as van Tuinen argues, 'to combine mannerism as historical conjuncture with mannerism as a torsion of historicity that takes the form of afterwardness (*Nachträglichkeit*): a history deferred and redoubled in relation to itself.'

This step helps us to think about the relation between mannerism and modernity – in the sense of why it is important to consider mannerism in thinking of modernity and in what ways it helps us in thinking about modernity. This remains a contemporary question not just in thinking about the present but also the future. It is true that the present situation of the Anthropocene perhaps is closer to mannerist art or that period of the sixteenth and seventeenth century where the attempt to overpower Nature is at a threshold, concerned not with the will of humans to overcome nature but in realising that nature has its own will. In this way, the mannerist artists like Archimboldo show how both nature and art (in the sense of artificiality as opposed to nature) are all *becomings* – one flowing into the other, such that this clear distinction is no longer possible. Excluded from art history and modernity, mannerism also depicts the situation of modernity in an oblique way – like a 'convex mirror.' It guides modernity although denied a part in its history. However, the point is not to go for a postmodern turn which would acknowledge this exclusion through something like the 'end of history'. Contemporary artists or rather 'artisans' depict a different way of thinking this, what the author calls 'metamodern', understood as among things – where practice is within the immanent material itself:

> Instead of the modernist 'new', the avant-gardist 'tomorrow', and the postmodern 'end of history', contemporary practice inhabits an a-synchronous present that we can call metamodern, where meta is understood in its etymological sense of 'among' a heterogeneity of (material, technical, social, political, digital) practices which, in their disjunctive togetherness, express and construct the contemporary.

As mentioned earlier, the author's aims are not restricted to thinking about mannerism in the arts and to finding its contemporary ramifications but also to consider ways or *modes* of being: to perceive manneristically but also to live in a mannerist way. This concerns the question of ontology and here we move towards 'modal metaphysics' – this is where van Tuinen reads early modern philosophers like Leibniz and Bruno but also modern philosophers like Henri Bergson, William James, Alfred North Whitehead, John Dewey, Étienne Souriau and Gilbert Simondon.

The author adopts an intriguing method in dealing with this diverse range of material. The book, divided into six chapters, hinges on the separation of manner and matter. Chapter 1 deals primarily with questions of art history and also shows what philosophy can provide art history. While mannerism remains a problem for art history, through philosophy we have a concept of mannerism, and it is through this gesture that we move from mannerism as an 'aesthetic object' to an 'aesthetic fact'. The second chapter provides us with the conceptual tools required to think of such a transformation. Deleuze and Guattari's work proves to be significant in thinking of a reversal of Platonism – to think without a model. The overturning of the logic of Platonism is not to reverse the hierarchy of the Idea and the object but rather to think difference as constitutive in all repetitions, that is, to think beyond representation. Modernism posits classical art as a break designating a unified style to it and in this way also legitimises it but this history is redoubled by 'a continuous series of metamorphosis of mannerism'. Mannerism is a latent transformation or translation of this original difference which makes our past ahistorical.

In this sense, van Tuinen's attempt is also to conceptualise mannerism such that it is both adequate to its historical time but also as an Event whose reverberations can be found across history. It is here that the concept of 'secondness' is important. Being second with regard to an established situation, mannerism is also a condition of the new and comes with a power of repetition which shows a new relation between matter and manner. However it is not only this incompletion but also a thinking of different modes of existence and it is with Souriau that the author argues for the pluralism of modes of existence which is the basis of any modal metaphysics, with a totality that exceeds these various modes.

It is a different reading of Leibniz that we find in chapters 3 and 4. Leibniz, the mannerist philosopher *par excellence*, situated between classicism and modernism, becomes a personification of the concept of 'secondness'. Leibniz provides us with a new theory of individuation and this separates him from the classicist Descartes. Leibniz's monad envelops the world, that is to say we cannot conceive an individual having attributes but have to rather think of predicates or events already enveloped in this individual. It is also that these monads in the world only understand a portion of it and hence we find a separation in Leibniz between this world of events (possible) and the existence of individuals (real). For Leibniz, God already creates the best world where the monads are compossible; God does not create Adam the sinner but the world in which Adam sins. The author contends it is 'manners' which brings the possible world and real individuals together. In the next chapter van Tuinen reads the concept of the *vinculum substantiale*, which remains a problem in the Leibnizian system, as a 'singularity or speculative problem.' The *vinculum* which is both a relation and a substance makes the Leibnizian system also think of divergences and contingencies. It seems that this reading provides us with a way to think of composition in the sense of a becoming or an incorporeal transformation and also leads to a new relation between theory and praxis, which is essential for any modal philosophy. This is also possible because of Leibniz's specific use of principles, which, as Deleuze notes, are 'reflexive.' The new world which is a witness to the fall of a theological foundation cannot be guided by a Law, but now principles must be invented for any object, and hence there is a proliferation of principles. In this sense, acoustics become essential rather than a narcissistic optics – to think of the echo or vibration.

The last two chapters reimagine the notions of art and artist through a mannerist reading. Art must be thought as design, which against both the Classical and Platonist version does not separate between the idea as transcendental and matter as immanent and separated from the Idea. Rather than stabilising, the mannerist conception reveals what appears beneath this stable design. This shifts the desire of the artist to be the second God by creating from 'nothing' and an artwork becomes only a realisation of forces which brings the three modes of matter (what), idea (why) and artist (who) in a surexistential mode of substantial union (how). It is this form of art or design that can be found in works of contemporary artists who now have to be understood as the 'cosmic artisans' who combine matter and manner, art and craft like that of alchemy where the desire is not towards reproducible knowledge but rather a speculative one.

Deleuze's interest in Leibniz incorporated the Leibnizian world, that is the Baroque world, into a thinking of Leibniz. In his 1980 seminar on Leibniz, we discover this interest – what is the world of Leibniz or rather what world does he create through his concepts? The same desire can be found in Sjoerd van Tuinen's book and this guides his study of the history of philosophy and of art. Our world, as Deleuze notes, is not the Leibnizian one but rather the world of Mallarmé and Nietzsche, a world of divergences, a game of chance. It is in this recognition that a philosophy of mannerism remains contemporary: to think of composition not as a capacity of God nor a property of nature but to understand it as artists do, where it remains immanent to the material without coinciding with it, where it is possible to think of disparate elements together. Such a philosophy also demands a creation of a world, and of existing in it. Our world which is 'a superdiverse world of incessant transformations' is where modality becomes the basic building block. Modal individuation gestures towards a situation where the subject and object are not discernable, and the political implication of such a project perhaps is in consideration of the question of labour in its division. The author's reference to Marx's idea of the division of labour in a communist society and its connection to Souriau's notion of modal individuation must be taken seriously in its political force where the question of existence through various modes takes the form of 'AND' rather than 'IS.' This indicates a new thinking of labour through a new understanding of existence as 'not substantial and analytic but processual and synthetic.' This also demands that we think of a new kind of subject. Separating himself from Classicism, and aligning with Mannerism, it seems that the author stands against a Cartesian subject based on a duality. So is this new subject of mannerism an interiorised one like something Deleuze conceives in Leibniz? This perhaps remains to be thought.

Debjyoti Sarkar

Healing collectives

Camille Robcis, *Disalienation: Politics, Philosophy, and Radical Psychiatry in Postwar France* (Chicago: The University of Chicago Press, 2021) 240 pp., £38.00 pb, 978 0 22677 774 0

In Camille Robcis' *Disalienation: Politics, Philosophy, and Radical Psychiatry in Postwar France*, the history of institutional psychotherapy in France begins at the site of the hospital at Saint-Alban and is aligned with resistance to fascism during the Second World War. Saint-Alban was the first but not the only source of radical psychiatric ideas and anti-fascist politics. The historical shift away from a conservative mainstream psychiatry to psychoanalysis, guided by Jacques Lacan's early insights into psychiatry's non-biological debts to the social, yielded influential modifications of key concepts such as the subject, the unconscious and transference that would animate the institutional psychotherapeutic project. The book provides a sound account of the transformative intent of institutional psychotherapy, the limits of its influence, and its enduring lessons. Although *Disalienation* speaks to a number of key institutions, events and philosophies, it is organised around a parade of male thinkers: François Toquelles, Frantz Fanon, Félix Guattari and Jean Oury, and Michel Foucault. Feminist literary critic and historian Joana Masó has made us aware that the story of institutional psychotherapy and its children can be told, alternatively, from the perspectives of the women who played key roles at St. Alban such as psychiatrists Agnès Masson and Germaine Balvet, as well as Frantz Fanon's colleague Alice Cherki, not to forget the later contributions of Liane Mozère and Anne Querrien in the research groups animated by Félix Guattari.

As Robcis shows, the intent to permanently reinvent the psychiatric institution was not aligned with the goals of the anti-psychiatry movement but, rather, remained more akin to an anti-anti-psychiatry. The double 'anti-' neither entails rejection of psychiatric treatment nor mental illness, but is a positive attempt to create the kind of caring institution that did not exacerbate the problems faced by patients. Félix Guattari, whose work is sometimes mistakenly aligned with anti-psychiatry, tells us in his critiques of the Oedipalism of some of the British strains of the movement, to be on the lookout for countercultural mythologising and reformist tendencies masquerading as fundamental change within anti-psychiatry.

The book's guiding concept of disalienation entails a refusal to separate the psyche from the social in psychosis; they must be always thought together, always doubled, and reparable through creative 'organigrams' such as the 'grid' of work rotations at Clinique de La Borde, perhaps the finest example, but one that changed shape over time. The effort to address psychic and social alienation by means of the practice of institutional psychotherapy, from Saint-Alban through the clinics at Saumery and to La Borde, begins with the effort to address the illness (deadening) of the institution itself, curing it of a tendency to seek 'concentrationist' forms. Alienation in the historical French psychiatric context arose from the application of fascist directives to caring facilities in occupied France that resulted in tens of thousands of deaths. Saint-Alban existed outside the occupied zone of France and enjoyed a relative degree of freedom, and it remained a model of vigilance for practitioners and theorists against ingrained fascist tendencies that survived the war. Robcis is interested in what the history and theory of institutional psychotherapy can contribute to a 'different political imaginary' applicable to contemporary predicaments. This means regaining the direct connection between the unconscious and politics, as well as reformulating concepts such as transference, so that they become mobile, transversal, 'burst', 'constellated', 'multi-referential' and 'dissociated'.

Over the first two chapters, the formative contributions of Tosquelles and Fanon are discussed in depth. For readers unfamiliar with the red Catalonian psychiatrist Tosquelles, his story is nothing less than miraculous. Tosquelles was rescued from a carceral French refugee camp after fleeing Franco's Spain, where he had set up a psychiatric service, by an enterprising doctor, director of Saint-Alban, Paul Balvet. Tosquelles was an early proponent of Lacan's 'structural understanding' of subjectivity, and the requirement of dealing with madness in its 'phenomenal totality', and a listed enemy of the occupying Vichy government, but the hospital's location deep in the Lozère in the free zone allowed it to temporarily house resistance fighters, artists and intellectuals on the level of Georges Canguilhem. This is the site at which the systematic disalienation of the institution would begin in earnest, through an analysis of the space, architecture, grounds, administration, clothing, regulations of control and logistics. Walls were demolished; uniforms were abandoned; a patient's club established, named after Balvet, a newsletter printed, ergotherapy established in order to 'revive the symbolic dimension of life'. As Robcis concludes: 'constantly evolving, adapting, and always revisable, institutional psychotherapy was meant as a permanent revolution of politics, society, and psychic life'. We are talking about 'revolution' here with a small 'r', a molecular level perfusion.

Fanon's decolonial adaptation of institutional psychotherapy forms part of the book's second chapter, which is devoted to his career as a psychiatrist inverting typical accounts that fail to grasp the radical character of his clinical practice, and the departure that his theory of the subject marked from traditional psychiatry, especially the role played by the ideas of Lacan in the development of the psychosocial thesis concerning 'North Africa Syndrome'. While the two pages devoted to Fanon's 'encounter' with institutional psychotherapy in Saint-Alban are limited, in part due to the fact that Fanon did not write about this period, Fanon brought the lessons of Saint-Alban with him to Blida hospital in Algeria where he first enjoyed success developing programming and practices, but only with a ward of Western European women, whereas a ward of Muslim men did not respond to the model of the 'healing collective'. Fanon grasped the 'violence' of his imposition of an imported sociotherapy and eventually adapted to the needs of traditional Algerian society. After he was expelled from Algeria in 1957, Fanon landed in La Manouba Hospital in Tunisia, where he continued to implement ideas from institutional psychotherapy. Robcis's conclusion is that 'Fanon took institutional psychotherapy as it was conceived in Saint-Alban one step further' by 'deterritorialising' it for the North African context. Whether this makes Fanon's transformations 'the most perfected example of institutional psychotherapy' is certainly a credible claim, but one that must be measured against the example of La Borde.

The monumental figures of Tosquelles and Fanon, and their constellations, linked through Saint-Alban, loom large in *Disalienation*, even if Fanon is exceptional in the history of institutional psychotherapy, which was, Robcis states, undertaken by 'mostly male and mostly white' doctors. Robcis should have addressed Tosquelles' own candid reflections about Fanon's arrival at Saint-Alban in the spring of 1952 as they do not neglect the question of race. Indeed, Tosquelles foils any effort to cleanly re-embed Fanon into the history of institutional psychotherapy in stating that 'nobody was yet talking about institutional psychotherapy' at that time. Certainly, Fanon's escape from the 'psychiatric desert' of his purely biological medical training in Lyon, and his experiences of racial profiling and harassment there by the police, again a concern of Tosquelles, makes Saint-Alban seem even more like a revelation. Fanon was quite active at Saint-Alban, especially in the patients' club, and he wrote for the newsletter (a remarkable example is reproduced, testimony to Robcis' deep research), fully exploring the 'hypothesis' posed by the hospital as a 'healing collective'. This sets up nicely the explication of Fanon's display of ingenuity in adapting institutional psychotherapy to a new sociocultural context in a difficult clinical situation in the Blida hospital that was nothing less than remarkable. Robcis writes, 'unlike the "assimilated psychiatry" that Fanon arrived with, this was a truly disalienated and disalienating psychotherapy'.

The unity of theory and practice in the *praxical* territory of La Borde is, for Robcis, a question of 'cosmology', a strange choice of term for chapter three about the clinic's disorganisational innovations such as 'the grid', the patients' club, the many precarious committees, publications, strange nomenclatures and creative events, all of which helped to produce new subjectivities. What is valuable in this chapter is Robcis's analysis of the extent to which Jean Oury tried to balance some of the methods of traditional psychiatry with psychoanalytic understandings of psychosis, using concepts borrowed from Lacan but adapted to the setting, such as a collective transference adequate to a 'shattered Symbolic', rather than being defined only as a product of the analyst-analysand dyad. Thus, Robcis states: 'The great invention of institutional psychotherapy was the possibility of implementing and working with this dissociated transference'. Unlike certain strains of anti-psychiatry, the clinicians at La Borde did not eschew shock therapies and anti-psychotic drugs.

Robcis explains that the publication of Deleuze and Guattari's *Anti-Oedipus* in 1972 created a number of schisms. It seems both a 'culmination' of Guattari's experience with institutional psychotherapy and his long-time working relationship with Oury, which becomes institutional analysis and then schizoanalysis; the latter types of analysis are either continuations of the former psychotherapy or breaks from it; as well as a rejection of Lacan's structuralism (wrapped in a rejection of a 'structural Oedipus' and any generalised oedipalisation of desire, as lack). Yet, these are announced without renouncing either Lacan or psychoanalysis altogether.

Certainly, Guattari's position seemed to push Oury away because of the manner in which it foregrounded desire, especially in the context of the treatment of psychotics (arguably elevating a *trans* Daniel Schreber to anti-oedipus himself). The ways it changed Guattari's approach to psychotherapy, especially in his private practice, is still a matter of debate. Certainly, it sharpened his understanding of how institutions, in the guise of the many groups and publications he was involved with before and after this period, can produce new, creative and less-alienated subjectivations, and he enjoyed a good deal of success in these adventures. Why Robcis resorts to tired misunderstandings here – 'schizoanalysis could not possibly mean that we should all strive to become psychotics' – is unclear, but perhaps necessary in a theoretical climate that tends to favour hyperbole and zealotry while ignoring clinical grounding, but her main point is more or less well taken: she does not see *Anti-Oedipus* as constituting a profound 'break with institutional psychotherapy in favor of anti-psychiatry', although this is a bit of a straw man argument. The harder question is the extent to which Guattari changed his therapeutic approaches once he had rejected so much of psychoanalysis and distanced himself from Oury and the 'Lacano-Labordian complex', while remaining critical of much of anti-psychiatry as reformist and mystifying. Still, Robcis's purpose is to rejoin Guattari and Fanon in the unity of a shared vision: not to depart from the fold, but to carry forward with ingenuity, adaptability and in the spirit of an unrelenting omnidirectional critique.

Turning to Foucault in chapter four, Robcis situates his early work in the context of a series of encounters with psychiatry and psychology in quite different settings, including his translation of Ludwig Binswanger and visit to the Münsterlingen asylum, and translation into French of Viktor Von Weizsäcker's book *Le cycle de la Structure* (1958), but with no mention of why this might be significant; to which may be added, the facilitating role played by Georges Daumézon (from Saint-Alban and a personal supporter), the publication of *Maladie mentale et personnalité* [1954], and his refusal to have it translated, his interest in psychosis, the connection made between criminology and psychiatry while at the Fresnes prison. There are openings to the vast terrain of phenomenological psychiatry that remain to be developed. The connection made between Foucault's *Maladie mentale* and *History of Madness* is resonant, and Robcis delicately threads together conceptual interests and figures that bring Foucault quite close to the concerns of institutional psychotherapy. It is with the publication and reception of *History of Madness* during and after 1968 – his preferred 'first' book – that the threads are unravelled, but in a controlled way. What Robcis discusses is the degree to which the book's reception as a 'manual for political activism, a "toolkit" for anti-authoritarianism', shifted its value onto the social movement of anti-psychiatry despite Foucault's statements that the writing of his project, and its timeframe, predated the existence of this movement. Praised by anti-psychiatrists R.D. Laing and David Cooper for an English readership, in translation the book became a 'guideline for antipsychiatry', which circulated back onto and influenced French debates about psychiatry during this period.

However, the key point that Robcis makes with great clarity is that anti-psychiatry and institutional psychotherapy were quite different; the latter held onto psychiatric treatments that were anathema to the movement, even if, as Robert Castel put it, it did so in a 'sublimated' way. Indeed, Foucault personally found himself involved in certain anti-psychiatric events, alongside his prison activism. And it was out of these encounters that his theory of power took shape, as well as a shift from institutions to disciplines. Ultimately, he endeavoured to map the 'many antipsychiatries' that had emerged, bringing his affinity with the political work of Guattari (and Franco Basaglia) of 'unmasking power relations' back into focus. It would have been useful here to clarify that Guattari's psychiatry engagements included the Réseau-Alternative à la psychiatrie, from the mid-late 70s, associated with Mony Elkaïm, an internationalist and social movements-focused initiative about creating other 'places' for living as a bulwark against the ravages of both hospitalisation and of mass deinstitutionalisation (the catastrophic legacy of anti-psychiatry's integration into mainstream hospital psychiatry).

Robcis identifies the struggle against fascism, both in the historical sense and in the sense of the fascism of the mind that Deleuze and Guattari's *Anti-Oedipus* sought to root out, but she declines to investigate the theory of microfascism, linked by Guattari through micropolitics to Foucault's microphysics of power after the latter's death, and this is one of the compromises in *Disalienation*. Instead, it is to Foucault's infamous introduction to *Anti-Oedipus* and thus to the non-fascist life that Robcis turns, with the idea of an everyday practice of living that releases personal and collective freedoms within the terms of institutional psychotherapy. However, this emphasis seeks the overlay of 'libidinal and political economy' that Guattari's antioedipalism exposed, but does not attempt to retrieve the aesthetic, as in the ethico-aesthetic paradigm, or the ecological praxes that bear a significant aesthetic dimension that helps Guattari develop a taste for the deepest ethical questions about future developments in the anthroposcene that would later take shape in his thought. Indeed, the recourse to Foucault's introduction, to the later American-English edition no less, is not justified. Why not refer to Deleuze's *Anti-Oedipus* lectures of 1971-72 in order to excavate fascism as a residual capitalist code and look at the advances from there in the theory of microfascism? Why can't we appreciate that capitalism searches for new models of molecularised fascism inside itself, in a fertile environment conducive to infestation and circulation? This is important because by the end of the book, when today's microfascist politics are finally broached, the bridge between historical and contemporary forms is simply given without explanation.

Disalienation jumps, then, to an epilogue without a conclusion proper. This is supposed to bring historical events into contemporary focus in the struggles against neoliberalism in the second decade of the twenty-first century, the political theory of 'instituent praxis' and the production of the 'collective subject', still a very relevant and very Guattarian project. The most recent return of fascism is situated in relation to the Trump presidency (it would be useful to note that Trump had been on Guattari's radar since the 80s). There are two ways to read her book, the author tells us. One, is to align the great figures of yesterday around the theory and practice of radical psychiatry in France. The other, is to read it as a work of 'critical history'. The question becomes how to map the influence of institutional psychotherapy for our world. The relevance of both fascism and psychosis for interpreting events unfolding today is unassailable. A molecular perspective on fascism would assist in the analysis of how historical phenomena never stop adapting and continue to proliferate in welcoming environments, setting up resonances among the many supercharged yet empty carriers of hate, disinformation, and recruitment of extremists, circulating virulently, forming a black hole into which even the most resilient subjectivities may be drawn.

Gary Genosko

Mario Tronti, 1931-2023
At war with the world
Matteo Mandarini

I met Mario Tronti for the last time in his office in the Senate, in the room adjoining the one where Galileo Galilei was tried for heresy over four-hundred years prior.[1] Thankfully, Tronti had nothing of the Inquisitor about him. If there was something clerical about him, it was that of a quiet but charismatic friar – a Dominican to Toni Negri's Franciscan one might quip. Having said that, he was not at all dour or intimidating. There was often a sense of amused knowingness, which I sense hid a certain shyness, certainly a reserve. He seemed entirely suited to the little monkish study, adorned with three lone Dürer prints, where he wrote in the Umbrian town of Ferentillo. That was where his family originated, but he was born and grew up in the bustling working-class neighbourhood of Ostiense in Rome. He kept a flat a few doors down from where he was born where he spent his time when he had meetings or wanted to use the library of the Senate. It was said that when he took the bus to the Senate wearing the suit and tie without which he could not gain admittance to his office, his embarrassment at sitting in formal bourgeois attire among the *popolo* of which he felt so much a part meant that he covered himself in a heavy overcoat in all weathers. It was as if he feared losing, even for the duration of a bus trip, that contact with the side to which he had asserted partisanship from the start.

That last meeting took place in late May 2022, after he sent me a touching email in memory of my father, who had died in March. Tronti and my father had known one another when both were members of the Central Committee of the *Partito Comunista Italiano* (PCI) in the 1980s. This was the declining phase of the party's fortunes, shortly before its public self-immolation at the start of the following decade, on 3 February 1991; only eleven months before the much more consequential dissolution of the Soviet Union on 26 December of that same year. The latter date marked, for Tronti, what he would soon call the twilight of politics, in his book of that name (*Il tramonto della politica*, 1998).[2] Despite Tronti's reservations regarding Eric Hobsbawm's talk of a 'short Twentieth century', for Tronti, the century of politics could be thought of as bookended by two events: 1917, when the great masses first came onto the scene of history, becoming its active participants, and 1991, when the dream of the alternative, the necessary utopian moment of 'great politics' – despite its corrupted form, which Tronti acknowledged – ceased to be. 1991 *not* 1989 was the crucial year. As he wrote in *The Twilight of Politics*: '1989 is not, will not be, an epochal historical date, despite the spectacle put in place by the pied pipers of the counter-revolution. Nothing begins in 1989, because nothing ended there. It took three years, from 1989 to 1991, to bureaucratically certify the death that had occurred many years before'.

From 1991 to his death, Tronti – the erstwhile 'father of *Operaismo*' – assumed what he felt was his responsibility: to wrest the memory of twentieth-century communism and communists from the 'miserable age of Restoration', or, as Walter Benjamin put it in Thesis VI of 'On the Concept of History', 'from the conformism that is working to overpower it ... convinced that *even the dead* will not be safe from the enemy if he is victorious'.[3] One must be careful not to read into Tronti's account a wistful paean to the world of yesteryear à la Stefan Zweig. His is rather an angry, Nietzschean denunciation of the self-satisfied smug onanism of the 'most contemptible person', the Last Man who is incapable of even generating the semblance of an ideal, of a desire that cannot be found on the shelves of a shopping mall.

I cannot hope to provide a full account of Tronti's development here. Instead, I will highlight certain moments without which one loses the breadth of this 'politician leant to the world of philosophy', remaining tethered instead to the brief and best-known phase of his political thought to which I shall turn first. *Operaismo* is the tradition with which Tronti continues to be associated, even when he declared that, as far as he was concerned, *operaismo* began circa 1960 with the journal *Quaderni Rossi* (under the leadership of Raniero Panzieri), and came to an end in 1967 with the final issue of the journal *classe operaia* (founded in 1964 by Romano Alquati, Rita di Leo, Negri and Tronti, amongst others, after a break with Panzieri).[4] While he never reneged on *operaismo*, his periodisation served to situate this body of thought and practice at the close of the period of what he would call 'great politics' (circa 1917 to 1968, after which, he suggests, politics continued until 1991 in a minor register). In short, *operaismo* took flight at dusk, when its moment had passed, like all great philosophies. That *operaismo* aimed to be so immediately tied to practice, to contemporary action, is what so tightly circumscribed its historical limits (practical and theoretical) to a time that was fast running out. This was, he argued, in part due the shifts subsequent to 1968: away from the immediate process of production and from the industrial worker as collective subject of the movement, moving from the workers' movement to many movements, from anti-capitalism to anti-authoritarianism, from revolution to rights – and to identity politics, one might add.

Perhaps the core tenet of *operaismo* was contained in the famous editorial, 'Lenin in England', from January 1964: 'at the level of socially developed capital, capitalist development is subordinate to working-class struggles; not only does it come after them, but it must make the political mechanism of capitalist development correspond to them'. This claim, Tronti later realised, was true not of capitalism *per se*, but only of a particular historical moment of the workers' movement, and so only a specific period of capitalist development, the one that ceases with the end of the Fordist-Keynesian compromise. 'The working class of the great industrial concentrations bore class conflict to the highest levels of conflict. Not the disappearance of industry, but the disappearance of large-scale industry was the critical discriminatory passage. The blunt fact was the mass worker. There, for the first time, dependency upon work freed itself from social subalternity. There, the potentially political working class was the emancipatory class'.[5] The 'mass worker' was not, for him, a sociological category, it was a political or organisational one – for the class only exists *as a class*, i.e., as something more than variable capital, when it is organised.

To put the issue of organisation in its most concise form, it concerned the relation of the working class to the party (as its form of organisation), on the one side; and, on the other, which is to say for capital, it concerned the relation of the capitalist class to its state (as its form of organisation). If the task of capital and its state is to reduce the worker to a fragment of capital (i.e., to variable capital, turning labour-power into a commodity via the wage system and then subordinating it through the system of machinery and managerial organisation), it is the task of the worker to refuse such a reduction (the 'refusal of work'), to reject labour's organisation by capital and to organise the working class as a class against capital and its state. Hence the famous phrase describing the Janus-faced character of the working class, in the central essay of *Operai e capitale*, as 'within and against capital': *within*, in that capital tries to increasingly reduce the worker to being a fraction *of* capital; *against*, the workers as a class, as an organised subject, forms itself in opposition *to* capital.

Whereas the individual capitalist confronts the individual worker on the labour market in buying the commodity labour-power, he can only avail himself of that commodity's use-value (to produce *surplus* value) by organising the worker in the process of production. In so doing, Tronti – in his rereading of Marx – shows how the worker never exists as an individual (other than on the market), but since the worker's labour-power is only bought in order to be organised in the process of production as cooperative, collective labour, workers are necessarily organised as a class. So, the working class does not precede capitalism, it precedes the capitalist *class*. It is only once the working class organises itself politically, which is to say *as a class* in the face of exploitation in the labour process, that the capitalist class too can take shape, without which capitalism could not survive. For individual capitalist competition can lead the system to ruination and only its political organisation as a class – as a collective capitalist or bourgeoisie – can constrain individual capitalists to save capitalism from itself.[6] For this reason, the 'working class *is* the secret of capitalism', as Tronti writes in an editorial from 1962 from *Quaderni Rossi* included in *Operai e capitale*.

This critical issue, the so-called 'problem of organisation', which is to say, 'the problem of the party' that existed in one form or another from the foundation of the journal *classe operaia*, would eventually bring *operaismo* to an end (or at least did for Tronti).[7] At this point, members of the disbanded editorial boards took a variety of directions. Many remained in the extra-parliamentary groupings and would eventually found others, such as *Potere operaio* and then *Autonomia operaia organizzata*. Many of these figures would later be imprisoned or flee into exile after the crackdown, often on trumped-up charges, following the killing of Italian Prime Minister, Aldo Moro, by the Red Brigades in 1978. Tronti, and a few others (notably the philosopher Massimo Cacciari and the literary and cultural critic Alberto Asor Rosa), would gradually make their way into (or back into) the PCI.

In 1979, Tronti, writing in the daily *Il Messaggero*, defended his erstwhile collaborator during the years of *Operaismo*, Antonio Negri, from the series of increasingly hysterical accusations that had led to his imprisonment. At the same time, Tronti demarcated the thinking of *operaismo* from that of *Autonomia operaia*, of which Negri was a leading light.[8] For Tronti, the core distinction turned upon the question of 'worker centrality': always face-to-face with the bosses, one standpoint against another, class against class in a binary logic of friend/enemy. Tronti accuses Negri and others of leaving by the wayside this core tenet of *operaismo*. The 'Autonomists' advanced the notion of a proliferation of new subjective forces, floating free from the immediate process of production, postulating not class confronting class directly at the core of industrial capital, but instead the spontaneity of proliferating antagonisms in conditions of marginality, generalised unemployment and fragmentation set against a state machine reduced to its apparatus of repression.

While Tronti was happy to accept that such a proliferation of social subjects was real, he refused *Autonomia*'s decision to turn these figures (the 'social worker' in the 1970s-'80s would be multiplied in later decades into 'immaterial workers', 'cognitive workers', the 'precariat', the 'multitude' …) into moments of *political* centrality, no longer linked – and often opposed – both to the industrial working class and certainly to the institutions of the workers' movement.[9] For Tronti, without worker centrality and the accompanying 'point of view' or 'partisan synthesis' that marked it, one had left *operaismo* behind.[10] This was a point at once political and epistemological, and without it *operaismo* ceased to operate theoretically or practically. For within capitalism, as declared in *Workers and Capital*, 'the whole can only be comprehended by the part'. Knowledge is tied to struggle. By contrast, the multiplication of subjects by the Autonomists followed a sociological, empirical definition of 'class'. By foregrounding their marginality, such subjects no longer thought of themselves as *within* but merely *against*, and capital collapses into the Moloch-like State machinery's repressive apparatus, thus encouraging a militaristic conception of struggle and losing any partisan epistemological advantage over its enemy. This

– Tronti implied – was a form of tailism in the guise of voluntarism, a 'political romanticism'[11] that abandoned the cognitive tools necessary for a revolutionary *politics*.

It is perhaps here that we begin to see the properly philosophical element that defines Tronti's thought: bringing together conflict and transcendence, marking the specificity of his anti- (mainstream, or Stalinist) Hegelianism. For him, conflict is not a moment of development, a marker of immanence's progressive mobility and flexibility, but produces dichotomies, contradictions, oppositions. Politics is a blade that slices and pierces through being, rupturing History's continuity, replacing unity with opposition, multiplicity with dichotomy, producing a caesura within the immanence of the technical-economic order and establishing contradictions, subjective standpoints at war.[12]

I recall a seminar in 2004 at the Fondazione Basso in Rome, where Giorgio Agamben, Roberto Esposito, Negri and Tronti were invited to speak on the issue of biopolitics. Tronti was the last to speak, and started by saying that he did not know why he had been invited, for the immanence embedded in the concept of biopolitics jarred fundamentally with his own thinking. In conclusion, Tronti made two fists that he ground against one another, slowly but forcefully turning knuckles against knuckles: 'For me it is all about class against class, at war'. It is important to note that this was no mere Marxist class reductionism, for without the 'weapon of organisation', class does not exist. If there is a reductionism in said remark, it is an inflationary one – of an almost metaphysical order. For what is sometimes ignored in Tronti's radical rereading of Marx – especially if contrasted to that which was dominant within the Italian 'national-popular' and historicist discourse of the PCI – is its embedding in a Nietzschean and Weberian re-reading of both Marx and Lenin. Against the 'Hegelian' tryptic (thesis-antithesis-synthesis), which ended in a pacific resolution of conflict in the whole, he proposed a 'dialectic' of the two in irresolvable conflict.[13]

Here, politics implicates a subject that rends the fabric of reality, a radical Nietzschean perspectivism, a Weberian world of infinite, chaotic multiplicity where 'points of view' cleave chaos and disassemble the mechanisms of immanence, of smooth exchange; and where order stems from the techno-economic unfolding of History or through Leninist decisionism. This is the same decisionism that would fascinate Carl Schmitt (who would become another reference point for Tronti from the 1970s), one that forms the subjects, the 'intensity' of whose conflict marks out the political as that which ruptures the dialectical progression of History in what the young Gramsci famously called a 'revolution against *Capital*'.

As Schmitt observed in *Political Theology II*: 'A conflict is always a struggle between organisations and institutions in the sense of concrete orders' constructed from conflicting subjects. 'Substances [or, collective subjects] must first of all have found their *form*'; Schmitt continues, 'they must have been brought into a *formation* before they can actually encounter each other as contesting subjects in a conflict, that is, as *parties belligérantes*'. So, the question of subjective organisation is a condition of conflict, but conflict necessarily accompanies the formation of contending subjects. This account of the irreducibility of conflict would accompany Tronti through to the end but would instantiate itself differently, assuming almost the status of a political ontology.

I think it is worth adding that Tronti's relationship to Hegel has yet to be adequately reflected on, with many too easily seeing Hegel as the 'enemy' or at least the foil against which Tronti's Nietzscheanism erected itself. It is in fact rare to find explicit critiques of Hegel in Tronti. It is far more typical for him to affirm specific aspects of Hegel's thinking. In a May 2017 interview with Podemos founder and former Spanish deputy PM Pablo Iglesias on his TV series, *Otra Vuelta de Tuerka*, Tronti is asked a series of concluding questions, one of which is who he considers to be a *maestro* (teacher, guide, mentor). After a brief series of remarks, in which he notes his distaste for thinking in terms of master and pupil, he says: 'From the theoretical point of view: the Hegel-Marx relation; together .... I always think of them together. For without Hegel there would have been no Marx. And Hegel would not have been what he has been for me, which is to say a lot, without Marx's critique.'[14]

The choice Tronti made *for* the Party – for the PCI, which he had never left but just stepped back from – in 1966-7, was driven by an acknowledgment of the expansion of the growing tide of workers' struggles, within but mainly outside the leadership of the institutions of the workers' movement. It was the very size of such a tide that meant it was beyond the coordinating capacities of what he called the proliferating 'groupuscules' through which the Italian 'New Left' had attempted to organise the tide. What was needed, he now declared, was organisational capacity on a vaster scale: from varieties of workplace struggle to the trade unions to a party seeking to govern the state and envisaging direct and indirect involvement in economic planning. This exigency led to a proposal that soon turned out to be no less tenuous or evanescent than that of those who argued for a spontaneous uprising of a multiplicity of revolutionary subjects (*Potere operaio*, *Autonomia operaia*, Negri, and so forth): the call for the creation of a cadre of militants in the factory who could be transferred into the Party, to change it from within.

In 1965 a debate had begun in *classe operaia* and beyond, on the need for the 'party [to be] in the factory',[15] which is to say, on the need to re-establish a link between the PCI and the working class, a link broken – it was argued – by the PCI's historicism grounded in a national-popular strategy of broad-based class alliance. Tronti now argued that the Party could only enter the factory if the factory had already entered the Party. Hence the call for the cadre to be built within the factory and then to find a way into the Party. Such an operation would then permit the 'autonomy of politics', which is to say, a two-pronged strategy where the Party would be free to make tactical decisions independent but in service of expanding struggles within the factory. At the same time, factory struggles could advance demands of their own without having to consider the tactical manoeuvring of the Party in its struggle to take command of the state, which would include a politics of class alliances not to be envisioned in the factory struggles themselves.[16]

The task of the PCI in this context, Tronti would argue, was to wedge itself between capital, the bourgeoisie and its state and so become the political fulcrum from which to manage the economic, social and political crisis within which 1970s Italy was caught. It was in these years that Tronti would begin extensive study of the entire history of the bourgeois state in order to learn how it might be turned into a tool against its class, resulting in a definition of the Christian Democratic party (DC) as the 'party of pure mediation'. In the end, the DC found ways to manage consent as a means to attenuate, absorb and reroute social conflict by reducing them to individual interests. In later years, Tronti would argue that it 'was not capitalism that defeated the workers' movement. The workers' movement was defeated by democracy'. 'This democracy', he declared in *The Twilight of Politics*, 'is the self-government of the last men. The extinguishing of politics', where atomisation and reduction of the demand for power to the demand for interests and rights undermines the political power of the large masses that alone can effect political change.[17]

The failure of this call for the 'autonomy of politics' is multifaceted. Tronti often blamed the fact that neither side, the PCI nor the extra-parliamentary left understood the call. Tronti also accused the PCI of always, in the words of Jamila Mascat, 'lagging systematically behind the demands posed at the social level (the factory struggles but also that of the youth movements), and thus always develops inadequate responses'.[18] But arguably there were objective as well as subjective conditions that were insufficiently grasped, not least of which was that the PCI's scope of manoeuvre was even more limited than the 'limited democracy' that characterised Italy as a whole.[19] A first draft of this systemic constraint was provided by the division of spheres of influence at Yalta, but by the 1960s-'70s this was not only a geopolitical question, but increasingly one of (un-)governability.[20]

As I mentioned at the beginning, when asked to write this obituary, now over a year after his death and as I try to work through the loss, my mind returned to the generous email Tronti sent me on the occasion of my father's death. One particular line returned to me, that I quote, not without some hesitation: '*Un esempio per tutti il compagno Francesco Mandarini, da operaio a militante a dirigente a governante. Gloria a lui!*' [Comrade Francesco Mandarini was an example to all, from [industrial] worker to militant to leader to governor. Glory be to him!]. What struck me, pride aside, was the path that Tronti traced here. In this short phrase, he provides the skeleton trajectory of the political subject that I have tried to outline: that is, of the political subject at the high point of modern politics, that of the mass worker that Tronti theorised as the bearer of a politics, without which politics would have been reduced to the mere administration of things as disposed by the techno-economic forces of History. From the struggle in the factory, in the immediate process of production, to the militant organisation of that struggle. Then political leadership through careful, tactical manoeuvring within the Party necessary to guard against the isolation of struggle behind the factory gates. And, finally, to the control of the tools of the state institutions. 'Glory', finally, operates as a concept marking the necessary moment of transcendence, the concrete utopian moment that refuses the reduction of change to innovation, refuses the *Gattopardismo* where '*tutto devo cambiare perché tutto resti come prima*' ['everything must change so that everything can remain the same'],[21] where one forgets that every innovation is a failed revolution, and where political realism would otherwise sink into opportunism. Glory, transcendence, is to be understood as an utterly material moment of politics, albeit sacralised, without which politics ceases, change is nothing but marketing, and the subject is hollow.

As Tronti writes at the end of his last, as yet unpublished final essay, taking for its title a famous phrase of Hegel's on the nature of Philosophy, '[one's] own time comprehended in thoughts':

> Approaching the way out of the desert, putting an end to exile, and taking up the path to the promised land is the task taken up by the modern proletariat, inheritors of all the insubordinations of the subaltern classes. A task that is to be rewritten in the most unfavourable conditions we have ever faced.... There is a theoretical miracle that only a sacred secularisation can see and so put into practice. It is anything but abstract, it is very concrete, a revolutionary politics that puts in play a "creative tension" between the City and the Temple, between the Temporal [*il Secolo*] and the Sacred. It is not difficult to translate these metaphors into slogans for the organisation of struggle. It has already been done after all. Written, engraved forever in the memory of the workers' movement are the past insurgencies that, albeit defeated, sought to storm heaven. From this memory of the past one must set out anew, to seek again to win a new tomorrow [*avvenire*].[22]

Hence, for Tronti, the era of modern politics ends with the defeat of the workers' movement.[23] But this never implies resignation and the accompanying wistfulness for bygone years, though I won't pretend that the shadow of nostalgia is entirely absent, whatever Tronti's protestations. What predominates, however, is a disenchanted, ruthless criticism of all that exists grounded in a subjective standpoint of conflict from within the domination of the forces of History. 'I must understand' was the later Tronti's categorical imperative. Not only must one understand that a great history can come to an end, that of the workers' movement, that of modern politics, and 'how it can end wretchedly' (*Dello spirito libero* (2015)). But more than this. The epistemological standpoint of conflict had to be reawakened and reasserted. At the heart of *Operai e capitale* was the working class as the subject within and against capital, a fragment of capital in conflict with it. Salvaging conflict is an epistemological and practical moment, a categorical imperative cutting through *bien pensant* 'common sense' by means of the patient, guarded, suspicious labour of extrication of the subject *as* conflict, resistant to pacification in the untroubled complacency of the Last Man.

Matteo Mandarini is Senior Lecturer in Organisation and Politics at Queen Mary, University of London and is the translator of Mario Tronti's The Twilight of Politics *(Seagull Books, 2004).*

Notes

1. The author would like to express his thanks to Sarah Kelleher, Elena Baglioni, Tariq Goddard, Demet Dinler and Alberto Toscano for commenting on earlier drafts of this obituary. Many thanks also to Brenna Bhandar for first proposing the idea.
2. The title of this obituary is drawn from the conclusion of his keynote lecture, 'Weber and Workers', delivered at the University of Kingston in autumn of 2019. The complete phrase is: 'At peace with myself, at war with the world.' The English translation, *The Twilight of Politics*, is published by Seagull Books (2004).
3. As he was to write almost two decades later: 'the past, once interpreted, subverts the present more than any imaginable future' (*Dello spirito libero*, 2015).
4. The so-called 'bible of *Operaismo*', *Operai e capitale* (1966, expanded 1971 and again in 2008), contains many of Tronti's principal editorials from the two journals, as well as essays written specifically for each edition. It was finally translated into English as *Workers and Capital* in 2018. I have critically discussed the shortcomings of that translation in a review published in *International Review of Social History* 65:3 (2020): 547–550.
5. Interview with Andrea Cerutti and Giulia Dettori, in *La rivoluzione in esilio. Scritti su Mario Tronti* (2021).
6. This is very evident in Keynesianism, but we have seen how capitalists can operate as a class in times of crisis in the various bailouts we have witnessed over recent decades. This was already clear from Marx's chapter on 'The Working Day' in volume 1 of *Capital*. There, Marx notes how state regulation emerges precisely as a means to curtail (or at least to alleviate) the hyper-exploitation of the workers in individual factories and has the further con-

sequence of forcing capitalists to innovate in the system of machinery since they can no longer exploit labour by extending the working day. In that sense, every innovation is a failed revolution.

7. Tronti later claimed that, for him, the party was always (if tacitly) the PCI. Tacitly, because many members of *Quaderni Rossi* and of *classe operaia* came from the *Partito Socialista Italiano* (most notably, Negri and Panzieri), and elsewhere. It was when Tronti increasingly felt that the turn towards the PCI was increasingly politically urgent, and resisted by most of his fellow editors, that Tronti decided to close *classe operaia* in the face of widespread opposition.

8. Tronti's demarcation of *Operaismo* proper from *Autonomia* shows the common collapsing of *Operaismo* into 'Autonomism', common in many Anglophone accounts, is both a theoretical and political choice that stands in profound contrast to Tronti's own understanding of *Operaismo*. For Tronti this is a *post-Workerism* whose relation to *Operaismo* might be said to parallel post-Marxism's relation to the Marxist tradition – not an internal critique, but a criticism that leads out of Marxism. For Tronti, *Operaismo* was always a strand of the workers' movement itself and of its dominant theoretical standpoint, Marxism.

9. In my last meeting with him in May 2022, he said: 'I think that those from *Autonomia* were more anti-communist than anti-capitalist'. By which he meant, anti-PCI and the institutions of the workers' movement more broadly.

10. This partisan standpoint would remain with him to the very end, as is attested to even in what must be his final interview with *L'Unità*, the daily founded by Gramsci, from May 2023. The title of the article was: 'Minimal Programme: To Recover Partisan Memory' ('Programma minimo: recuperare la memoria di parte').

11. The accusation of 'political romanticism' of those who understood capital in terms of the State Moloch savaging human rights, is one that Tronti levelled in his lecture, 'Lo Stato del capitalismo organizzato'. This was delivered at a two-day conference on the State and Capitalism in the 1930s at the Gramsci Institute in Rome in November 1979.

12. One can trace a direct line from the theory of the 'point of view' of *Operai e capitale* – itself echoing if not overlapping with the early Lukács's reflections on the standpoint of the proletariat – to the repeated call to 'partisanship' of the later years: 'One needs a point of view from which to look at the world and life. One needs a part of the world and life to which to ascribe one's own thought .... The history of the workers' movement has left us a bequest, you must go and seek your side [*parte*] with patient intelligence, with passion, thinkingly, tearing it almost day-by-day from the narrative that has buried it; piercing the veil of dominant ideas that have left it for dead, and then allowing it to be glimpsed from afar, with vision, allowing it to be touched close by, with realism, ever mindful of being and operating behind the bars of an iron cage' (Tronti, *Per la critica del presente* (2013)).

13. I put 'Hegelian' in scare quotes for it seems to me that Tronti took aim here not only at Gramsci's historicism but also at the Soviet philosophy of Diamat. In critical comments on the dialectic, he was, for the most part, much less engaged in a concerted philosophical confrontation with Hegel himself. Arguably, one might claim that this is true in much of French anti-Hegelianism as well, from Louis Althusser to Gilles Deleuze, where it was Diamat and the PCF that were the principal objects of critique. It might be useful to note that Tronti's only real, substantive text on Hegel (who actually appears throughout Tronti's writings) – *Hegel politico* (1975) – was composed in the period of his call for the 'autonomy of the political', for which Hegel was, to his mind, a precursor. This was a Hegel that proceeded from the subject, a subjectivity 'replete with political realism', i.e., a step towards a 'political class dimension' that breaks the purported but absent 'autonomy of the economic' (as he declared in a lecture on 5 April 1975).

14. The interview is available on YouTube, in Italian and Spanish, accessed October 12 2024, https://www.youtube.com/watch?v=xzKymyIsj50&list=PLU8WjOORJXltNmKcUkant0ljJLTa1On03&index=20

15. For a very useful discussion, in English, see Andrew Anastasi's excellent collection – and very useful introduction – to *The Weapon of Organization: Mario Tronti's Political Revolution in Marxism* (Brooklyn and Philadelphia: Common Notions, 2020).

16. The 'infamous' lecture, 'L'autonomia del politico', took place in 1972 but was not published until five years later. (An English translation is available online at *Viewpoint Magazine* with the title 'The Autonomy of the Political', https://viewpointmag.com/2020/02/26/the-autonomy-of-the-political/.) It was infamous for a number of reasons. The most important of which, I would argue, is that it never made explicit that the struggles in the factory should be autonomous from the Party. And so, it was read by many, particularly those from *Potere operaio* and, later, *Autonomia operaia organizzata* – who felt they were remaining true to *operaismo*'s primacy of the antagonistic subject – as granting the PCI *carte blanche*, permitting it to act opportunistically, without an eye to the struggles in the factory. Hence, it was considered as a betrayal of the tenets of *operaismo*'s class against class standpoint, by Tronti's erstwhile and now-'Autonomist' collaborators, and was greeted with stony silence by the PCI intellectuals and institutional hierarchy, which was the intended audience. (It is likely that Tronti did not highlight the autonomy of the factory struggles, simply because his audience was the party establishment.) Andrew Anastasi and I have tried to answer the accusation of betrayal in 'A Betrayal Retrieved: Mario Tronti's Critique of the Political', in *Viewpoint Magazine*, https://viewpointmag.com/2020/02/25/a-betrayal-retrieved-mario-trontis-critique-of-the-political/.

17. The critique of democracy would become a rich vein of research tapped by Tronti over the subsequent decades.

18. Thanks to Jamila Mascat for allowing me to read a draft of her insightful forthcoming paper, 'Mario Tronti e il partito come problema: Fenomenologia del PCI e metafisica del politico'.

19. These 'limits' were posed by the unwritten but well-known block on the PCI ever assuming democratic command of the state. This was imposed in a number of ways by the USA and its allies: enforced through the US's direct interference in Italian domestic politics (the State Department website shows the near daily communications with ministers in the Italian government throughout the postwar period); the intimate relationship between the Italian and US-NATO security apparatuses; the various 'stay behind' organisations, the full extent and reach of which were not entirely uncovered until the parliamentary commissions of the 1990s; and the established relationship between organised crime, the security services and elements of the Vatican.

20. Consider, for instance, The Trilateral Commission's Report, *The Crisis of Democracy: On the Governability of Democracies* (1975). See also Grégoire Chamayou, *The Ungovernable Society: A Genealogy of Authoritarian Liberalism* (Cambridge: Polity, 2021).

21. Literally, 'leopordism', referring to the famous phrase uttered by Tancredi Falconeri in Giuseppe Tomasi di Lampedusa's *The Leopard*.

22. This long essay, which is shortly to be published in Italian, was one Tronti had been working on, on and off, for some years and was still working on shortly before his death. It is unclear whether this would have been the final version.

23. That the best one can hope for from what goes by the name of 'politics' today is to act as *katechon*, a withholding power 'of the new modernity that kills the ancient greatness of the modern' (*The Twilight of Politics*).